European Architecture
in India 1750–1850

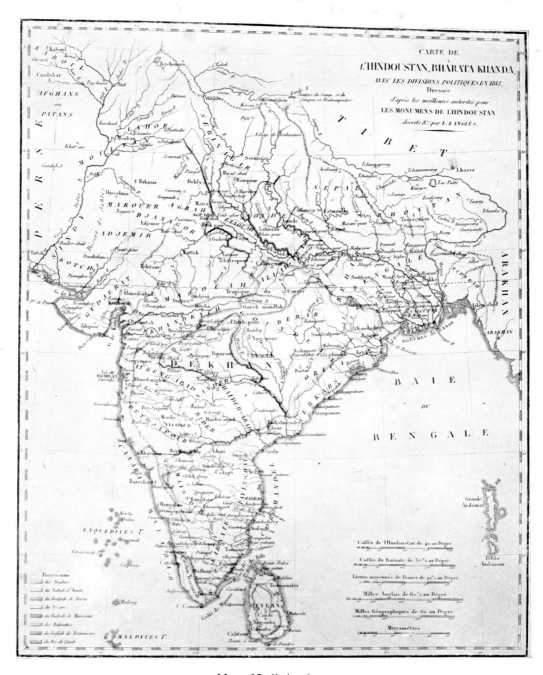

Map of India in 1812.

European Architecture in India 1750–1850

STEN NILSSON

Taplinger Publishing Company
New York

First American Edition published by
Taplinger Publishing Co., Inc., 1969
© *1968 by Sten Nilsson*

Library of Congress Catalog Card Number 69–11074

Printed in Great Britain

To my wife CARIN

Acknowledgements

This study of the type of architecture developed in India between 1750 and 1850 by the Danes, French, British and, to a certain extent, by the Dutch and Portuguese, is based on a number of lectures delivered in London, Copenhagen, Stockholm and Lund. The Swedish edition of this book was presented as a doctoral thesis in May 1967 at Lund University, Sweden.

Now that the English edition is to appear, I would like to extend my thanks to all who have helped in the various stages of its publication: Mildred Archer and her husband, W. G. Archer, have read the manuscript and made several valuable observations; Sir John Summerson has done me the same favour and has, in addition, shown me the very great kindness of writing the Foreword; Dorothy Stroud has found an idiomatic form for the numerous architectural terms of the translation; the editing and production staff of Faber's have always been most understanding and helpful.

My researches have brought me in contact with still more people without whose help and understanding my efforts would not have advanced very far. I should, therefore, also like to thank the following persons and institutes:

In Denmark — the Office of the Comptroller of the Royal Household of Amalienborg Castle and the late superintendent of H.M. the King's Private Library, H. F. Kjaer; Ib Andersen, Fredensborg; Inge Mejer Antonsen and Ole Feldbaek, Copenhagen; Steen Eiler Rasmussen, H. H. Engqvist and Hakon Lund of the Academy of Fine Arts, Copenhagen; the staff of the Royal Library, of the Library of the Academy of Fine Arts and the Library of the Royal Navy, Copenhagen; the staff of the Commercial and Maritime Museum in Kronborg Castle, Elsinore.

In Norway — the staff of the Ethnographical Museum, Oslo.

In England — the Institute of Royal Engineers, Chatham; the staff of the various departments of the British Museum, London; the India Office Library, London; the Drawings Collection and the Library of the Royal Institute of British Architects, London; the Swedish Embassy, London.

In Holland — the staff of the Koninklijk Institut voor de Tropen and of the Tropenmuseum, particularly Londje Dobbelman of the above Institute in Amsterdam.

In France — Roderick Cameron, St. Jean Cap Ferrat; A. Meunier of the Bibliothèque de la Section Outre-Mer des Archives Nationales, Paris; Bibliothèque de l'Institut des Hautes Etudes d'Outre-Mer, Paris; Musée de la France Outre-Mer, Paris; and the Swedish Embassy, Paris.

ACKNOWLEDGEMENTS

In the U.S.S.R. — the Department of Preservation of Buildings in Leningrad.

In Australia — Thomas Inglis, Perth.

In India — K. Deva, Deputy Director General of Archaeology in India; Sourin Roy of the National Archives of India; M. Mujeeb, Vice-Chancellor of Jamia Millia Islamia and B. Grover of the same institute; the staff of the National Gallery of Modern Art, New Delhi; Baron Henrik Ramel, then of the Swedish Embassy, New Delhi, and Rasmus Rasmusson and their families; the Secretary to the Governor of West Bengal; the Secretary and Curator of Victoria Memorial Hall, S. K. Saraswati, Calcutta; and the Secretary of the Turf Club, Calcutta; P. K. Menon and family, Madras. Pondicherry's grande dame, Yvonne Robert-Gaebelé; the missionaries, Ellen Nordmark in Usilampatti, Hildegard Klein in Poreyar, Olle Johnson in Coimbatore, and Bror Tiliander in Madura and Lund; The Governor of Maharashtra, His Excellency, P. V. Cherian; P. M. Joshi, Director of Archives & Historical Monuments, Bombay; D. S. Palande, Municipal Architect, Bombay; the staff of the library of the Asiatic Society, Bombay.

In Sweden — I should like in the first place to acknowledge a debt to the Indian Embassy in Stockholm, and also those who at various times have taught me art history; the late Ragnar Josephson; Sven Sandström; Sigurd Wallin; Sten Karling and Oscar Reutersvärd. I should also like to express my thanks to Rudolf Zeitler and the mission of the Church of Sweden, Uppsala; Göran Lindahl and John Sjöström of the architectural department of the Academy of Fine Arts, Stockholm; Dagny and Holger Arbman, Anna Lisa Centerwall, Hallgerd Dyrssen, Agnes George, Inger Sondén- and Karl Reinhold Haellquist, Arne and Eleonore Zettersten, Lars Österlin and the staff of the University Library, Lund.

Photographs of architectural drawings and other material in collections and publications are reproduced by courtesy of:

The Royal Household Department, Amalienborg; The Royal Library and The National Archives, Copenhagen; The Commercial and Maritime Museum in Kronborg Castle, Elsinore; The Secretary of State for Commonwealth Affairs, London; The Trustees of the British Museum, London; The Royal Institute of British Architects, London; The Courtauld Institute of Art, London; Messrs. Hutchinson & Co. Ltd., London; Institution of Royal Engineers in Chatham; The Department of Preservation of Buildings, Leningrad; The Trustees of The Victoria Memorial Hall, Calcutta.

S. N.

Contents

CONTENTS

Illustrations

ILLUSTRATIONS

14

27b. Government House, Calcutta. (Department of Prints and Drawings, British Museum.)

28. Government House, Calcutta. Detail of one of the gates facing Council House Street.

29a. Government House, Calcutta. One of the gates facing Council House Street.

29b. Syon House, Middlesex. (Engraving from *The Works in Architecture of Robert and James Adam*, London, 1778–1822.)

30a. Government House and Banqueting Hall, Triplicane, Madras. (Aquatint published by Edward Orme in 1807. Department of Prints and Drawings, British Museum.)

30b. Government House, Triplicane, Madras. (Architectural drawing from India Office Library, London.)

31a. The park of Government House, Triplicane, Madras. (Drawing from India Office Library, London.)

31b and c. Banqueting Hall, Triplicane, Madras. Details from the interior.

32a. Plan of a palace, projected for the Nawab of Murshidabad. (Architectural drawing by Edward Tiretta, British Museum.)

32b. Plan of a palace, projected for the Nawab of Murshidabad. (Architectural drawing, British Museum.)

33. Serampore College, plan of the first and second floors. (The Private Library of His Majesty the King of Denmark.)

34. The Banqueting Hall of the British Residency in Lucknow.

35. The Banqueting Hall of the British Residency in Lucknow. Part of the interior.

36. House in Clyde Road, Lucknow, showing mixed European and Indian decoration.

37a. The British Residency in Hyderabad.

37b. The British Residency in Hyderabad. (Aquatint from *Scenery, Costumes and Architecture*, London, 1826–30.)

38. The British Residency in Hyderabad. Details from the interior.

39a. Staircase of Home House (now the Courtauld Institute), Portman Square, London.

39b. Staircase of the main building of the British Residency in Hyderabad.

39c. Staircase of the main building of the British Residency in Hyderabad. Detail showing the bannisters.

40. Town Hall, Calcutta. (Photograph by Bourne & Shepherd, Calcutta.)

41. The Mint, Calcutta.

42. Town Hall, Bombay.

43. Town Hall, Bombay.

44a and b. Town Hall, Bombay.

45. Town Hall, Bombay.

ILLUSTRATIONS

68a. The 'main street' of South Park Cemetery, Calcutta.

68b and c. Tombs designed by William Chambers. (Engravings from *Treatise of Civil Architecture*, London, 1759.)

69a and b. Tombs in South Park Cemetery, Calcutta.

70a, b, c and d. Tombs in South Park Cemetery, Calcutta.

71. Tomb in South Park Cemetery, Calcutta.

72. Fragment of a marble slab showing Thanatos motif, South Park Cemetery, Calcutta.

73. The Old Cemetery in Patna.

74a and b. 'Two European officers being entertained at a nautch in an Indian house'; b, 'A European presiding over a musical performance in his house'. (India Office Library, London.)

75a. House of a distinguished Indian, Serampore. (The Commercial and Maritime Museum in Kronborg Castle, Elsinore.)

75b. Indian houses in Chitpore Road, Calcutta. (Detail of an engraving from *Oriental Scenery. Twenty-four views in Hindoostan*, London, 1797.)

76. Indian palace showing influences from European architecture. (The Drawings Collection of the R.I.B.A., London.)

77. Sawai Man Singh Town Hall, Jaipur, erected about 1790.

78a. Acroterion, made of terra-cotta, Panjim.

78b. Veranda with a cast iron railing, probably from the 1820's, Serampore.

79. Window with shutters composed of wooden laths and oyster-shells, Panjim.

80. Limestone columns from a Portuguese building in Old Goa.

81a. Cast iron columns from a Portuguese building from the middle of the 19th century, Panjim.

81b. Balusters made of terra-cotta and filled with mortar, Barrackpore.

82. Fragments of columns and walling composed of Indian burnt bricks, Lucknow.

83a. Figure showing the composing of neo-Classical elements of brick and mortar to be covered with plaster. (From *Outline of a Course of Practical Architecture, compiled for the use of Junior Officers of Royal Engineers*, Chatham, 1826.)

83b. Fragment of a column composed of 'column-bricks' and mortar, Tranquebar.

84. Wooden screens in the Governor's Bungalow, Malabar Point, Bombay.

85. Screens cut out of sandstone slabs. Tomb of Imam Zamin, Delhi.

86. Portico of a house in Kongens gade (King Street), Tranquebar.

87a and b. 'Tatties' in the verandas of Government House, Triplicane, Madras.

88a. Doorways of the basement storey, the 'godown' of a house in Fort St. George, Madras.

88b. Doorway of the basement storey of a house in Fort St. George, Madras.

89. Doorway of the house No. 9 Russell Street, Calcutta.

ILLUSTRATIONS

90a, b and c. William Hickey's House, Calcutta; the same house with verandas added by Hickey; and Hickey's country residence at Chinsura. (Sketches from W. Hickey's *Memoirs*, London, 1925.)

90d. Part of Lall Bazar, Calcutta. (Detail of an aquatint from *Scenery of Calcutta and its environs*, London, 1824–26.)

90e. Terrace roofs in Pondicherry on the Coromandel Coast. (Detail of photograph by Bourne & Shepherd, Calcutta.)

91a. Wooden verandas of a house in Marine Street, Bombay.

91b. Tiled sloping roofs in Panjim.

92a. Guest bungalow attached to the Residence of the Governor of Maharashtra, Malabar Point, Bombay.

92b. Bungalow in Fraser Road, Patna.

93a. 'Curvilinear huts', bungalow and European country residence in Bengal. (Detail of an aquatint by H. Merke, published by Edward Orme in 1805, Victoria Memorial Hall, Calcutta.)

93b. 'Double-roofed house' in a European housing area near Calcutta. (Detail of a painting, Victoria Memorial Hall, Calcutta.)

93c. 'Bungalow attached to the House of Maharajah Mutrefeyt Singh'. (India Office Library, London.)

93d. Bungalow in which to deposit rice, Tranquebar.

94a. Detail of a bungalow in Fraser Road, Patna.

94b and c. Bungalow with *pucka* columns and a complicated wooden construction supporting the roof, Tranquebar.

95. Bamboo window in a Bengal house.

The photographs of the actual structures were all taken by the author while travelling in India in 1964–65.

ILLUSTRATIONS IN THE TEXT

1a. Centralized town plan. (From Pietro Cataneo, *Quattro Primi Libri di Architettura*, 1554.)   *page* 41

1b. Daman on the west coast of India, founded by the Portuguese in 1558. (Drawing after Manuel de Faria y Sousa, *Asia Portuguesa*, Lisboa, 1674.)   41

2. Dannemarksnagore, the first factory founded by the Danes in Bengal in 1698, and abandoned in 1714. (Drawing after a plan in Asiatisk Kompagnis Arkiv, National Archives, Copenhagen.)   42

3a. Madras in 1688. (Plan from L. Langlès, *Monuments anciens . . . de l'Hindoustan*, Paris, 1821.)   43

18

Several of the older maps and plans have no scale. I have, however, tried to show the approximate scale whenever possible.

S. N.

FOREWORD by Sir John Summerson

WITH one exception, it seems that nobody before Mr. Nilsson has thought it worthwhile to describe categorically the architecture which the Danes, the French and the English brought to India in the great century of Imperial increase and consciousness between 1750 and 1850. The exception is the all-seeing James Fergusson who devoted nineteen pages of text and five wood-cuts to the subject in Chapter I of Book VIII of his *History of the Modern Styles of Architecture*, published by John Murray in 1862.

Fergusson, of course, was a special case. In early life he went into the indigo business and was employed by a firm in Calcutta. His curiosity about architecture was aroused by the architectures of ancient India. From the study of these he developed views on the aesthetics of architecture generally and in the course of forty years investigated and described nearly the whole architectural product of the civilized world. Looking back to India, the structural deposits of the conquering races could hardly be omitted from such an encyclopedic work. The contributions of the Portuguese, the Spaniards, the Dutch and the French were dealt with in turn. 'The French', he says, 'probably would have done better than the other colonists' if they had had the chance. He admired the town-plan of Pondicherry and alluded to the vanished fortifications whose gateways Mr. Nilsson describes.

There was no false patriotism about Fergusson and when he comes to the English performance he is pretty rigorous. He had a horror of Greek Doric columns, 'built up as mere ornaments, and generally so as to obstruct ventilation, without keeping out the heat, and arranged in such a manner as to be as unlike a truly Grecian design as was possible with such correct details'. He particularly instanced the Town Hall at Bombay and the Mint at Calcutta which, in Mr. Nilsson's sympathetic photographs, look so calm and splendid and so truly Greek.

Government House at Calcutta Fergusson admired. The derivation from Kedleston was 'singularly happy' and Mr. Nilsson is able to endorse his view that the five articulated masses combined convenience with perfect ventilation. 'Altogether', continues Fergusson, 'there are few modern palaces of its class either more appropriate in design, or more effective in their architectural arrangement and play of light and shade, than this residence of the Governor-General of India.' Fergusson's estimate of Kedleston itself in an earlier book was scarcely as enthusiastic.

But one of the pleasures of reading Fergusson is the unaccountable originality of his verdicts. Faced with General Martin's extravaganza at Lucknow, which Mr. Nilsson understandably finds hard to classify, one might suppose him either disgusted or dumb. Not at all. It earns two appreciative paragraphs. It is 'a far more reasonable edifice than the rival capriccio of Beckford, at Fonthill; and . . . really does contain the germ of a very beautiful design.'

It is now more than a hundred years since Fergusson, at his desk in Langham Place, pondered these things. I have said that he was a special case. We have had to wait a long time for another special case — one, as it turns out, of a totally different kind. For a Swedish scholar, the architectural enterprises of the French and British in eighteenth- and nineteenth-century India must surely wear a veil of almost mythical remoteness; and it is my guess — not, I hope, impertinent — that romantic singularity in time and place was one of the things which drew Mr. Nilsson, of the University of Lund, to the subject he has now so sharply and delightfully profiled for us.

Could an English scholar have written this book? The answer is 'yes', but the fact is that no English scholar did; and the reasons for that might have to be sought in the embarrassing load of apprehensions, prejudices and inhibitions about India and about imperialism which most educated Englishmen still carry around with them. Mr. Nilsson is free of such impedimenta — a roving northerner coolly observing the collisions and contortions of architectural style in the currents of world history. Fergusson put the matter rather well. 'Where the round hat of the European is seen,' he wrote, 'there the "orders" follow eventually', (meaning, of course, the orders of classical architecture). Of this fine generalization in its Indian application, Mr. Nilsson demonstrates the truth.

One · The Approach

1 · Projections of Greece and Rome

WE shall approach the architecture which is our subject in the same way as the travellers of the Romantic Age did — from the sea. After a long sea voyage round Africa and across the Indian Ocean, they finally saw the towns of India emerging before the bowsprit. To be sure, they had already broken their journey in Cape Town, and some were bound even further east, for Batavia, Singapore or Canton, but none of these were destined to leave the strongest impression. The buildings in Cape Town were nearly all in the Dutch style, and would be scarcely a surprise to travellers coming direct from Europe. There is no reason to suppose that Batavia at that time would have any more imposing effect than Singapore, where the European influence was considerably less. The impression of Canton approached via Bocca Tigris, and of the line of factories along the harbour, has been preserved in a number of paintings which record the presence of European architecture in a distant land, but give no hint of any passionate involvement.[1]

But the towns of the Coromandel Coast and of Bengal these travellers saw in quite a different light. There they discovered buildings in brilliant settings and with strong associative values. They were dazzled by what they saw — and what they thought they saw. What first met their eyes was not a characteristically oriental milieu, but a familiar classical world, an architecture which had its roots in Greece and Rome.[2]

Eliza Fay's first contact with India, in 1780, was anything but easy, but she forgot some of the hardships she had endured when she finally reached Madras. She described the buildings that lined the waterfront as follows:

'Many of the houses and public buildings are very extensive and elegant — they are covered with a sort of shell-lime which takes a polish like marble, and produces a wonderful effect — I could have fancied myself transported into Italy, so magnificently are they decorated, yet with the utmost taste.'[3]

Mrs. Fay herself has been described as 'a work of art', and the portrait of her reproduced by E. M. Forster in his Introduction to *Original Letters from India* does not gainsay such a description. In it she appears in Egyptian dress, as befits a romantic traveller aware of those parallel changes in apparel and background that current aesthetics approved. Her confusion of India and Italy should be seen in the same context.

William Hodges came to Madras in 1781, the year after Eliza Fay. He saw the same townscape as she had, and experienced the same admiration and the same sense of recognition:

'The English town, rising from within Fort St. George has from the sea a rich and beautiful appearance. The stile of the buildings is in general handsome. They consist of long colonades, with open porticoes, and flat roofs and offer to the eye an appearance similar to that what we may conceive of a Grecian city in the age of Alexander. The clear, blue and cloudless sky, the polished white buildings, the bright sandy beach, and the dark green sea, present a combination totally new to the eye of an Englishman just arrived from London, who accustomed to the sight of rolling masses of clouds floating in a damp atmosphere, cannot but contemplate the difference with delight.'[4]

This same city of marble, the projection of the Mediterranean cities of classical antiquity, is to be found in Maria Graham's notes, at the beginning of the 19th century:

'I do not know anything more striking than the first approach to Madras. The low, flat sandy shore extending for miles to the north and south. . . . The public offices and store-houses which line the beach, are fine buildings, with colonades to the upper stories, supported by rustic bases arched, all of the fine Madras chunam, smooth, hard, and polished as marble.'[5]

It may seem paradoxical that travellers of the neo-Classical period should find their dream of Greece realized so many miles east of the Bosphorus. But there was justification for such an experience. Behind the projection there appeared a very real architecture with rows of columns 'supported by rustic bases'.

The landscape artist, Hodges, had seen Madras as a scene in an atmospheric dream. The descriptions of Eliza Fay and Maria Graham are more precise; together they give the same impression as the water-colours of John Gantz of Madras in the 1820's. Here the buildings form a magnificent sea-front; the wind blows over the wide promenade, the sky is light blue and the colonnades dazzling white.[6] It is understandable that the sight should surprise someone accustomed to the fogs and the dark brick façades of London.

Calcutta's neo-Classical architecture was still more ostentatious than that of Madras, but did not present itself so directly. If we follow the author of *The Oriental Voyager*, James Johnson, on his journey across the Bay of Bengal, we approach it gradually. First we come to Diamond Harbour, where the East Indiamen usually anchored to load and unload their goods. After that, the trip up the River Hooghly is rather uninteresting until Falta is reached, 'when chateaux as well as cottages begin to peep out from the umbrageous foliage that skirts the banks of the river. It is at Garden Reach, however, that the most striking and beautiful prospect presents itself to the view.'[7]

So far we have only been able to see fragments of the residential districts outside Calcutta. The description of the city itself we shall leave to another traveller, Leopold von Orlich:

'Viewed from the Hooghly, Calcutta has the appearance of a city of palaces. A row of large superb buildings extend from the princely residence of the Governor-General, along the Esplanade and produce a remarkable striking effect.'[8]

Von Orlich first came to Calcutta in the 1840's, and his remarks were actually a repetition of what many had said before him. The 'city of palaces' was already a conventional description of Calcutta. Those who had perhaps contributed more than most — more, in fact, than the architects — to the origin of this idea were the artists, Thomas and William Daniell, who had drawn Calcutta from 1786 onwards and published their work in the collections entitled *Views of Calcutta* (1786–88) and *Oriental Scenery* (1795–1808).

The Daniells provided detailed pictorial records of all the great monuments being erected at the time. But, in addition to fulfilling this practical function, they were also travellers with a keen appreciation of the picturesque — and in particular, landscape painters. Many of their contemporaries shared their aesthetic attitude. However, it may be sufficient to quote Lord Valentia, who passed the English country houses along the Hooghly in 1803 and wrote of them:

'They were in *themselves* [my italics] picturesque being white, with extensive porticoes to the south, and the windows closed by venetian blinds painted green.'

It is possible that Lord Valentia borrowed his impressions from the artist Henry Salt, who accompanied him on the journey.[9]

The person who gave the most original description of neo-Classical Calcutta was Bishop Heber, who visited it in 1823. He wrote to his friend Charles W. Williams Wynn on 29th October of that year:

'The impression made by the appearance of the European houses which we passed in Garden Reach, — by our own apartments, by the crowd of servants . . . was that of the extreme similarity of everything to Russia. . . . This impression was afterwards rather confirmed than weakened. The size of the houses, their whiteness and Palladian porticos, the loftiness of the rooms, and the scanty furniture, . . . all reminded me of Petersburgh and Moscow; to which the manner in which the European houses are scattered, with few regular streets, but each with its separate court-yard and gate-way, and often intermixed with miserable huts, still more contributed.'[10]

Bishop Heber re-iterated this comparison when he saw the public buildings in the centre of Calcutta, the Town Hall, Government House and so on. He even went so far as to talk about roubles instead of rupees!

Heber had visited St. Petersburg in 1805, when the Alexandrian architecture was beginning to dominate the scene. The immense Kazan church was being erected; private and public buildings in a strictly neo-Classical style were being built throughout the city. Heber was greatly impressed by this architecture, by its heroism and magnificence.[11] We may take it that the dominant tone of Calcutta in the 1820's was much the same. But the resemblance went further, concerning not only the basic lay-out of the town, the size of its houses and the brilliant final effect, but also the material of the buildings and the effect it gave. In this respect, St. Petersburg was reminiscent of some of the new parts of London also.

'There is indeed nothing more striking than *the apparant instability of the splendour* [my italics] of this great town; houses, Churches, and public buildings are all of plaistered brick; and a portico worthy of a Grecian temple is often disfigured by the falling of the stucco, and the bad rotten bricks peeping through.'[12]

This was also true of Calcutta. In his criticism, Heber touched upon a very sensitive spot in the aesthetics of neo-Classicism. The person contemplating the architecture might well be conscious of the fiction behind the structure. But he could easily be deceived by an architectural façade, if it had sufficiently strong associations. Christian Elling has told how the poet Oehlenschläger, for instance, recalled his Italian journey on a summer's day in Denmark. The Roman monuments he remembered best, and which he brought into a poem, were the temples of Aesculapius, and of Antoninus and Faustina, two imitation antiques erected by Alessandro Albani. In the same way the painter, Eckersberg harked back to the Egyptian entrance-pylons in the Villa Borghese.[13]

But this aesthetic experience could be shattered, so to speak, if the façade showed too large cracks. Heber's feeling of instability and badly applied make-up was shared by other travellers. James Johnson admired the *chunam* stucco on façades in Madras and Calcutta, so long as the strongly polished surface was intact and gave the impression of marble. When it began to scale and the brickwork could be seen, the houses acquired 'a beggarly appearance'. The contrast reminded him of certain Portuguese whom he had seen, with shining swords and ragged clothing: 'complete emblems of pride and poverty united.'[14] The Dane, Steen Bille made the same observation when going round the streets of Calcutta. The houses were actually built in different styles, but they had one feature in common; they bore the mark of being built in a material which could not stand the strain of climate and time. In their appearance they were very different from the architecture of the ancients, which they were supposed to emulate.[15] This last remark is important. It indicates a focal point, a deep note that lies at the heart of all classicism, but is especially characteristic of neo-Classicism. The antique was admired because it had survived, these buildings manifested their monumental character by continuing to exist. The consequence of these thoughts, if we transfer them to a plane where form and substance are united, was a devotion to the monolith. This was often expressed, but we can content ourselves with quoting from one of Sir John Soane's lectures to the students of the Royal Academy: 'The Ancients, in order to render their Works eternal, were not satisfied with using immense blocks of granite and marble; entire buildings were sometimes formed of a single stone.'[16]

John Soane and his contemporaries were familiar with monolithic works of art in Egypt and Italy; the obelisks were hewn in one block as were the columns of the Pantheon in Rome. But these were also found in quite a different part of the world, in India, where interest in the rock temples on Elephanta and Salsette and in Mahabalipuram now greatly increased. Knowledge about them spread to Europe by means of pictures, amongst others those of the Daniells.[17]

It is against this background, that we must regard the travellers' criticism of the decaying houses in Calcutta and Madras; they saw their deterioration as a breach of convention.

There was, however, one final possibility for the buildings to rise again in the aesthetic scale of values, and that was their collapsing so completely that they could be regarded as ruins. That sort of change was quite in accordance with the taste of the time. A ruin was usually regarded with reverence, even if it were only a few decades old. The remains of Ghiretty House, a stately building on the banks of the Hooghly outside Chandernagore, which was still inhabited at the beginning of the 19th century, were beheld by Bishop Heber in 1824. 'It has at present a very melancholy aspect, and in some degree reminded me of Moreton Corbet having like that the remains of Grecian pillars and ornaments, with a high carved pediment.' . . . A writer in *The Calcutta Review* in 1845 expressed the view that: 'If there be any other place in Bengal, after Gour, with its ruined palaces and mosques, which presents an air of the most melancholy desolation, heightened by the remembrance of its former beauty and cheerfulness, it is the country house of the French governors of Chandernagore.'[18]

Not even the country house of the Marquis of Wellesley at Barrackpore, which could scarcely be regarded as a ruin, as it had never actually been completed, escaped such contemplation. Maria Graham wrote:

'Its unfinished arches shewed by the moon-light like an ancient ruin, and completed the beauty of the scenery.'[19]

The beauty was not disturbed by the corpses which floated past on the river.

The Frenchman Laplace gave the most grandiose description of ancient ruins under the Indian moon. He came to Tranquebar, the small Danish colony on the Coromandel coast, during his voyage round the world at the end of the 1830's. He stayed on his frigate, which was anchored a short distance from the coast, and from it he saw houses with yellow and white plaster and the fort with its red and white flag fluttering in the breeze. At nightfall he went into the town and through the large gateway up Kongens gade (King Street):

'j'aperçus à la clarté de la lune deux rangées de maisons dont les façades, ornées de colonnades et bariolées de couleurs brillantes, étaient surmontées de terasses qu'entourait une balustrade élégamment découpée. Tous ces édifices n'avaient que de très-petites dimensions : peut-être même qu'à la clarté du jour ils ne m'auraient présenté rien de remarquable ; mais leur architecture quasi grecque, l'absence complètes de lumières à leur fenêtres, les ombres que toutes ces petites colonnades projetaient sur notre chemin enfin la solitude profonde et le silence qui régnaient dans la rue que nous parcourions, me rappelaient l'impression inexprimable à laquelle j'avais été en proie lorsque, huit années auparavant, je visitai Pompéia, cette cité romaine exhumée du sein des cendres que le Vésuve répandit sur elle comme un linceul, il y a seize siècles passés. Un semblable rapprochement paraîtra extraordinaire, je le crains, et pourtant il y avait sans doute quelque ressemblance entre les deux cités, puisqu'elle saisit à la fois mon âme et mon esprit. Ici, de même qu'au sein de la voisine de Naples, ces demeures des hommes étaient debout et paraissaient ornées, peintes, sculptées comme au temps où une foule agissante remplissait leurs murs. . . . enfin, la clarté brillante du ciel et la douce température de l'air avaient achevé l'illusion.'[20]

I THE APPROACH

1. *Projections of Greece and Rome:* Notes

1. James Johnson writes thus of Cape Town in *The Oriental Voyager*, London 1807, p. 49: 'The flatroofed houses of Cape Town, disposed into formal clumps, appear like those fabrics which children are accustomed to make with cards.' J. C. Stavorinus *Reise nach dem Vorgebürge der guten Hoffnung, Java und Bengalen*, Berlin 1796, p. 185, actually calls Batavia 'die Königin der Städte des östlichen Indiens', but that was 1770, when the English towns were still relatively small. Mirza Abu Taleb Khan had a different basis for his judgment. He sailed *westwards* and was more and more impressed by every European town he saw. His ranking list was: Calcutta, Cape Town, Cork, Dublin, London — 'ces villes s'éclipsant toutes progressivement en beauté et splendeur'. *Voyages de Mirza Abu Taleb Khan*, Paris, 1811. C. P. T. Laplace describes Singapore in his *Voyage autour de Monde ... pendant les années 1830, 1831, et 1832*, Paris, 1835, vol. 1, p. 337. Cf. T. H. H. Hancock, 'Coleman of Singapore', *Architectural Review*, March, 1955. By pictures of Canton and Bocca Tigris I mean the paintings on canvas, rice-paper or glass which were taken home to Europe as souvenirs, a large number of which are preserved in museums and private collections. One or more of such pictures probably served as prototype for a print, published in 1805, and an oil-painting by Thomas Daniell, No. 983 M, Victoria Memorial Hall, Calcutta.

2. The attitude of the travellers towards the strange environment has been elucidated by George D. Bearce in *British Attitudes towards India 1784–1858*, Oxford, 1961. passim.

3. Eliza Fay, *Original Letters from India 1779–1815*; first published 1817, London, 1925, with an introduction by E. M. Forster. Forster's characterization and the portrait of Mrs. Fay are to be found in this edition.

4. Of Hodges as an architectural theorist see below, p. 33. Quotation from *Travels in India during the years 1781, 82, 83*, London, 1793, pp. 1 f.

5. Maria Graham, *Journal of a Residence in India*, Edinburgh, 1812, p. 123. *Chunam* was the characteristic white plaster used for facing buildings.

6. John Gantz's water-colours, WD. 1362 and 1363, India Office Library, Commonwealth Office, London; the latter, dated 1822, has been published by Mildred Archer in 'Company Architects and their influence in India', *R.I.B.A. Journal*, Aug. 1963. The townscape of Madras at that time — like that of Calcutta — is described below in the section about the urban patterns, p. 65.

7. James Johnson, op. cit. p. 97.

8. Leopold von Orlich, *Travels in India*, London, 1845, vol. 2, p. 175.

9. George Annesley, Viscount Valentia, *Voyages and Travels to India, Ceylon ... in the years 1802, 1803, 1804, 1805 and 1806*, London, 1809, vol. 1, p. 60. Cf. Mildred Archer, 'Forgotten Painter of the Picturesque, Henry Salt in India 1802–1804', *Country Life*, Nov. 19, 1959, and M. & W. G. Archer, *Indian Painting for the British 1770–1880*, Oxford, 1955, pp. 3 ff.

10. Reginald Heber, *Narrative of a Journey from Calcutta to the Upper Provinces of India; from Calcutta to Bombay 1824–25*, London, 1828, vol. II, p. 287.

11. Reginald Heber, *The life of Reginald Heber by his Widow, together with a journal of his tour in Norway, Sweden, Russia, Hungary and Germany*, London, 1830, vol. 1, pp. 116 f. Re the

Russian buildings, cf. G. Quarenghi, *Edifices construits à Saint-Pétersbourg*, St. Petersburg, 1810; and G. H. Hamilton, *The Art and Architecture of Russia*, The Pelican History of Art, 1954, pp. 203 ff.

12. Reginald Heber, *The Life of Reginald Heber* etc., London, 1830, vol. 1, p. 106.

13. Christian Elling, *Rom, arkitekturens Liv fra Bernini til Thorvaldsen*, Copenhagen, 1956, pp. 462 ff.

14. James Johnson, op. cit. p. 99.

15. Steen Andersen Bille, *Beretning om Corvetten Galathea's Reise omkring Jorden 1845, 46 og 47*, Copenhagen, 1849–51, vol. 1, p. 192. The material in the European buildings is treated more specifically in a special section below: p. 167.

16. Sir John Soane, R.A., *Lectures on Architecture*, Publication of Sir John Soane's Museum No. 14, London, 1929, p. 121.

17. Ibid., p. 19. The lecturer refers here to the Daniells.

18. Reginald Heber, *Narrative of a Journey* etc., London, 1828, vol. I, p. 85. *The Calcutta Review*, vol. IV, 1845; cf. W. K. Firminger, *Thacker's Guide to Calcutta*, Calcutta, 1906, p. 243 and below, p. 122.

19. Maria Graham, op. cit., p. 142. Cf. below, p. 124.

20. C. P. T. Laplace, *Campagne de Circumnavigation de la frigate l'Artémise pendant les années 1837, 1838, 1839 et 1840*, Paris, 1842, vol. II, pp. 190 ff.

2 · The Requirements of Climate

WE now know, from the narratives of travellers, the general features of India's European architecture. During the last decades of the 18th century and up to the middle of the 19th century it showed a very clear neo-Classic character. The connection with the European prototypes was so strong that Bishop Heber could confuse Calcutta with St. Petersburg and Laplace could experience a Pompeian atmosphere in Tranquebar. People in the Romantic era were quick everywhere to make such comparisons, but in India such comparisons were, in spite of everything, close at hand.

In Europe, the neo-Classical architecture was temporarily subjected to severe criticism, especially when adopted in countries north of the Alps. Here the climatic requirements were different from those of Greece and Rome, and the purely practical problems which this transfer incurred were much discussed. But this was not the only reason: in the background was the more metaphysical climatology characteristic of Montesquieu, a theme which was varied in a number of philosophical writings during the 18th century. The Swede Ehrensvärd represented both these aspects in a very extreme way. When he stayed in Berlin during his Grand Tour in the beginning of the 1780's, he formulated his criticism in an aphorism: 'The eye would seem to see more columns here than in Rome, but asks everywhere: Columns, what are you doing here?'[1] The attack was aimed at eclecticism, imitation without principles, structural elements without functional contact with each other and their surroundings. When one has seen a circular temple filled with snow during a Swedish winter, one can also understand one of the basic reasons for these contemplations on climate.

Lodoli had lodged similar criticism; and in England Sir John Soane warned his pupils:

'Before (therefore) we apply the Orders of Architecture in the exterior of buildings for domestic purposes, we shall do well to pause for a moment and reflect that they were first used in Climates where it was desirable to exclude the too powerful rays of the Sun, and to produce Shade and fresh air about the building.'[2]

The Indian climate would seem to be far more congenial to antique and neo-Classical architecture. Here, elements acting as sunbreakers, such as porticos and colonnades, function in the same way as in their original setting, and to judge from the notes made by William Hodges, Eliza Fay and Maria Graham, the sky, the sea and the landscape formed a perfect frame around the white buildings.[3] However, their statements only show one side of the question; we must be conscious of the fact that there are more than one. In India too, classicism was criticized from climatic points of view.

32

THE REQUIREMENTS OF CLIMATE

Lord Valentia criticized the buildings from a practical aspect; he considered that the elevation of the colonnades was much too high for effective protection against the sun in the morning and in the evening, and that during the rainy season these large openings were even more vulnerable. 'The more confined Hindoo or Gothic architecture would surely be preferable.'[4]

Steen Bille criticized the Mint in Calcutta, a large Doric construction, as it seemed far too massive under the tropical sky. He also gave some sort of alternative:

'Now and again one sees a house which shows prosperity and comfort and which is correctly adapted to the country and its climate. In these cases, the hut or the house is always built of bamboo rods and covered with straw, it has a beautiful veranda running outside the rooms; the veranda is plaited in artistic ornamental designs and grown over with leaves and brilliant flowers.'[5]

Neither Valentia nor Bille were trained art historians and we cannot expect of them appreciation with very direct reference to the relevant debate of that time. However, the statements which I have cited here indicate some of the cardinal points in architectonic theory of Romanticism.

Valentia preferred a style more in line with the native Indian architecture; one gets the impression that it should combine Oriental and Gothic features in the same way as *The Stones of Venice* or the monumental structures which were erected in Bombay towards the end of the 19th century. Bille's comments, on the other hand, point in a different direction.

The theorists of the 18th century liked to talk about the 'hut', but they did not regard it specially suitable for a dwelling and initially they did not grant it any picturesque value. They dealt with it reverently, since they saw in it the prototype of the Greek temple and, as a matter of fact, of all architecture. It merely consisted of supporting and supported elements taken directly from nature. From these primitive constructions the most perfect forms had developed with time: the wooden supports had changed into columns, the branches of the roof into ceiling and pediment. The frontispiece of Laugier's *Essai sur l'Architecture* shows this first model of architecture, and William Chambers presents in his treatise of 1759 its entire hypothetical progress of development.

These are well-known facts, but I repeat them as they, together with Steen Bille's idea of the hut as the 'climatically correct building', form the basis for the architectonic theory of William Hodges.

In 1787, Hodges published a dissertation on architectural prototypes. As a treatise on architecture, this work is perhaps not very important; however, the background is original and for us this book is especially interesting as it is directly connected with India. Hodges was actually a landscape painter and, as such, a pupil of Richard Wilson. In architecture he had an almost encyclopaedic fund of experience, as he had taken part in one of Captain Cook's voyages and studied landscape and buildings in nearly every corner of the earth. The treatise was written on the basis of another tour, this time with Warren Hastings, through Bengal and up to the Northern Provinces of India. His conclusion was extremely tolerant:

THE APPROACH

'it [the building] should, and must be adapted to all the climates and countries which mankind inhabit, and is variously, more than any other, influenced and modified by their nature and materials, and the habits and pursuits of their inhabitants.'[6]

On the basis of his wide knowledge, Hodges criticized the prevalent idea of the Greek hut as the only correct prototype. For Oriental architecture different laws must apply, and for it he found other models: grottoes which were reproduced in the rock temples and the pointed rock formations which led to the construction of pyramids, spires and minarets. Hodges also described how different climatic conditions forced men to choose a suitable type of dwelling. Where the moisture in the soil is considerable, combined with the risk of sudden floods one could build high up in the trees as on the banks of the Orinoco, in Guiana and in the inner parts of Surinam. In very cold parts, men dug their dwellings in the ground in order to get protection against wind and snow. In the north the huts were made of seal skin or reindeer hides, or of felt and matting in Arabia and Tartary.

The conclusions drawn from these ideas as to the characteristics of the various countries and the harmony between architecture, climate and living conditions would, it appears, eliminate the thought of a neo-Classic architecture in India. Here, a Doric building is definitely out of place; it does not, to use Bille's words, correspond to the tropical sky. In any case, it stands out strikingly from everything in its surroundings. But Hodges does not voice any such criticism and instead presents us with an important 'precedent' when he says:

'When emigrations to foreign climates take place, their prototype will follow the colonist, and, by its own rule, genius will, and may at last stretch and improve it to the highest degree of perfection.'[7]

The general value of this theory may be left open and we may merely state that this is what actually happened in the European colonies in India as well as in Java, the Caribbean and all other places to which classical architecture was transferred and where it was forced to function. Naturally, no 'highest degree of perfection' was ever achieved. The result cannot be found in a definite formula, but in a series of solutions, some of which we will now consider.

2. *The Requirements of Climate:* Notes

1. *Carl August Ehrensvärds Skrifter*, published by the Swedish Society for Belles-Lettres, Stockholm, 1922, 23 and 25, p. 107.

2. Sir John Soane, R.A., *Lectures on Architecture*, Publication of Sir John Soane's Museum, No. 14; London, 1929, p. 153.

3. Cf. above, p. 26.

4. George Annesley, Viscount Valentia, *Voyages and Travels to India, Ceylon . . . in the years 1802, 1803, 1804, 1805 and 1806*, London, 1809, vol. 1, p. 240.

5. Steen Andersen Bille, *Beretning om Corvetten Galathea's Reise omkring Jorden 1845, 46 og*

47, Copenhagen, 1849–51, vol. 1, pp. 191 and 196. Indian houses of this primitive type are dealt with in a separate chapter, 'The Origin of the Dwelling-House', below, p. 186.

6. William Hodges, *A dissertation on the Prototypes of Architecture* etc., London, 1787, p. 2.

7. Ibid., p. 3.

Two · The Structures

1 · Urban Patterns

THE prerequisites for the architecture seen and described by the travellers in the Romantic period had been created at an early date. Most of India's European towns were founded in the 16th and 17th centuries. They were, from the start, places of very limited area, but they functioned as fixed points in a system of waterways by which the Europeans were able not only to dominate trade, but also to make far-reaching political claims.[1]

In the slow European conquest, several nations in turn played a dominant rôle. As we know, the Portuguese were the first on the scene. Already in the middle of the 16th century they had driven the Moslem merchants from their old trade-routes and soon dominated an area in which Macao in China, the towns on the west coast of India, and Ormuz and Aden were some of the key-points.

In about 1600, several other European nations began to play a part in the game. East India Companies were formed in Amsterdam, London and Copenhagen and the Portuguese monopoly of the spice trade was broken by force. In the beginning of the 1660's the Dutch conquered many of the Portuguese possessions and founded new colonies themselves.[2] Some decades later the Dutch, British and French were all fighting for the control of South-East Asia.

In the middle of the 18th century the areas conquered by the Europeans were still only small spots on the map, but then an expansion occurred which took in large areas of land and gave the British hegemony over the whole Indian sub-continent. The destruction of Chandernagore in 1758, the battle of Biderra in 1759, the destruction of Pondicherry in 1761 and the battle of Buxar in 1764 were some of the landmarks in the British assumption of political leadership and were at the same time the beginning of the end of the power exercised by the Dutch, the French and the Mughal rulers.

We shall consider merely fragments from this context, and, to start with, the pattern of the towns.

In order to convey something of the dynamics of the events, I shall go somewhat outside the actual period of time covered by this book in an account of some of the first enclaves and their composition. By means of one example, the Danish Tranquebar, we can follow in detail how a rudimentary town formation grows — and stagnates, owing to economic changes produced by European wars. A comparison with construction in Copenhagen gives us an idea of the contrast between the mother-country and the colony in the field of architecture.

THE STRUCTURES

In changing the scene to Calcutta, we step right into the middle of British expansion. The political conditions which stopped the development of Tranquebar turned Calcutta into the capital of a growing empire. Even the look of the town has an air of expansion and dominance. Near it lie a number of small places which gradually came to function as suburbs of the new metropolis, among them the Danish Serampore. The rise of the cantonments, which were formed on the model of a spacious camp, is also part of the urban changes around Calcutta and other towns.

To sum up briefly, these structural changes, which are anything but homogeneous and straightforward, can be said to have developed from enclosed towns, into formations that can no longer be defined in simple architectural terms such as a wall or a boundary, but where the scattered character points towards the possibility of even further expansion.

Thus the change could also be described as a development from the static to the dynamic. On the other hand, one should not be tempted to identify this last pattern with the general attitude towards the foreign environment. The Europeans in the enclosed towns might show greater receptivity to Indian impressions than those in the 'open' towns. The scattered pattern of the cantonments might become as much a symbol of uncompromising militarism, as the citadel or the fort.

The survey also contains information on racial and sociological conditions. Unfortunately, Indian points of view are rarely expressed. The book deals with the structures of the Europeans and therefore must be dominated by the white parts; from the Indian point of view it may be regarded in the same way as a photographic negative.

i The Enclaves

With the conquest of Goa by Albuquerque in November, 1510, the Portuguese gained a foothold in India. A few years previously they had established their first factory and their first fort in Cochin.[1] These early structures and their nearest successors all had a provisional character. Resources were limited and any building material available had to be used. Fort St. Emanuele in Cochin was erected of wood, as was the palisade around the town of Chaul. The historian, Gaspar Correia, records in 1521 the construction of a palisade of palm trunks — 'de palmeiras cortades e grossa madeira' — around the trading area of Chaul.[2]

The character of these structures, however, changed when wood was replaced by stone. The change started in the middle of the 16th century, when the towns of Diu, Bassein and Daman were erected in the form of fortresses with heavy bastions. These towns were all fortified according to the European pattern. The lay-out of Daman was the most distinct and its town plan can be traced straight back to the ideal projects worked out in Italy by Renaissance and Mannerist architects. In this case, the master-builder was also an Italian, Giovanni Baptista Cairato. He had entered Portuguese service after coming to India in 1583, and was employed in many places (probably also on Malacca).[3]

40

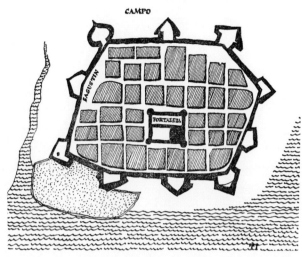

1a. Centralized town plan.

1b. Daman on the west coast of India, founded by the Portuguese in 1558.

The earliest pictures of Daman show a decagon. The walls are of considerable thickness and at the ten corners there are triangular or heart-shaped bastions. The plan is not regular. The wall almost forms an oval and the centre of gravity of the town is not in the actual centre. Furthermore, the various blocks form a pattern which is also not quite regular. However, in spite of these deviations, we can trace the prototype, i.e. a centralized lay-out of the type presented, for example, in Pietro Cataneo's *Quattro Primi Libri di Architettura* (1554). I shall not go into details of the lay-out, but will only emphasize items that are of fundamental importance for this survey. This town, with its combination of a fortified polygonal wall and a chess-board plan is the first of a large number of similar European settlements in India. The fort in the centre is also a recurring feature, although not of such a medieval design as here, but based more on modern and strict patterns of fortification. The function is likewise determined. In Daman, the walls already enclose a town in miniature; here we find the house of the commander, the church, the college, the prison and the factory.

North of Daman, further up the west coast of India, lies Surat, which was likewise a centre of early European colonization. Here not only the Portuguese, but also the British in 1612, the Dutch in 1616, and the French in 1668, built factories. The development of the colonies followed the same pattern. The provisional enclosures of clay and wood were in due course replaced by strong walls of stone and brick. The fortification was usually effected with the consent of the Indian princes from whom the territory had been acquired.[4]

The enclosed areas were small and the factories, or 'lodges,' looked more like private mercantile houses.[5] An engraving shows the Dutch factory in Surat as it looked in the beginning of the 1630's.[6] Around a courtyard a number of long, low buildings have been

41

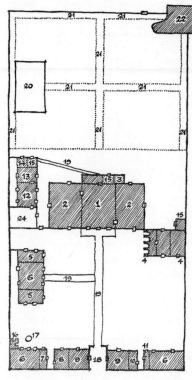

2. Danmarksnagore, the first factory founded by the Danes in Bengal in 1698, and abandoned in 1714. Plan showing: 1, vestibule (above this space lies a big hall); 2, rooms; 3, staircase leading to the hall; 4, the office; 5, godown; 6, store-room; 7, sergeant's room; 8, guard-room; 9, watch-room; 10, powder-magazine; 11, armoury; 12, kitchen; 13, larder; 14, privy; 15, warehouse; 16, room for brahmins; 17, flagstaff; 18, main gate; 19, paved footpath crossing the courtyard; 20, fish-pond; 21, alleyways; 22, bastion.

grouped, which function both as dwellings and warehouses. The houses face inward into the courtyard. The outer walls are high and of simple design. There are only a few very diminutive windows, and in some we can trace gun-barrels in the openings. Nevertheless, the engraving would seem to show the second stage of the factory. The first construction was probably even simpler. A perspective drawing of the Achin factory in Indonesia shows only a collection of small huts within a low palisade.[7] The huts have thatched roofs and are built exactly like the huts of the indigenous population. The only typically Dutch feature are the dovecotes which look like the gabled houses in Amsterdam or Leyden. The factory in Surat shows similar 'ideal models', conveying an association with the mother-country.

The detailed lay-out of such a factory is known through a plan which was made around 1720 of the Danish trading centre of Danmarksnagore in Bengal, which had eventually to be surrendered after repeated attacks by its militant neighbours.[8] The plan is similar to the Dutch centre in Surat. It has a rectangular shape with a garden at the far end. Avenues of trees frame an open square and a fish-pond. Through the gate, which is flanked by warehouses, guard-houses and dwellings for the small garrison, we reach a stone-paved path leading straight to the main building. The central section of the latter has two storeys. The staircase up to the 'hall' lies at the back of the house. To the

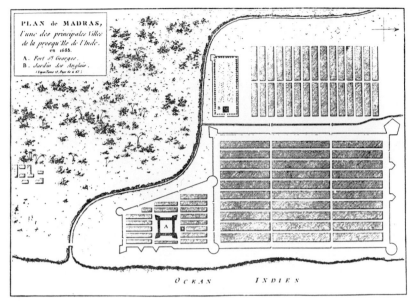

3a. Madras in 1688.

right there is the 'office' and to the left the warehouse, with small rooms for the employees in the gables, and a kitchen wing. The drawing is very simple and only shows the plan and distribution. However, in front of the office an arcade is suggested. The small bastion in the corner of the garden is the only item of fortification.

The British established a small trading station on the Coromandel Coast in 1639. Five years later, a fort was erected and the following year, 1645, British ownership of the territory was confirmed by the last Rajah of Vijayanagar. In a charter dated 30 December, 1687, the place is constituted as 'the town of Fort St. George and City of Madrassapatam'.[9] This became the first British municipality in India and was later called Madras.

We may presume that in the 1680's, the town looked approximately as it is presented on a map in Langlès' *Monuments anciens . . . de l'Hindoustan*.[10] The eastern boundary is determined by the coastline on the Gulf of Bengal, and to the west and south the town is enclosed by the river Cooum. The fort is situated in the bend of the river; it has a square plan and triangular corner bastions and is surrounded by a number of regular rectangular quarters. All these structures are in turn enclosed by a wall which forms a triangle with the apex abruptly cut off. The wall is fortified most strongly towards the sea. Towards the land and the north it has two gateways. This must be the town of Fort St. George, as mentioned in the charter. Attached to the wall on the north lies the city of Madrassapatam which is also enclosed by fortified walls and divided into rectangular quarters. This part of the town was later called 'Black Town' and here the Indians lived.[11] West of a narrow canal which has been drawn from the river lies a new block with rectangular quarters, probably an 'extension area', and an English garden.

43

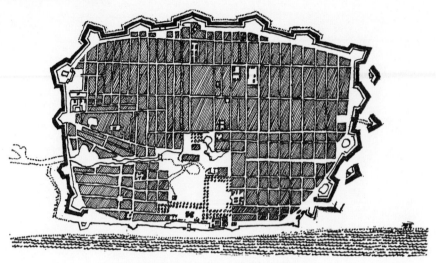

3b. Pondicherry in 1778. (1 : 16000)

The sketch is only a skeleton drawing. The streets in Black Town probably never formed such a geometrical pattern as shown here. However, the main features of the plan can still be discerned in the modern town of Madras.[12]

On account of its schematic character, the town plan of Madras gives a clear picture of the division into white and black, European and Indian. We can study the plan together with an almost contemporary map of Pondicherry,[13] the main French property on the Coromandel Coast, which was founded in 1674. Pondicherry is also built up along the coastline. Here the fortification system is far more complicated and *ideal* than in Madras. Radial streets connect the bastions of the fort with a five-sided space in the centre. The whole lay-out strongly recalls a French town like Rocroi, which had been planned after an Italian model, but which was remodelled by Vauban.[14]

Around the citadel of the fort the European quarters are grouped, with straight streets and open squares. Here we find the Capuchin church and monastery. To the west the Jesuits have their church, together with other buildings and a garden, and around the 'foreign missionaries' premises we can see their mission field, Black Town, where the division into quarters also indicates a separation into occupational groups. Thus the carpenters live along the street which is marked 'NNNN' on the plan. Also in this case, a canal divides the Indian part of the town from the European. Nearest to the canal there are a number of ponds, probably for the extraction of salt, as well as a 'pagoda' as a religious alternative to the mission church. South of the river and west of the fortified boundary of Black Town, two Pariah villages have been indicated. Near one of them, isolated from all other houses, as is also the case in Madras, lies the garden of the Company.[15]

Pondicherry went through an important period of development during the years 1721–35 when Lenoir was governor. But already prior to this, the town would seem to have been thoroughly altered. The individual parts of the town have, at least on the map, been united to form an urban whole within the wide *enceinte*.[16] The earlier town had been added to, and was changed into an irregular oval through the incorporation of the open fields on the southern bank of the river. Thus the river now runs *through* the town, and across the entire town plan lie two roads which cross each other communicating with the surrounding country to the west, south and north and with the sea through a sea-gate to the east.

The improvements credited to Lenoir include — amongst other things — the planting of avenues of trees along the straight roads, and a social policy which was surprisingly daring and modern, but which was hardly followed up. He attempted to mitigate the system of privileges of the Hindus by allowing everybody to go beyond the boundaries determined by the caste: 'Le Roi, disait-il, ne veut faire aucune distinction entre ses sujets, quellesque soient leurs croyance, leur race, leur richesse ou leur pauvreté; par conséquent un chacun peut, à cheval ou à palanquin, emprunter pour rentrer chez lui les nouvelles voies percées.'[17]

In the north, Bourreau-Deslandes had founded the Bengal factory of France, Chander-nagore, in 1690. In Langlès' *Monuments Anciens . . . de l'Hindoustan* we find an engrav-ing which is said to show the factory as it looked in 1656.[18] The year must be wrong, but it is feasible that the plan for the factory was prepared in advance in France and not, as was usual, by military engineers on the spot. The engraving shows a very well worked out composition which differs in its architecture from what we have seen so far. The rectangular plan measures about 229 × 153 yards and a high wall encloses the whole. Through a monumental portal we reach a stone-paved path leading straight to the main building which consists of two storeys and has a gable on the long side, to emphasize the centre. Two warehouses form detached wings and in connection with the main building and the wall there is a chapel, several out-offices and dwellings for the servants. There is even a water reservoir, in the form of a tank, within the enclosure. The whole construc-tion is of almost military heaviness. The arcades are rusticated and have Tuscan columns in front. In the *Porte principale* these are replaced by gun-barrels. The garden at the back is designed in strict parterres.[19]

The main part of this project would seem to have actually been realized. A plan, dated 1722, also showing a view of the factory, corresponds with the proposed con-struction even in details.[20] Here we can see rows of trees planted to the north and between the factory and the river to the east.

Chandernagore was completely destroyed by the British in December 1758. Only a few houses were spared in which the widows of the fallen soldiers were allowed to live. According to the Treaty of Paris, which concluded the Seven Years' War, the French were not allowed to construct any fortifications nor to keep any garrisons there.[21]

Some miles south of Chandernagore, farther down the Hooghly, the British founded a trading centre at the end of the 17th century which in the course of time was to grow and finally constitute the centre of the British Empire in India. I refer to Calcutta which

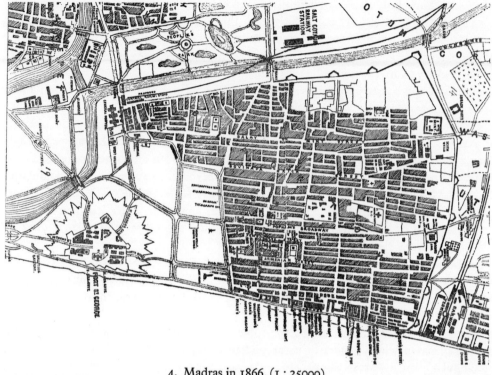

4. Madras in 1866. (1 : 25000)

originally consisted of three Indian villages let to the British by Azim-us-Shan, grandson of the Emperor Aurangzeb.

The beginning was very humble. In August 1690, the British made a list of all the buildings which would be necessary for opening trade in Bengal. The list included a warehouse, a room to sort cloth in, a house for the agent, the secretary and the servants of the Company. All these separate small houses were erected with clay walls and straw thatched roofs and can best be regarded as temporary buildings, used until the colonists obtained the ground on which they built a factory.[22]

A political incident soon hastened development. In 1696, war broke out between the Indian principalities west of the Hooghly and the Mughal Empire. In this connection the British were permitted to protect their trading centre with fortifications. In Kalikata, one of the three villages, John Goldsborough founded the first Fort William. It was planned near the bank of the river and contained the residence of the Governor as well as dwellings for the factors and the writers, as related by Alexander Hamilton early in the 18th century.[23] The fort looked approximately the same as Fort St. George, Madras.

The actual factory building had two storeys, a long, low house with projecting wings and a colonnade towards the sea-gate.[24]

Towards the middle of the 18th century, the town extended beyond the enclosure.

Private individuals, merchants and officers acquired residences which were wedged into the hitherto entirely Indian quarters. In the course of time this led to the formation of an irregular ring of European houses beside the fort and around the park and the Large Tank (the area around the present Dalhousie Square). Alexander Hamilton continued: '... everyone taking in what Ground best pleased them for Gardening, so that in most Houses you must pass through a Garden into the House.'[25] The type of building indicates that the people living there were more prepared for trade and peaceful living than for defence. This attitude soon proved to be over-optimistic. At a far too early stage the protective position behind the walls and bastions had been abandoned. When Siraj-ud-daulah attacked the town in 1756 it had to surrender after a short siege.[26]

ii The Growing Towns: Tranquebar

The Danish enclave, Tranquebar, was founded about the same time as the first factories at Surat.[1] On 19 November, 1620, the Naik of Tanjore transferred a small part of his land to the Danish East India Company for a yearly tribute and gave them permission to erect a fort there.[2] The place was a fishing village with the Tamil name of Tarangambadi and was situated on the delta of the Cauweri river on the Coromandel Coast. The position, more exactly, was 10° 51′ N. A Danish soldier, Mouritz Christensen, described the climatic conditions to which he and his fellow countrymen were unaccustomed:

June: very sharp and burning heat, so strong that the wind drives the sand. It is best to sit in the earth cellars; nowhere else is there a spot where one is not made faint and consumed by the sun and the heat of the air. The sand flies strongly and penetrates into the stone houses. Now is the expensive season for water, which we drink instead of beer.'[3]

The first thing the Danes erected on the site was a fort whose strong walls gave protection against both the heat of the sun and other enemies. It was a simple structure with four corner bastions. The architect is unknown, although the name of Ove Gedde, who led the expedition, has been suggested. All the buildings of the colony were placed inside the walls and built by Indian workmen under Danish supervision. These included the church, a large 'palace' used as the house of the Commander and also as court-room, council chamber and office. There was also a large kitchen building and a well.[4] The small garrison lived by the south and west walls.

In these premises we find the patterns recognizable from other quarters: a rudimentary town crowded into a small area and enclosed by strong walls. The place was called from the start not 'Tranquebar', which is a distortion of its Tamil name, but simply 'Dansborg', after the fort itself.[5]

The situation changed in the middle of the 17th century. When the Naik of Tanjore did not receive the agreed tribute for several years, he started a war against the Danes and besieged their area. The Danes then began to construct a polygon of embattlements and a moat round a large area north and west of Dansborg.[6] The outlines thus effected, which from then on marked the boundaries of the town of Tranquebar, are reproduced

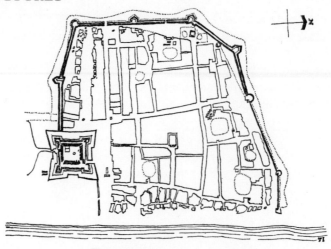

5. Tranquebar in 1671. (1 : 10000)

for probably the first time on a map dated 1671.[7] This map shows a series of partly planned or provisionally built wall sections which are joined by circular and triangular bastions. The wall goes as far as the west moat of the citadel and is continued, so to speak, on the other side by a section which goes right down to the shore. The result is complete protection on the land side. There are gates at the south-east, towards the water and on the west towards the land.

In planning the area inside the walls, consideration was paid to the already existing buildings. All the Hindu temples and the large mosque were thus allowed to remain and to continue to function as religious centres, while the area around them was changed. A number of straight roads were made. The most important were Kongens gade (King Street), which led from the largest gate on the side facing inland to the parade ground in front of the fort, and Dronningens gade (Queen Street), which bisects the former and divides the town in a north–south direction.

Thus the Indian buildings were incorporated in a European road system. Tranquebar acquired the appearance of a Danish provincial town, which in fact it was, although it was an outpost 70° east of its Scandinavian counterparts. It is true that the plan was not so finely set out as in Fredericia or Christianstad, as it was necessary to take into account existing buildings, but generally speaking, Tranquebar belongs to the Dutch-inspired fortified towns founded by Christian IV of Denmark.[8]

The map of 1671, which I am still following in my description, shows that the main part of the Danish colonists at that time were still living in the fort. Not far from its walls, however, we find a couple of godowns, or warehouses, and a customs-house; farther inside the town, near the mosque, lies the Admiral's house and garden, and on King Street a private house inhabited by Eskil Andersson Kongsbakke, formerly Commander and promoter of the fortifications.

When Eskil Andersson laid out his *enceinte*, there were only a few Danes in Tranque-

48

bar, and in 1669 he could report that he was quite alone.[9] Although reinforcements arrived and the area was extended in 1670 with a hinterland consisting of the villages of Poreyar, Tillaly and Erkutanchery, the trading centre grew rather slowly during the following decades.[10] Work on the *enceinte* continued; parts which had been erected earlier as a palisade of palm trunks were replaced by stone. Thus on 1 January, 1696, three hundred and fifty-nine day labourers and fifty-six water-buffaloes were working on behalf of the Company.[11] Before the turn of the century it would seem that the system of fortifications was completed. In 1704, however, the ravelin in front of the portal on the land side was added.[12]

Some Indians moved into the town, but there was no spectacular architectural progress. In a census taken in 1702 there proved to be a total of 381 stone houses, but more than double that number of clay houses, straw houses and 'huts'.[13]

The most important events at the beginning of the 18th century were the erection of two churches, which came to occupy a prominent place in the town centre. The first, which was provided for the Danish members of the colony and thus replaced the old church in the fort, was erected at the corner of the parade ground with its long side on King Street. The structure is simple; it consists only of a large hall for services. But the façade is brightened by pilasters and quoins. The upper part of the building — a parapet with pinnacles — and the roof show purely Indian features. The roof is vaulted in the same way as the Hindu temples in the town; its section looks like a pointed arch. This is undoubtedly a strange borrowing, when one thinks of the old symbolism of church building, where the vault represents the heavens, but the reason is, of course, purely practical: the Indian craftsmen were allowed to use the vaulting technique to which they were accustomed.[14] The square tower has an original top. Above a frieze and a parapet corresponding to those of the nave rise a vault and a small spire decorated with hanging festoons.

'Zion's Church' was consecrated in 1701;[15] sixteen years later a mission church was erected on the opposite side of King Street, a little farther down towards the gate leading inland. It was called 'New Jerusalem'.

The mission in Tranquebar started in the summer of 1706, when Bartolomeus Ziegenbalg and Heinrich Plütschau landed on the shore near the fort. They had come direct from Copenhagen, where they had been ordained as missionaries, but they actually came originally from Halle, and they therefore founded the German–Halle Mission in South India.[16] Merely a year after their arrival they were able to open their first small church which was called 'Jerusalem' and which lay near the shore. In spite of set-backs of various kinds, their congregation grew, and it was mainly to get more space that the 'New Jerusalem' was built ten years later. Naturally this transfer from modest surroundings to the street which in future was to be the finest in Tranquebar was also a sign of progress.

Ziegenbalg and Gründler, a German missionary colleague, have related how the new church was built. The site they had been allotted was best suited to a central church, and the plan was therefore made like a Greek cross. First Lieutenant Claus Krøckel, who is said to have designed some buildings before, was employed as architect. The bricks were made on the site, and so was the lime for which shells from the shore were used. Floor flagstones were fetched from the Dutch town of Sadraspatnam and other stone from St. Thomas Mount, a little outside Madras.[17]

The result was a simple exterior with deep window-splays; the altar was placed at the east end. The façade was enlivened by clusters of pilasters forming projections in the horizontal mouldings. Over each window was a small pediment and on each arm of the cross a large pediment was outlined with alternating acroteria and S-shaped volutes. The general impression, which is mainly produced by the high gable sections (the top angles are comparatively small) and the effect of the pilasters, which are of a strange hybrid form, could possibly be characterized as Euro-Indian Baroque.

The congregation which held its services in the 'New Jerusalem' was recruited from both caste-Hindus and untouchables. The cross shape of the building was used to divide these classes;[18] they were placed in different arms of the cross, a paradoxical way of trying to bridge traditional differences!

Strangely enough, the newly erected churches had little place on a perspective map drawn in 1773 by First Lieutenant Gregers Daa Trellund.[19] In other details also one must question the exactness of his reproduction. Nevertheless, the map gives us a survey of the town and shows the main features of the changes which had taken place in the first decades of the 18th century. The fortifications are complete; the side towards the sea has been fortified in addition with a low enclosure and bastions. The fort protects the town.[20] The parade ground, part of Queen Street and the road along the wall on the land side are planted with shady trees. The cemetery and the Admiral's garden are completely green areas, and near the latter stands the mosque. The street system seems to be planned in a spacious and rational way. All the buildings are inside the walls except for a few godowns which were erected on the so-called 'Holmen' (small island) outside the south-east bastion of the fort.

We know from a report that in about 1730, Tranquebar had 476 stone houses and 172 huts with straw roofs. Thus the stability of the town had increased since the census of 1702.[21] On Gregers Daa's map all the houses — with four exceptions — are shown as having tiled pitched roofs. The houses are simply designed and arranged in small groups. They look as if they had been arranged by a child who had only one kind of brick to build with. The majority of the houses are very small. One building stands out from the others — the Commander's two-storey house which lies at right-angles to Prince Jørgen's Street. In front of it a small square has been formed, Nytorvet (New Square), actually a widening of Queen Street where the latter joins the parade ground. The Commander's house has a dormer over the entrance and there is a construction that looks like a veranda on the ground floor. This is, however, doubtful. As stated, the drawing has been done naively; the vertical elements represented as straight shafts between dice-shaped pedestals and capitals may not necessarily be detached, but may lie against the

50

walls as pilasters. Thus it is difficult to decide whether the arrangement is decorative or
if it actually functions as a shade from the sun. The Commander's house is still standing,
although it has been altered. Remains of cornices, quoins and other details suggest an
original exterior which does not really agree with the picture given by the map.

Some of the other houses also show signs of a pronounced articulation of the walls;
this is the case, for example, with the four buildings I mentioned above as 'exceptions'.
These have flat roofs and high pilasters. One of them is the Admiral's large
house.

The question of the functional significance of the various elements is of great importance for the following investigation. This is because it shows how the building is adapted
to the climate. As we shall see, Tranquebar was changed into a *neo-Classical* town during
the 18th century. The block-shaped houses with their pitched roofs were rebuilt or
replaced by structures that functioned better in the foreign environment. Thus the type
of construction which dominated the townscape on Gregers Daa's map was abandoned.
But the change did not take place immediately. Prior to it there was a period which was
more undefined, both from the architectural and commercial point of view. Nevertheless,
the start seems very decided and promising.

In the beginning of the 1730's an attempt was made in Denmark to improve the
economy of the country.[22] During past decades Denmark had suffered greatly from the
long Nordic War and the general depression which followed it. The founding of the
Danish Asiatic Company was one of the measures taken; the charter of the old Company
had expired in 1729. In April 1732, the newly formed company, which was to carry on
trade both in China and India, finally received a royal charter stating its trading privileges.
This it was to possess for more than forty years.[23]

In Copenhagen the new Company made an impressive start, both architecturally and
artistically. In 1739 their premises on Strandgade at Christianshavn were erected — a
baroque building with the character of a *palazzo*. The central part was crowned with a
segmental pediment where Neptune and Mercury flanked a globe; the gods of Trade
and the Sea would together guarantee that the valuable cargoes from the East came home
safely and were sold at a good profit. The architect was Philip de Lange.[24]

Behind this building, in the quarter near the harbour, another of Denmark's well-
known architects, Nicolai Eigtved, erected a four-storey warehouse with a row of
dormers along the façade facing the dock.[25] Here those imports were stored for which
no customs duty was required.

The Company's most expensive artistic project was not, however, intended for its
own premises, but to honour its royal patron, King Frederik V. Homage was paid to the
King in the form of a monument, an equestrian statue made by the Frenchman Saly
and erected in Frederiks-staden, that is, the part of Copenhagen which was changed in
the middle of the 18th century into a homogeneous rococo district. The equestrian statue
was placed at the focal point in the centre of the octagonal square called Amalieplads,

which was in general the creation of Eigtved. The base of the statue was set up there in 1760.[26]

We shall now see what was happening at the same time in India. According to the royal charter of 1732, the fort of Dansborg and Tranquebar — that is to say, the town shown on Gregers Daa's map — was handed over to the Danish Asiatic Company.[27] Thus the Company also took over responsibility for the buildings. This task was tackled quite differently from the way in which the buildings in Copenhagen were approached.

One is struck by the contrast, when comparing the Asiatic Company's artistic policy in Denmark with the policy they simultaneously pursued in India. There is no comparison whatsoever between what was built at home and what was built in the colony. The extravagant gesture towards the mighty ones in the capital seems to have created a vacuum in Tranquebar. Here there were no famous architects at work. Nor were designs sent out from Copenhagen to be used as models, a course of action which would have been possible. The unsophisticated engineers who built in India had to rely on their own constructions and the buildings they had to erect were very simple. They worked, so to speak, in the dark, and in the face of circumstances which limited their building activity to an absolute minimum.[28]

One of the reasons for this was that trade with China was more profitable for the Company at that time. After all, Tranquebar was only a small trading post; the surrounding area was unimportant and the Governor's economic resources limited. There was no basis for a policy of the type, for example, carried out by Dupleix in neighbouring Pondicherry.[29]

When one studies the building work in Tranquebar in the middle of the 18th century, one realizes how modest conditions were. To begin with, the fortifications were falling down; there were, in fact, no funds for maintaining them.[30] The dilapidation was obvious even when the new Company took over responsibility. In 1739 the palisade towards the sea was completely destroyed and the town lay exposed in that direction. The condition of the fort was bad. In 1747 the Town Council finally requested that an engineer should be sent out to estimate the extent and cost of fundamental repairs. An engineer actually arrived in 1749, Lieutenant Kyhn, who, after his examination demanded 10,000–11,000 rixdollars for the reconstruction. The money eventually arrived, and in 1755 the fort was repaired. The restoration of the fortifications on the side facing the sea presented a special problem. Here the large breakers destroyed everything that was built. Kyhn tried to keep them back with pilework and heavy foundations, but in vain. The sea ate its way farther and farther in and broke up the bastions.[31]

The civil buildings scarcely fared better. To start with, the Company had done away with a number of properties, but even those remaining could not be kept in good condition. The hospital began to collapse and was demolished in 1735. The year before, the Admiral's house was in a similarly dilapidated state; that also was allowed to fall into decay. A commission which had been sent out, reported in 1749 that the warehouses were being destroyed by rats, termites and damp.[32] Among the few architectural drawings left from Tranquebar there is one for a warehouse made in March 1755 by C. A. von Passow, who had come out as assistant and successor to Kyhn.[33] The warehouse, in Queen Street, consisted of several one-storey buildings arranged round a rectangular courtyard. There was an entrance door from the street. All the buildings had pitched roofs, except one which was flat, and not tiled like the others. The front of one consisted of a series of arcades; otherwise the exterior was articulated with broad mouldings which ran along the base of the roof and formed cornices over doors and windows. This scale drawing was probably made in connection with changes in the warehouses; as already mentioned, these were badly in need of repair.

As regards contemporary private buildings, we can do best by considering the actions of the Protestant mission. In 1740, a large school building was erected on Admiral's Street; the main building is strongly reminiscent of the New Jerusalem Church, the same kind of Euro-Indian baroque being used. But here small ogee arches have been introduced over the windows.[34] The New Jerusalem was also a prototype for a church in Poreyar, the largest village in the Danish area. It was built between 1743 and 1746 in the shape of a cross with triangular gables crowned with volutes.[35]

Among the rural districts, we also hear of Tillaly, where the Company had a property. This was used for resting on the way home from the official visit to the Prince of Tanjore in 1753.[36]

The area of Tranquebar was extended in 1739 to include the villages of Catechery and Anacoil.[37] The extension which took place in 1755 in Bengal, when Serampore and Akna were bought from the Nawab of Murshidabad, was of more importance. The project was directed from Tranquebar.[38] So was the bold attempt to conquer new territory for Denmark through colonizing an island group in the Bay of Bengal. In 1755 an expedition to the Nicobar Islands was fitted out. An engineer, Tanck, led the undertaking, and building materials were shipped as part of the expedition. The attempt was not successful, but for decades the Nicobar Islands were to figure as a Land of Promise for the Danes who dreamed of progress in the colonies.[39]

In 1772 the charter of the Asiatic Company expired; it was prolonged for twenty years, but after only a couple of years there was a reorganization that changed the basis of its activity. The Crown took over its real estate in 1777. After 1772 trade was also open to private enterprise.[40]

Trade and economic activity were extremely good. Among other things the Danes could take advantage of their neutrality in various war situations. Trade with India entered on the phase called 'Den Florissante' (the prosperous) which, on the whole, lasted until 1807, when the position of Denmark in European politics changed as a result of Napoleon's blockade of England.[41] This was a crippling blow to connections with Asia.

The prosperous period, the decades between 1777 and 1807, are therefore the most active and interesting for the present investigation. During this period Tranquebar was transformed into a neo-Classical town.

In connection with the Crown taking over the Company's possessions in India, a detailed list of buildings and other property was made.[42] In it Tranquebar occupies a considerable space, but mainly owing to the large number of names of all the small villages belonging to the area, not because the town as such was regarded as specially valuable.

The buildings within the town walls were few in number: the fort, the Admiral's house, the powder-magazine, the royal bazaars and several stores, one of which was newly erected. The houses in the Indian villages were very small; a *larger* house is mentioned, for instance, as being $16 \times 4 \times 5$ ft in size and a smaller one $6 \times 5\frac{1}{2} \times 5$ ft. In Tillaly is the governor's old country residence called 'Sorgenfri' (Carefree); it was assessed at only one-tenth of the value of the newly erected storehouse in the town.

Among the items we note especially that there is no official building for the Governor. This is because, although there *was* a building, it was still private property belonging to Governor Brown, who in turn had taken it over from Edward Stevenson, a merchant of Tranquebar. In the purchase-deed the property is described as 'a dwelling House with several Godowns, Offices & Garden & other Grounds . . . being situated opposit to the Citadel of Tranquebar, Bounded by Mr. Halkier's House to the West & a Pagoda to the East.'[43] This property, which will be dealt with more in detail later, was bought in 1784 and replaced the governor's old apartments in the citadel.

The buildings which the Crown took over were naturally only a fraction of those in the town. Together with these, the churches, mission buildings and schools and a number of private merchants' houses formed the material which the 'prosperous' period inherited from the preceding one. The same was the case with the town plan, which was to be kept to a considerable degree unchanged. The contour line of the built-up area was still based on the *enceinte* and the street system as originally laid out. In the year 1800 Tranquebar looked practically the same as in 1700, if one chose a sufficiently commanding view.

We shall soon make an analysis of the changes, but first it may be relevant to touch briefly upon the town's *social* structure. A census roll, drawn up in 1790, gives a good idea of conditions.[44] In that year the population of the town totalled 3,722. Near the parade ground lived the governor; in King Street lived two missionaries, a principal assistant secretary, a major etc., and in New Street likewise a few Danes, but in both streets lived also Indians and 'Portuguese', i.e., Eurasians. Religion differed as much as colour of skin; the inhabitants were Catholic, Protestant or Reformed Church, but in all cases *Christian*. The same is the case with those who lived in South Wall Street, Dübens Street, Cat's Lane, Prince Jørgen Street, Prince Christian Street and parts of Queen Street and Admiral's Street. All these streets lie near each other; therefore a collection of Christian quarters was formed in the south-west part of the town, where the churches also were situated. A division was made on religious grounds; race seems to have been less important.[45]

The Moslems of the town also lived near their religious centre; most of them lived in the streets round the mosque. Such an arrangement seems to be quite logical, and also holds good for the Hindu (and far the greater) part of the population. But here the places of worship were considerably more numerous and the pattern more ramified. Several castes were represented in Tranquebar. In Brahmin Street lived a number of Brahmins, all of whom were priests; otherwise there was a certain mixture: members of Chelpa, Wellala and Edien, for example, lived together with an occasional Christian from the mission in Queen Street (after No. 99). The population was also mixed as regards occupations; there lived, for example, in Pyntador Street, a few *pyntador*, i.e., craftsmen who put the patterns on the white cotton material, which formed an important part of the goods exported to Europe.[46] In an instruction issued in November 1777, there was promulgated in Point 4 a 'mild' policy to encourage artists and craftsmen from other places to move to Tranquebar; Point 21 in the same regulations says that craftsmen should be given land to build a house, 'so that there should be no deserted place or unused sites'.[47]

The changes which occurred in Tranquebar during the 'prosperous' period mainly affected the Christian or European part of the town. Owing to the trade boom, conditions were created which made it possible for private merchants to build and live with a certain splendour, and this was also the reason for the construction of the state buildings. The central figure in this connection was the Norwegian, Peter Anker. He came out as governor in 1788, to remain until 1806, and thus was in control of the colony during the greater part of the period dealt with here.

Owing to his background, Anker also had possibilities of influencing development. He had studied in England and France; in 1773 he became Danish Consul in Hull and ten years later was appointed Consul General in London.[48] In this position he made contacts which were to be of importance to him in his post as governor. At that time the British were laying the foundations of their empire in India; their dominion was growing. In 1790 they took over the administration of Tanjore and thus became the Danes' nearest neighbour.[49] Anker's correspondence with the ruling powers in Fort St. George shows that he was anxious to maintain good relations with his neighbours, which is very natural owing to the relative political strength of the two countries, but there were also personal reasons. Among other things, during his time in England Anker had made the acquaintance of Cornwallis.[50]

After his arrival in India, Anker's first contribution to architecture was also in an English style. In October 1788, work was started on converting the old country residence in Tillaly into an official recreational house for the Governor. Much building material was used, and after the changes the residence was 'as if newly erected'.[51] We know its appearance from a drawing by Anker himself; in addition to his other qualities he was a good draughtsman, with a special talent for architecture, a gift which proved to be of importance.[52]

In Tranquebar itself, the fort and the fortifications had been repaired in the middle of the 1780's. In 1789, the whole of the dilapidated barracks in Prince Christian Street were rebuilt. This work was led by an engineer, Braun, who was replaced in 1791 by Mattias Mühldorff, an engineer officer on whom Anker came greatly to rely.[53]

THE STRUCTURES

In 1791, Mühldorff had erected a gate for his own house between King Street and New Street.[54] On the orders of Anker he built a similar gate, but considerably larger, at the main entrance to the town on the west. It is dated 1792, according to the royal monogram in the pediment, but the accounts show that its construction was started the year before, and a drawing that has been preserved — by Anker or Mühldorff — is also dated 1791.[55] The gate was a heavy structure. The Danes had clearly taken as model Bélidor's well-known *La Science des Ingénieurs*, two copies of which were in Mühldorff's small library.[56] In connection with the entrance gate were also built two tollbooths. Here the important inland tax on goods brought into the town was collected. When all this was completed, Tranquebar had an impressive entrance gate similar to that in nearby Pondicherry, where the engineer La Lustière had erected a couple of large gateways in 1788 (also after models from Bélidor).[57]

At that time the main entrance to the citadel towards the parade ground was adorned with a large gate. Once again a heavy and somewhat antiquated design was used: Tuscan columns in couples support a high pediment. This is baroque Classicism of a kind that had been in fashion in Denmark during the 1730's, when Lauritz de Thurah built his portal for the Archbishop's Palace at Roskilde.[58] Nevertheless, this late addition to Dansborg does not seem to be out of place. It shows up excellently against the solid walls of the fort.

On the other side of the parade ground opposite the fort lay Anker's own house which was bought by the State in 1784.[59] We know how this building looked at the beginning of the 1780's, during the time of Brown, through a ground-plan and façade sketch which was probably made in connection with the purchase.[60] The building covers a considerable area; it consists of only *one* storey, and thus the rooms are joined together like dominoes. The façade towards the parade ground actually gives no clue of this. It shows only a veranda and behind that a door opening and three pairs of windows.

The space behind the façade consists of three large units — the residence of the European family; dwellings and working rooms for the servants; a large department for cattle, cowsheds and stables, grooms, coachmen and so on. In the centre of each section is a courtyard. There is also a large garden laid out with parterres. The central path in the garden, which is formed as a pergola, runs in the same direction as the axis of the house and thus indicates the 'backbone' of the actual residence of the governor. The other premises lie to the right (east) of this, and they are entered from Calnein and Wexler Streets. With its system of courtyards and its spacious grouping of the various parts, the residence recalls a South Indian, Hindu house.

Anker converted the façade of the governor's building facing towards the parade ground. Among his drawings is a picture of Government House which is quite different from the one we have just studied.[61] It shows the structure with a *double* veranda in the centre curving outwards in a semicircle and with steps on each side. The large door is shown open and through it can be caught a glimpse of the garden and further architectural details. The drawing is dated 1793; it must be regarded as a plan for the changes which were made in May of the following year. The Engineer's accounts for that month

56

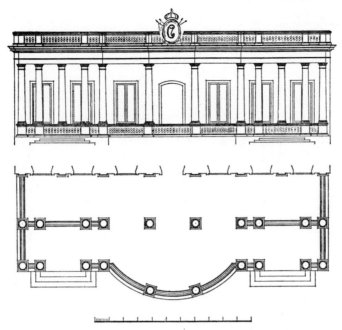

6a. Houses in Tranquebar: Government House. (scale of metres)

include much material, among other things over 14,000 bricks and almost 4,000 'column stones' which were used for making 'a new veranda for the General's house'.[62]

Undeniably the appearance of the house was improved by the changes. The large number of stones were bonded together to form high Tuscan columns which support a massive entablature and a balustrade on top. In the centre of the latter Anker placed Christian VII's crowned monogram. Parts of the building behind the façade were reconstructed during the following years, and a collection of magnificent fittings and furniture was acquired for the governor's residence and bought by the State when Anker was relieved of his office in 1806.[63] The Danish governor could in this way reside on about the same level as the governors in the other European settlements.

I have now indicated three important features in the European part of Tranquebar where architecture took a more representational direction during the first part of Peter Anker's governorship, probably by his direct intervention. These changes are symptomatic of the period that followed: more and more buildings had their appearance improved in the same way as Government House. We read in the accounts of the use of many column stones and balusters.

The change gives a new uniformity to the European quarters. The façades which face the parade ground are now dominated by verandas and straight rooflines crowned with balusters. In King Street, which became the main thoroughfare leading from the gateway on the land side and forming a connecting link between the gate, Government House and the citadel, porticos project from almost every house and together form a row of light

57

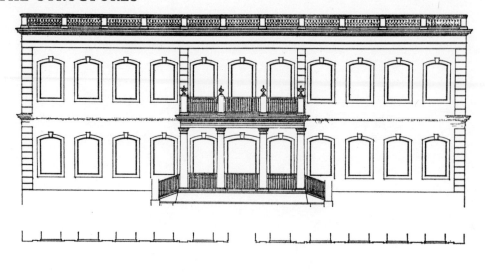

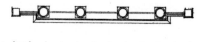

6b. Houses in Tranquebar: 'Old Hospital', in Kongens gade (King Street).
(scale of metres)

colonnades.[64] In the wider New Street an avenue of trees has been planted that shades the entrances to the houses. On the south side of this street a number of large villas were built by foreign merchants who availed themselves of Tranquebar's neutral position.[65] After the conquest of Pondicherry by the British in 1793, this was the only accessible port on the Coromandel Coast.

The changes were made for *climatic* reasons. The porticos and verandas were added to function in the same way as the cloth cover did which the soldiers of the colony had worn from 1786 over the crown of their hats 'to break the sun's rays'.[66] And the fenced-in flat roofs behind the balustrades were splendid places for walking towards sunset, when it was cool and the breeze from the sea could be enjoyed. On several roofs a cube-shaped room was built which could be used as a bedroom or as a belvedere.[67]

However, the metamorphosis also followed the laws of style; *Baroque changed into neo-Classicism.* This effect was often produced very simply. We shall consider some individual examples in order to see both the actual change and the result.

The houses we shall examine more closely are in King Street. We know the houses through measurements and detailed reconstructions made by the Danish draughtsmen and architect, Ib Andersen, in 1948–49.[68]

One of the houses is the so-called 'Old Hospital' or 'Governor Hansen's house' (Hansen was Tranquebar's last governor, from 1841–45). It lies on the north side of the street, beyond Zion's Church and the 'Elders' House', coming from the parade ground.

58

The general impression is dominated by the two rows of windows running in uninterrupted horizontal lines along the façade. Like the doors, the windows are framed by flat mouldings, and in the upper members the key-stones have been indicated. As in the case of Zion's Church, the façade is enlivened by quoins. Thus the centre part of the building is given an effect of projection, but is actually in line with the wall.

The emphasis on the centre part is considerably strengthened by the portico which was added in 1800. This really formed a *plastic* addition, a move towards the street which catches the eye and changes the whole façade. It was given the same width as the centre part, and the verticality of its outer columns is continued, so to speak, by the quoins in the upper storey. The columns rise from a balcony at first floor level. They are Tuscan, but have an entablature of almost Corinthian character.[69] The mouldings include a fine dentil cornice which may originally have continued on either side of the façade to mark the dividing line between the two storeys. The upper storey has been finished with a prominent moulding, from which rises a balustrade. Thus again a horizontal effect, but now with the accent on dividing lines and contours: neo-Classicism instead of Baroque.[70]

The 'Convent', which lies nearly opposite the Old Hospital, has in general the same characteristics. The wall surfaces, which have windows with segmental tops, are framed by rustic chains at the corners and by powerful cornices. A colonnade runs along the entire lower storey on the most westerly part of the house. The long eastern part of the building has a small portico above the steps and is so low that the supports, which were placed on pedestals, have almost the character of colonnettes. Above the roofline on both these façades rises the high, square John's Tower, called after a missionary who was active in Tranquebar in Anker's time.[71]

If we pass from the whole to details, we again find a number of baroque features, but the neo-Classical character predominates. The Tea Club, a short distance from the Convent down towards the gateway on the land side, has a triglyph frieze which corresponds to the simple Doric order of the columns, but there is also a dentil in the entablature which breaks the system and the pilasters in the upper storey carry an entablature with corresponding projections. On the other hand, the house opposite on the north side of the street has had a beautiful meander pattern in the frieze and above this an elegant row of projecting gargoyles. This fine decoration has now vanished, as many other ornaments which were difficult to maintain must have done.

In this connection we may recall the thorough reconstruction by Ib Andersen of 'Mr. Jørgensen's House' at the corner of King Street and Queen Street.[72] The long veranda towards the parade ground has been given capitals adorned with acanthus leaves corresponding to the richly carved octagonal bases of the columns, but the order does not in general show any decoration; the cornice and balustrade appear to be of the same type as on the other houses. Thus it is easy to suppose that many of the structures had richly formed features, and that these have been destroyed either by monsoon rains or ignorant hands. The urns which adorned the roof lines of the buildings undoubtedly formed an element which has disappeared. Such urns were, for example, on the

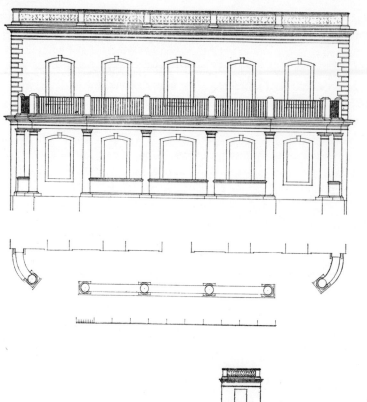

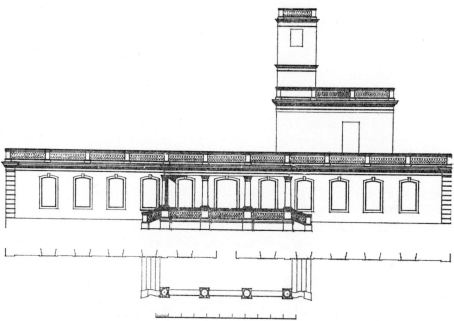

7a and b. Houses in Tranquebar: a, The Convent in Kongens gade (King Street), western part; b, The Convent, eastern part. (scales of metres)

gateway of the fort and on the gateway which was erected in 1802 beside Mr. Jørgensen's House but which stands on another level and obviously does not belong to it. The latter is, however, in keeping with the other gates in Tranquebar, having coupled pilasters which support a Doric entablature. The composition of the design is complicated and baroque in character; even the urns may be regarded as a baroque element.[73]

These examples of elements and deviations in style must suffice. The final effect was not determined by details. The baroque elements came also to play a part in a new connection. As we have seen, they were integrated in the façades, were disguised and incorporated in a whole which was impressive owing to its *bold features*, its outlines and its colour effect in yellow and white. The buildings must also be regarded as parts of a larger unit: a flexible street system starting inside the large gateway on the land side and stretching to the parade ground, where the scene is enormously widened and where the roar of the breakers may be heard.

The formation of Tranquebar's main street may appear to be quite natural if the climatic and stylistic conditions are considered. One gets the impression that it could not have been conceived in any other way. It is therefore interesting to compare this town centre with a contemporary Danish one in another part of the world: the town of Christiansted on the island of St. Croix in the Caribbean. Instead of colonnades there are long arcades forming shady passages along streets and squares.[74] One feels almost transported to Weinbrenner's Karlsruhe. Here it is sufficient to emphasize the difference; we know the motive force behind Danish architecture in India; we cannot go further into detail about the background of the West Indian architecture, but one more decisive difference should be noted; it is rather a question of economic geography and does not concern the town itself, but the district around it.

The Danes worked plantations on the islands of the West Indies. The land was divided up into large estates and the planters lived on their estates in villas. Thus the houses were extremely scattered — spread over the whole area of the colony.[75] In the hinterland of Tranquebar, the Indians themselves cultivated the soil. The Europeans lived in the town; some of them had a 'garden' a little way out in the country, but that was all.[76] There was never any important European settlement outside the town itself or the centre of the village of Poreyar.[77] Apart from the governor's official country residence at Tillaly there were no private estates in the country.

The comparison with the West Indies makes us realize, however, that colonial architecture must be studied on the basis of its special conditions, which are not always to be found in the mother country. As regards Tranquebar, the proximity of the richer English and French possessions must have been very significant. Large garden houses of the kind that were erected on New Street would have been altogether unthinkable without the structures which were built in Pondicherry and Madras at the end of the 18th century.[78] Correspondence which has been preserved, and also the inscription-tablets in the Tranquebar cemetery tell of connections both with Englishmen and Frenchmen. As I have already mentioned, Anker's personal relations with his British colleagues were very important. This was specially the case in 1801, when the British occupied Tranquebar.[79] It is certainly not by mere chance that the main streets created during Anker's period as governor recall the perspective of Fort St. George bristling with columns. But the private houses were simpler, possessed another breadth, stronger features of intrinsic Baroque. Nevertheless, the change had the same character as the one taking place simultaneously in the provinces of Denmark.[80]

It has been possible to observe an occasional connection with *Indian* models during earlier periods in the history of Tranquebar, when the churches and mission schools were built, or when the later Government House was designed. It would seem that neo-Classicism with its strongly purist features is quite foreign to such borrowings, at least if they are of a purely stylistic nature. Nor can many examples of a mixing of styles be quoted. On the contrary, the last decades of the 18th century were the years when European architecture very clearly dissociated itself from Indian.[81] But on Prince Christian Street there stands a small house with Ionic pilasters. In a panel between them is a window in a cusped arch which, of course, *could* be the result of a later alteration. A number of houses in Tranquebar have been modified in a similar way: in some of them the original columns have been exchanged for wooden supports which have been painted blue, red and yellow.

In 1805 Tranquebar was mentioned by James Johnson, the author of *The Oriental Voyager*, as a flourishing town.[82] In 1806 Peter Anker left his post as governor and returned to Norway.[83] In 1808 the repercussions of the great European wars began to be felt and the Danish territory in India was occupied by the British. For the following eight years the colonies were completely cut off from the mother-country.[84] This was the beginning of the end for Tranquebar, as a trading centre and an entrepôt for Asiatic trade. It caused it to stagnate and decline as regards architecture also.

During the eight years of occupation very little was done to keep the buildings in good condition. But after liberation we again find in the accounts annually recurring charges for repairs to the governor's house, the citadel, the warehouse, the prison, the hospital, the doctor's house, the admiral's house, the guardrooms, the customs house, the thirteen royal bazaars and the powder-magazine on the Laaland bastion.[85] From 1829, the Crown assumed responsibility for the mission buildings, churches and schools also. Thus an attempt was made to keep up the appearance of the European part of the town. According to a census in June 1835, 235 people were living there; many of them were pensioners.[86] The decline in trade had left clear traces. The European merchants went away to more active trading centres; they gave up their houses, the storehouses were empty and remained so. In the Indian part of Tranquebar many houses soon lay in ruins, as the craftsmen who lived there could no longer find work.[87] Thus the small Danish town was reduced to a shadow of its past, a deserted place which, looked on with romantic eyes, could be confused with Pompeii. It was, in fact, built in the same way, of the same substance and according to the same principles of style. In its ruin it gave an almost *authentic* impression; we remember the description at the end of the 1830's of the traveller, Laplace, that emphasized this air of classicism and phantom-like reality.[88]

Nor did the Danes see any possibility of rousing the town into life. Business was anything but good; the colonies in India were a constant source of loss in those years. It was therefore natural that the thought was entertained of disposing of them. As early as the 1820's, there were negotiations with the British about a possible purchase, but it was not until twenty years later that the plan took more definite form.[89] In 1840, the definite decision to sell was made. The conditions were finally agreed upon; the treaty was signed in Calcutta on 22 February, 1845, ratified by the Danish king in Copenhagen on 30 May the same year and by the East India Company on 2 July. Thus the town of Tranquebar with its land area, its fort and all other buildings passed into the possession of the British.

Because of the annual repairs, the public buildings were in good condition and so the last Danish governor, Peter Hansen, ventured to propose to Lord Auckland that the British administration for the whole district be transferred to Tranquebar.[90] Thus the town could have been roused from its torpor and given a new function and importance. The Collector of Tanjore, Montgomery, who formally took over Tranquebar on behalf of the East India Company, also considered such a transfer to be very possible,[91] but other powers intervened, and Tranquebar remained in its state of inertia. Steen Bille, who was sent out to superintend the transfer of the colony to the British, aptly quoted Laplace when he saw the streets and squares overgrown with grass.[92]

iii The Growing Towns: Calcutta

In the chapter on the enclaves I indicated that Calcutta in the middle of the 18th century was particularly vulnerable. When Siraj-ud-daulah and his troops swept in over the area, they could use the first houses they took for firing on Fort William, where the English colonists had retreated.[1] From positions in the stoutly built church, in the Company's building and in the houses of Mr. Eyre and Mr. Cruttenden, which were all beside the walls of the fort, they were able to concentrate the attack and compel the English to take flight or to surrender. This happened in June 1756, and the siege was followed by the controversial episode of the Black Hole of Calcutta.

In his summary of the events after the siege, Captain Grant stated that the best way to prevent it would have been to pull down all houses outside the walls of the fort and protect the latter by a ditch and sloping bank.[2] Undoubtedly a radical suggestion, which must be regarded against the background of what had just happened.

In fact, long before the attack of the Nawab, the necessity of strengthening the positions had been recognized, and a certain Colonel Scott had presented a proposal for a defence system including ditches, drawbridges, etc. which should encircle the bounds

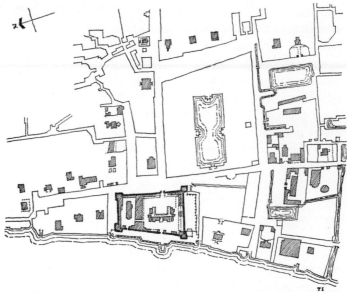

8. Calcutta in 1753, the area around Old Fort William. (1: 12500)

of Calcutta. This plan was never put into practice. However, there were some rudiments of such a defence boundary, a long ditch behind which both the houses of the British and the Indian villages in that area should lie. At the start of the 1740's when an invasion of the Mahrattas was feared this ditch had been begun. The intention was to make the ditch seven miles long, but only three miles were completed.[3]

The effectiveness of the Mahratta ditch in case of attack was never tested. However, it was to play its part in the development of Calcutta; the ditch was added to and constructed to its full length and was for a long time the boundary of the actual town. To-day, it is marked by the Circular Roads.

The continuation of the digging of the Mahratta ditch was one item in the reconstruction after the siege. The town had been recaptured by the British as early as 1757. New precautions were taken against future military attacks. The badly damaged fort was repaired and was again to function, though not as a fort, but as a customs house from 1766. Instead, a gigantic new fort was constructed, of which the architect was Captain Brohier.[4] As building supervisor he was soon succeeded by James Mace, newly-appointed chief engineer. The construction of the new fort implied activity in many fields. In March 1757, building materials such as *chunam* and bricks were advertized for, and some workers (bricklayers and carpenters who could act as instructors for the Indians) were recruited directly from England. The new fort became, to a greater degree than the old one, a European construction from the outer plaster to the inside. In addition, it was considerably larger. The central point inside its walls is St. Peter's Church; the distance from the church to the outermost point of the system of ramparts is almost one-sixth of a mile.[5]

9. Calcutta in 1784. European areas are marked with diagonal lines. (1 : 60000)

The new Fort William necessitated substantial alterations in the town plan of Calcutta. In order to obtain space for the large fort, it was necessary to clear away the Indian dwellings along the river bank, and in order to have a free view and firing space, large areas towards the inland were also cleared. This is the motivation behind the Maidan, the enormous open space which extends from Tolly's Nala and Lower Circular Road in the south to Esplanade Row in the north, from the bank of the river in the west to Chowringhi in the east. To judge from maps available and the Daniell engravings, it was largely finished in the middle of the 1780's;[6] but only a few years previously, Warren Hastings had been forced to take himself through jungle in order to reach his country seat in Alipur, about one mile south of the fort. Jungle and marshy ground had originally covered the greater part of the area and it took, of course, some time to drain and clear this wilderness.[7]

In addition to the military origin of the Maidan, it was also to have at least one other function. When the grassy plain was finally cleared, it functioned aesthetically, as a significant space, an enormous vista which created a perspective for the splendid buildings which were erected in Chowringhi and along the Esplanade.

Along the latter a number of official buildings were erected at an early stage; on Upjohn's map from 1794, Government House, Council House, the Accountant General's Office and the Supreme Court lie beside each other. Some ten years later, they are replaced by yet more splendid structures. At that time, the scene was dominated by Wellesley's Government House, built between 1798 and 1803, and a town hall, completed in 1813. These buildings will be dealt with in detail in connection with other individual patterns.[8] The concentration of large houses along the Esplanade appears to be quite intentional. The aim was to create a front where all the wealth and power of the town were concentrated. In this way, the vision of the travellers, of which I talked in my introductory chapter, was 'encouraged'.[9] Several towns in India were changed along similar lines at that time. Madras acquired its sea front, Tranquebar its parade and Serampore its picturesque waterfront along the river bank.[10]

THE STRUCTURES

In the area behind the Esplanade there was a considerable number of European buildings even after the siege. Construction work according to the old pattern was continued; each house was erected in its own compound, often surrounded by a garden.[11] In fact, this lay-out is characteristic of Indian towns, which are never dominated by large-scale plans. There are no uniform quarters and districts of the type which develop in London and other English towns. The reason for this was to be sought in the different social and economic situation. There seems to have been a certain speculation in sites and houses, but it was always a question of *individual* structures.[12] There was only a small number of Europeans and each of them demanded attention and space for himself.

With reference to the type of buildings in Calcutta, William Hodges comments in 1783: 'It adds greatly to the superb appearance that the houses are detached from each other, and insulated in great space.'[13] Thus the area around the old fort was built up fairly whimsically. On maps from the 1780's we can, however, discern some attempts at a more strict arrangement in this part of the town. This arrangement was achieved by means of emphasizing certain streets and buildings. The broad Court House Street turns at right angles from the Esplanade and parallel with it runs the somewhat smaller Council House Street. Between these lies Tank Square, one long side of which is entirely dominated by Writers' Buildings, erected in 1780.[14] From the corner of the latter runs Lall Bazaar and its continuation, Bow Bazaar as far as the Mahratta ditch. The Esplanade continues into Durumtolla Street. These pronouncedly *non-Indian* perspectives represent the actual theme of the engravings of Calcutta by Daniell, James Baillie Fraser and others.

Naturally, every new large building contributed to the change in the picture of the town, but only a few can have affected the plan *outside* their compound. One exception was Wellesley's Government House. Here the longitudinal axis of the structure was in due course continued through the quarters in front of the building and up to Tank Square, later Dalhousie Square. In this way an axis was formed from the portico of Government House to the centre of Writers' Buildings. This change is documented by a map from 1832.[15] Now the Old Court House has also been replaced by St. Andrew's Church which with its portico and tall spire forms an impressive termination of (Old) Court House Street.[16] And in another part of the town, in Strand Road which was constructed in 1823, the new Mint is the dominant feature in the area with its heavy Doric order which was borrowed from the Parthenon.[18]

So far we have dealt with the centre of Calcutta, which was also the centre for the surrounding province and for the expanding British Empire in India. The growing commercial life was directed from the large buildings on the Esplanade, the wharfs, ghats and customs house on the bank of the river, trading firms and bazaars in the area around the large Tank Square. The architectural wealth is a direct result of this gradual expansion. More and more Englishmen came here; increased profits — and an increased contraction of debts — made it possible for them to build and reside with great splendour. In 1752, the number of Europeans in Calcutta was only between two and three hundred;

66

in 1876 this had increased to nine thousand,[18] and during this time parts of the original Indian villages with their houses of clay and straw had been turned into a 'metropolis of brick and stone'.[19]

The Calcutta of the Europeans was an area strictly concentrated on the bank of the river and a few extensions to the east along Bow Bazaar and Durumtollah. This was the city of palaces behind which such travellers as Bishop Heber and C. A. Bluhme discerned a quite different reality. Heber wrote in a letter of 1823:

'These are, however, the front lines; behind them ranges the native town, deep, black and dingy, with narrow crooked streets, huts of earth baked in the sun, or twisted bamboos, interspersed here and there with ruinous brick bazars, pools of dirty water, coco-trees, and little gardens, and a few very large, very fine, and generally very dirty houses, . . . the residence of wealthy natives.'[20]

This statement does not suggest any intimate knowledge of the Indian way of living. It only tells us superficially about a milieu which the Europeans tried to keep at a distance, and at the time of Heber's comment, they had succeeded in this endeavour.

In order to get sufficient space for the erection of the new Fort William, many Indian houses had been cleared away at the end of the 1750's, as mentioned previously, and the Indian inhabitants of these houses had been moved.[21] The Indian settlements were gradually forced out of the central parts of the town. Price says that in '1782, when Mr. Hastings came to government he divided the black and white town into 35 wards, and purchased the consent of the natives to go a little further.'[22] That the British actually went farther has already been shown.

Disasters of all kinds cleared the way for alterations. In 1780, fifteen thousand straw houses were destroyed by fire.[23] Storms and floods took their toll. Naturally, their effects were greatest in the densely populated Indian parts of the town. In order to cope with a particularly heavy flood, a great scheme for the improvement of Calcutta was worked out in 1803. This took place during Wellesley's period as governor. A special committee was ordered to clarify the situation, and we can read in the Minutes, among other things, the following:

'The increasing extent and population of Calcutta, the capital of the British empire in India, and the seat of the supreme authority, require the serious attention of Government. It is now become absolutely necessary to provide permanent means of promoting the health, the comfort, and the convenience of the numerous inhabitants of this great town.

'The construction of the public drains and water courses of the town is extremely defective. The drains and water-courses in their present state neither answer the purpose of cleansing the town, nor of discharging the annual inundations occasioned by the rise of the river, or by the excessive fall of rain during the south-west monsoon. During the last week a great part of this town has remained under water, and the drains have been so offensive, that unless early measures be adopted for the purpose of improving their construction, the health of the inhabitants of Calcutta, both European and native, must be seriously affected . . . In those quarters of the town occupied principally by the native inhabitants, the houses have been built without order or regularity and the streets and lanes have been formed without attention to the health, convenience, or safety of the inhabitants.'[24]

To start with it might be worth while noting that this welfare programme, like everything else in Wellesley's policy, would seem to have been drawn up to strengthen the position of Calcutta. The improvements were intended to help make Calcutta a more worthy centre for the future empire. It is difficult to determine how far-reaching and effective these improvements were. There are scarcely any means of making an evaluation of this kind.

An interesting, though not contemporary aspect of the problem is supplied by H. V. Lanchester when commenting on the ideas of Patrick Geddes on Indian town planning. He writes: 'The British began by cutting straight roads through the more congested areas, regardless of the protests of those who were displaced. . . . Much of this work was in the hands of officers not trained for it, who did not realise the sociological aspects of the problems, and whose views on hygiene and sanitation were too largely based on European traditions.'[25]

From our standpoint, the work of the British engineers appears both dilettantish and one-sided; this attitude, based on an understanding and knowledge of the true conditions, does not in turn eliminate the possibility though that the work carried out by these engineers might have been useful at that time.

Summarizing part of the above, we are able to say that the changes which took place in Calcutta from the middle of the 18th century include several new aspects of town planning. In spite of negative experience with another type of town, the principle of the enclosed town has been abandoned and deviations from the strictly regular take place; components like the Maidan and the scattered buildings around the central square are created. The prerequisites for these are, in the first place, of a defensive and social nature; the aesthetic effect is quite clear, but of secondary importance. We can also discern a third important factor, namely the climate.

An observer writes as follows: 'The Climate of Calcutta may be inferred from its situation in a damp hollow, on the banks of one of the largest rivers in the world. Each season has its peculiar dangers . . .'[26] As for the danger, we have already heard about the heavy rain and floods during the time of the monsoon. The hot season was equally difficult, especially in the Ganges basin, where the humidity of the air is great. By placing the houses wide apart and clearing a large area such as the Maidan, something to counterbalance the heat was obtained. The evening breeze could sweep through the wide spaces and provide coolness.[27]

The reasons that lay behind the most radical breach in the earlier pattern of the town were also climatic and military. The conception of the town as a clearly defined unit was finally abandoned and the houses were allowed to extend into the river basin. The character of the town became that of a ganglion knot. Roads were laid and in connection

68

with these, groups of houses were built which in time were combined and formed real suburbs. The great number of Indians moving into the town resulted in an extensive erection of shanties. This was the origin of the complex composition of the modern town of Calcutta.[28]

To start with I shall deal with Chowringhi, the most central of all the residential quarters which were formed. In 1761, a suggestion was made of acquiring a house 'for the Refreshment of the Governor when the Load of Business will permit him to retire.'[29] The house which was decided on stood in Chowringhi, that is in the south-eastern part of the enclosure formed by the Mahratta ditch. The house was fairly isolated. At the end of the 1760's this area was still considered to be outside the town. On maps from the 1780's it can be seen that the built-up area is slowly advancing towards the Esplanade. In 1794, we find twenty-four houses here, all large and standing in large compounds.[30] The Daniells state in 1797 that Chowringhi, 'though formerly separated, may now be considered as making part of the town of Calcutta.'[31]

One of the largest streets in Chowringhi was South Park Street which led to the European cemetery that was opened in 1767.[32] The forming of the Maidan was, as pointed out previously, of significance for the aesthetic effect of the area. The Daniells' engravings convey a clear idea of the magnificence of this group of spaciously arranged residences, a counterpart to the official splendour as displayed on the Esplanade.

The road from the town centre to Chowringhi was old and much used. It continued to Tollyganj in the south and to the famous temple in Kalighat. We can read about other roads which were to lead to places far beyond the Mahratta ditch. The roads to Dum Dum and Baraset are mentioned in 1747 and 1757. Some ten years later, Dum Dum was to become a cantonment; Baraset, which was situated in the jungle, was used for pig-sticking and other country sports. Around 1780 there were garden houses in Ballyganj, to which the bodyguard of the governor moved in about 1800, in Russapagla, Baitakhanal and Alipur, where Warren Hastings lived.[33] From the 1770's onwards, Barrackpore was developed into a cantonment.[34] The country residence of the governor-general was erected there, and Wellesley is said to have planned to connect this building with Government House by a fourteen-mile-long esplanade, forming an axis between these two seats of power.[35] Barrackpore Trunk Road marks this imaginary line fairly exactly.

The most important means of communication to the north through the actual city of Calcutta was Chitpur Road which joined the road to Dum Dum. In 1823 a broad new road was constructed along the banks of the Hooghly. Five years later this Strand Road continued southward to Garden Reach via Kidderpur.[36]

Furthermore, the old British territory of Hooghly, Chinsura and Serampore may also be considered as suburbs of Calcutta. These areas were acquired from the Dutch East India Company and the Danish Crown in 1825 and 1845 respectively, but in practice had already become an organic part of the British dominions. As a result of the Napoleonic Wars they had been occupied for several years by the British.[37]

A large map which was printed in 1841 shows the River Hooghly from Bandel to

Garden Reach with Calcutta in the centre of its wide system of suburbs.[38] The writers and artists who travelled in a spirit of Romanticism presented us with a version of the same phenomenon, but with more feeling. They saw the white buildings embedded in the green vegetation of the river banks. They particularly admired the 'enchanting' Garden Reach, but — as we recall — they encountered the first ramifications of the town as far south as Falta.[39]

The recreation areas around Calcutta helped the Europeans to adjust themselves to the sub-tropical climate, but they could not, of course, abolish all inconvenience. The hot season was still oppressive. It seems natural then that the Europeans, when it became possible, went to places with better climatic conditions. During the first decades of the 19th century, therefore, they moved up into the hills where agreeable temperatures were obtained at heights of between four and seven thousand feet.

The first Englishmen scaled the Himalayas as conquerors and cartographers. Some subaltern officers built the earliest cottages in Simla after the surrounding area had become British after the Gurkha War of 1814–16. From the middle of the 1820's, a small colony was formed there, with buildings made mostly of wood.[40]

It might appear irrelevant to mention Simla in this connection, but the origin of this hill-station was to be of great importance for Calcutta; it was soon to be its most remote and also its most popular 'suburb'. Several governor-generals preferred Simla to Calcutta, and towards the end of the 19th century, Simla was to become India's official capital in the summer. In the same way, alternative recreation places for Europeans in Madras and Bombay were created near Ootacamund in the Nilgiris and Mahabaleshwar to the west of the sub-continent.[41]

iv Suburban Changes: Serampore

In the middle of the 18th century, a Danish factory was added to the European trading centres already in Bengal. This factory was erected on the river Hooghly, south of Dutch Chinsura and French Chandernagore, and only fourteen miles from British Calcutta. The vicinity of Calcutta was to be of significance for the Danish area; it was, in due course, subjected to growing British influence and finally functioned merely as a suburb of its powerful neighbour. The territory which the Nawab at Murshidabad ceded to the Danes in September 1755 and which was enlarged in 1759 was called by them Frederiksnagore after King Fredrik V; however, its international name became Serampore, which will also be used here.[1]

The setting up of the new factory marked the continuation of the Danish attempts at colonization which had been begun much earlier, but which had been badly shattered in 1714 when the Danes were obliged to give up Danmarksnagore.[2] It was hoped to re-open a profitable trade in Bengal; the province's richness in cotton and silk was especially tempting, as well as the possibilities of marketing opium and saltpetre from Bihar (a Danish factory was erected in Patna in 1770).[3] It was, however, a long time before

70

these hopes were fulfilled. The start was rather unsuccessful, as it coincided with the political disturbances in Bengal during the years 1756–57, the struggle between Siraj-ud-daulah and Robert Clive.[4] On the whole, the first decades of the factory were a failure from a trading point of view.

Likewise the architectonic start was humble; some simple buildings were erected within a similarly simple compound. The first managers of the factory express their regret when referring to the houses, which were of straw, and the enclosures which fell to pieces, thus making gaps for tigers and worse enemies of man.[5] As opposed to Tranquebar, Serampore never became a fortified town. Kay Larsen said that the town's best protection was for a long time its insignificance.[6] And the first picture we have of the factory well bears out such a statement; it is a mere basic lay-out. Around the small triangle which marks the factory a square has been sketched which in turn is flanked by two long bazaar streets, and beyond this lies a compact group of uniform rectangles, the quarters for the 'large castes'.[7] This plan may, however, have existed merely on paper; as in Tranquebar, the Danes took into consideration the already existing Indian settlement. Later maps show that the latter had a far more differentiated pattern.

It was, in fact, a series of disasters which caused the architecture of the colony to develop. They obliged the inhabitants to increase the stability of their constructions. In the middle of the 1760's, a hurricane destroyed houses and flooded a large part of the territory. During the subsequent reconstruction, bricks were used instead of bamboo and clay for the most important buildings.[8] On 2 December, 1770, the house of the manager fell in for no apparent external reason. The situation was dramatic, as a great number of the members of the colony were in the building when it collapsed. This happened on a Sunday shortly after church service. A wall gave way and the roof followed in a cloud of clay-dust and broken pieces of wood.[9]

In the following year, the manager's house was reconstructed in the form of a *pucka* building, a single-storey rectangular with a high portico on the east front that faced the river and the gateway of the factory. The Ionic columns of the portico convey an impression of grandeur. Above each window there is a heavy cornice; the roof is flat and topped by a balustrade. The architect is unknown, but the construction corresponds to those of the British country residences which were then starting to be built in the vicinity of Calcutta. The house was, in fact, situated like a country seat, surrounded by a large garden.

Of private contemporary buildings we know the Catholic Church best, which was built a little nearer the river than the manager's house. It was finished in 1776, and resembled a long 'barn' with a splendid Doric order supporting an enormous segmental pediment. It represents a dramatic piece of architecture. Its designer possibly came from Calcutta, where the necessary money was actually collected.[10]

When the colony was taken over by the Crown in 1777, the manager's house was the most highly evaluated house of all, including those of Tranquebar. The houses near it — a storehouse and a *corps de garde* — were also estimated at large amounts. The surrounding wall was, however, of clay and the appearance of the factory can hardly have been impressive.[11]

At that time the situation changed; the war between the British and the French favoured the neutral Serampore and trade there entered upon a boom. This formed the basis for urban expansion, and during the following decades Serampore changed considerably.[12] As in Tranquebar, the manager of the factory was the driving force behind the changes. His name was Ole Bie, a Norwegian like Peter Anker. He took up his post in 1776 and held it with some intervals until 1805. However, the motivation behind Bie's actions is not as obvious as in the case of Anker; a pronounced striving for personal prestige can be discerned behind his actions, even if they are said to be taken 'for the good of the colony'.[13]

On the initiative of Bie, in 1780, a strong brick wall was erected around the factory. The old enclosure of clay and straw had been destroyed by the rains and in his reconstruction proposal Bie pointed out to the Board of Trade that the dilapidated condition might arouse ridicule and cause 'unfavourable reflexions' amongst Europeans living nearby, and that it would particularly harm the nation's reputation with the Indians, who liked to see political power visibly manifested in order to believe in it.[14] Similar arguments were later to be used by other people who, like Bie, were struggling for a position in the Indian scene.[15]

In 1782, there were sixty fairly large stone houses outside the factory enclosure. All of them stood near the river, an area which Bie laid out by making a number of wide roads.[16] These roads continued into the Indian quarters and were to form a pattern like the veins in a gigantic leaf. Thus the entire area had acquired an urban character and Bie was able to say in 1783 that the place, which six years previously had looked like a desert, was now a fine town. He could watch new dwelling-houses and godowns being erected daily.[17] The houses were usually made of bricks and mortar and fitted with window-panes obtained from Calcutta. However, we can read about many additions made from simpler materials. Bamboo, straw and 'mats' were used for bungalows and verandas, and split bamboo for screens, so called 'tatties'.[18]

Three large constructions can be connected directly with Bie: a bazaar, a Protestant church and a prison. In the beginning, the bazaar was used by Bie himself, who conducted considerable private trade, but it became the property of the Crown in 1797.[19] The construction of the church took a long time and was rather involved. In 1798, a collection for the necessary money was organized on the initiative of Bie and building was commenced in 1800. In 1805, when Bie died, the church was partly finished, but had neither tower nor veranda, and if we are to believe a contemporary description, it looked like a warehouse![20] Fifteen years later its architectural features were more emphasized and the church was completed with the help of the British.[21]

The plan for the new prison and 'catcheri', which was signed by B. Wickede in 1803, suggests a tolerant attitude.[22] The various religions in the colony had, so to speak, been accepted together with their ritual requirements and the building had been designed

72

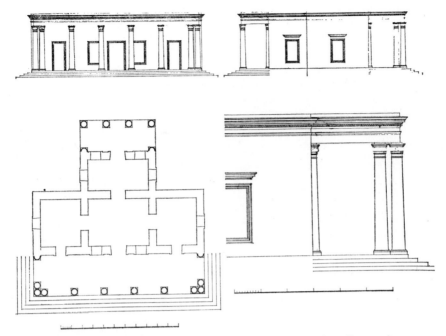

10. 'The House with the Monkey', Serampore. (scales of metres)

accordingly. Europeans, native Christians, Moslems and Hindus were placed in different compartments and the same applied to men and women. In the enclosed courtyard there was a tank for religious ablutions beside the 'catcheri', i.e. the court. A special small room was reserved for 'turbulent and drunken' individuals.

After 1777, when the colony was taken over by the Crown, Indians and Europeans had equal rights, that is, on paper but hardly in practice.[23] It is thus of interest to encounter this model institution, where all would appear to have the same chance in spite of their being criminals.

A fine example of private buildings in Serampore of the time of Ole Bie was measured in 1949 by Ib Andersen.[24] The house is the one standing nearest the church in the compound and enclosed by a wall; it is called here 'the House with the Monkey' after its last inhabitant.[25] It has a veranda along the entire façade and a portico facing the courtyard. It is a single-storey construction under a flat roof. The rooms are arranged strictly symmetrically, three in a row, and with doors leading on to the veranda. The lay-out has been made with special reference to the climate. When studying the style of the building we find that its appearance is determined by the colonnades and the bold cornice which runs like a ribbon round the whole structure. On the inside, the walls are whitewashed with shallow panels outlined in the plaster.

As mentioned above, the private buildings as well as those of the Crown in Serampore are in the area near the river. In the beginning, this arrangement need not have been

73

intentional, but in due course the situation was recognized and utilized aesthetically. The houses were not merely situated near the river; they were *facing* it. Together they formed a waterfront similar to that which was created at the same time in Madras.[26] This tendency can be observed as early as 1790 on a water-colour painting by Peter Anker; the row of façades was, of course, not so long and impressive as in the large towns.[27]

In fact, Serampore's long waterfront on the Hooghly is more reminiscent of Dacca than of Madras. The houses alternate with green vegetation, thus forming a picturesque festoon along the bank of the river.[28] It was also this picture that travellers like Lord Valentia described in the Romantic era.[29]

Lord Valentia, who travelled in Bengal in 1803, also pointed out that Serampore was completely surrounded by British territory. This was a situation which would have favoured an anglicization of the Danish town, even if the situation had not changed; however, a change took place which led to an even stronger anglicization. To start with, Serampore was occupied by British troops in 1801 and 1808–14, and English law was introduced.[30]

During the course of the last long occupation, the buildings became greatly dilapidated. After 1814, a certain rehabilitation could be noted and, amongst other things, the main gate of the manager's house was rebuilt.[31] The gate was not designed as martially as its counterparts in Tranquebar. Coupled Ionic pilasters support a triangular pediment with the monogram of King Fredrik VI. The cornice above the arch of the portal is 'broken'; there are consoles on the sides as well as crowning urns. All this implies that the outer character of the portal is still rather in the Baroque spirit.[32]

However, the greatest building activity during these first decades of the 19th century was not developed by the Crown, but by the church and mission.

The Baptist mission in Serampore was started in 1799, when William Carey, Joshua Marshman and William Ward arrived. The reason why these Englishmen came to the Danish colony was that they were permitted to carry on evangelical work there. They soon started a printing establishment and a paper mill, and their productions became widespread.[33]

In 1816, William Carey is said to have broached the idea of establishing a college to teach young people 'Eastern Literature and European Science'. In 1819, a memorandum was printed concerning the college in which we can read, among other things of a proposal that: 'A building for the College shall be erected on a convenient spot in Serampore, to contain Rooms for the Library and the Museum, a Hall for the various College Exercises, and such other rooms as may be found requisite.'[34]

The mission was allotted a large site on the outskirts of Serampore near its other properties, but there was uncertainty as to the style of the new building. In fact, a dispute would seem to have arisen which anticipated other and more important European quarrels. The question was what style would be suitable. Bishop Middleton had chosen Gothic for his college in Calcutta; however, the missionaries in Serampore were opposed to this idea, in the first place for climatic reasons.[35] The alternative was a classical building and the college was erected as such in the Palladian manner, closely adhering to the English pattern. The designs on which the building was based were English, consisting of a fine drawing (unsigned) for the façade, and more simple ground-plans and sections with naïve features in the conception of the perspective, which suggest that a Bengal master-builder had assisted.[36]

In its design, Serampore college recalls the palace of the Nawab of Murshidabad which was planned by British architects around 1804.[37] It consists of a main building with a projecting apse on the south and two wings. The structures are connected by low walls. The centre of the main building is occupied by two large halls. The vestibule contains an iron staircase which was cast in Birmingham, and the fanlights of the doors are likewise of iron.[38] The entrance is protected by a very high portico with Ionic columns and rich mouldings in the entablature. As usual, the façades of the wings are less elaborate. The centre is emphasized by a low attic and the windows are arranged in pairs which gives a certain variation to the construction without spoiling the homogeneity. In fact, only the main building and the east wing were erected and no walls connect these two.[39] When one sees them lying there like two big blocks beside a green field, the impression conveyed is of a sharpness of detail and a desintegration.

Major Wickede was responsible for the actual construction work; he was employed for all the larger construction work in Serampore during these decades.[40] It was also Wickede who completed the Protestant church. In this case, too, he followed an English architectural drawing, signed 1806 by 'Lt. Armstrong', and he changed the 'warehouse' into a building crowned by a steeple deriving from a design of James Gibbs.[41] The model was, of course, to be found on British territory, to be more precise, in Calcutta.[42] It is, however, interesting to note that the same pattern was used at a very early stage in Copenhagen, where Vincent Lerche, a distinguished amateur who had Gibbs's *Book of Architecture* in his library, influenced the design of *Vor Frue Kirke* in 1730.[43] Nevertheless, St. Olav's in Serampore was given an appearance which recalls the architecture of the mother country, Denmark. In this connection I refer particularly to the pediment, broken at the base, above the portico, a feature which can be observed on many Danish houses in the 18th century, and which we have also observed above the entrance of the manager's house.

The funnel-shaped square in front of the church would seem to have been designed in conjunction with the completion of the church in 1821. It provides the space necessary to appreciate the tall façade as a whole.

The spire could be seen at a great distance and it gave the town silhouette a bold feature when seen from the river.[44] It completed the waterfront which had been developing since Ole Bie's time. The college was also erected with an eye to the same pictorial effect, and for this purpose a great number of Indian rowan-trees were cut down to clear a space for an uninterrupted view of the façade towards the river.[45] In the upper edge of a map showing the entire Danish territory, James Thompson drew a view of

Serampore in 1827.[46] Here we can see the waterfront in its full length with the college to the far left, the paper-mill, the printing works, Dr. Marshman's house, several large private residences and several ghats, the Catholic church, the government godown and high above these light-coloured outlines the flagpole and the spire of the Protestant church. The artist states that he sketched the view from the river. It is more likely that he stood on the opposite bank in Barrackpore, where the best view could be obtained. Serampore appears to have had decided leanings towards England, even in this concrete way.[47] It could first of all be seen from the country residence of the governor-general; and it is significant that Wellesley gave money for the building of the church, and discussed its completion during an audience he gave to Kraefting, Serampore's governor.[48] In the same way, his successor, the Earl of Moira (Lord Hastings) acted as patron of the college.[49] Serampore already formed an indirect part of their territory.

At the same time the Danish element was *de facto* weakened in Serampore. Trade ceased. In 1818 the last East-Indiaman left Copenhagen and in 1834 the last boat from China returned to Denmark.[50] Together with trade other activities ceased. The godowns were emptied and the dwelling-houses became depopulated, as in Tranquebar.[51] Serampore became for some time a sleeping town. It was kept neat and clean and became a popular place for excursions for people seeking quiet and recreation. The transfer into English hands in 1845 took place practically unnoticed.[52] In fact, Serampore had for a long time formed a suburb of Calcutta. And this is its position to-day, though now forming an active part of the new India.

v Suburban Changes: the Cantonments

One of the suburban changes that took place at the end of the 18th century was the development of the cantonments. They constituted an alternative to the forts when the latter could no longer guard the large areas which came under British control. The political changes which were to take place required a new type of strategy demanding rapid troop movements and open deployment. Therefore the fortifications were moved from the centre of the town to its periphery; and instead of an enclosed strongpoint these cantonments, with their extremely scattered buildings, were developed as the most spacious of all urban patterns.

The cantonments interest us especially because of their function and structure. Winston Churchill gives us, in passing, some information about these two factors when describing his arrival in India in the middle of the 1890's. He says concerning Bangalore:

'The British lines or cantonments are in accordance with invariable practice placed five or six miles from the populous cities which they guard; and in the intervening space lie the lines of the Indian regiments.'[1]
and concerning Poona:

'we passed our second night after landing in large double-fly tents upon a spacious plain.'[2]

76

Owing to their character as additional means of defence, the cantonments could easily be placed wherever military control was considered necessary. They did not require difficult changes in the already existing patterns, and thus were suitable instruments in the hands of the occupying power. Their function determined their structure. They may be compared with the army camps of military states such as the Romans in Europe or the Vijayanagar in India.[3] Their origin can be sought in a strictly arranged camp, a 'moving city' suited to a hot climate.

Churchill's description may be used as an introduction, but in the following we shall not consider either Bangalore or Poona, but look at some similar garrison towns in Bengal and especially near Calcutta. In this way we can fit the analyses into the context which we have already sketched in the section about the growing towns.[4] Dum Dum, which became the headquarters of the Bengal Artillery in 1783, and Chinsura, which functioned as a British frontier station from 1825, when it was taken over from the Dutch East India Company, are two examples of such military suburbs. The buildings here, however, bear the stamp of the nearness of Calcutta: the messrooms look like the clubs of the city, the barracks are heavy buildings with a simplified version of the façade of the town houses. The arcade on the ground usually supports a loggia or veranda.

The change-over from a camp to a permanent garrison establishment is better illustrated by another military base near Calcutta, Ballyganj, to which the governor-general's bodyguard was transferred about 1800. A water-colour of this period shows the Marquis of Wellesley inspecting his troops, which are drawn up on an open field.[5] In the background a flagpole rises in front of two fairly symmetrical buildings, probably mess houses. Round the field lie uniform bungalows for the soldiers, 'double-roofed houses' with verandas on three sides.[6] It is certainly difficult to call the camp at Ballyganj an urban formation; a 'standing camp' would be more correct, but it contains a couple of the elements which were to characterize later cantonments: separate houses for officers and soldiers and a large parade ground.

Few maps, and only of comparatively late date, exist of the cantonments. It was not until the middle of the 19th century that the establishments were properly surveyed and drawn. We shall study the details of two such maps, both from 1851, thus showing how the garrison towns were built up. Now one can really talk of urban development. These settlements contain most of what could be required of a town at that period, but everything serves a military purpose. The basic element is still the camp, even if most of the buildings are now of brick.

The map of Barrackpore shows an establishment which did not originate all at once, according to a uniform plan, but which developed gradually to meet new military requirements. In the middle of the 1770's, it consisted of merely a few bungalows which were used by the officers (while the soldiers presumably lived in tents). Seventy-five years later it covers a widespread area by the Hooghly, north-west of the country residence of the governor-general.[7] The officers' houses lie very near the river and are fair-sized buildings following the usual pattern of country houses in the Calcutta area. They lie apart, each in its own compound surrounded by offices and often separated from each other and from the road by low walls. The houses form part of a very regular road system; the drives leading up to the porticos of the houses form characteristic figures on the map, like bulls' horns.

In the officers' quarter lies the church. A wide, straight road separates this part of the cantonment from the parade ground and the sepoys' lines. The distance between the different compounds is considerable.

The Berhampur cantonment grew up in much the same way as Barrackpore. The first barracks were built as early as 1767. A couple of decades later, the establishment had developed into a large brigade station. The map from the middle of the 19th century, however, gives an impression of great uniformity and precision.[8]

The British military camp lies between two Indian villages which creep right up to the outer lines. There is a marked difference between the dense and irregular building in these areas and the large open spaces dominating the European settlement. A considerable area has been cleared to make room for a parade ground with a racecourse and a large European quarter. The whole area is intersected by a fine network of roads and ditches. The ditches, like the system of large tanks, show that the place is liable to flooding, and a note on the map also tells of a flood as the result of heavy rain. From the way the tanks are arranged they would, however, also seem to fulfil a fortifying purpose. They protect the most important part of the area on the one side, as the river does on the other.

The area between these two water-lines is occupied by a large regular square: the barrack square. Around this lies a strictly symmetrical quarter for officers and soldiers. In an outer ring temporary barracks for subalterns, messrooms, guardrooms, detention barracks, a cold-store and a coal-godown near the anchorage on the bank of the river are spread out. On the other side of Lall Diggee is a Catholic chapel. A mission hall has been placed on the north side, near the Indian village of Kudye. Near the latter several large residences are grouped, presumably for the civil servants of the station.

On the opposite side of the parade ground we find the sepoys' lines, which have a special hospital. Officers and men have separate cemeteries; segregation is strictly observed. The European hospital lies by the river north-west of the main settlement, on a large open space; this is said to be 'the site of Clashi Bazar cleared away during 1857' — the map was, to be sure, made in 1851–52, but shows changes and improvements up to May, 1859, when the unruly 5th European Regiment was stationed there. It had replaced the 19th Native Infantry which had mutinied and marched on Calcutta.[9]

The occurrences at the end of the 1850's changed the cantonments into battlefields. The rigorously drawn boundary lines of the areas were pierced and disrupted. The officers' residences and barracks were shot to pieces and burned. The violence of the events indicates great conflict of ideas and a strain that had been latent for many decades

What the Indians rose against was not, of course, the military towns as such, but the political system which had created them.[10] But for a time the pattern of the map was also changed.

II THE STRUCTURES

1. *Urban Patterns:* Notes

1. This introduction draws partly on two books by M. Edwardes, *Asia in the European Age 1498–1955* and *A History of India, From the Earliest Time to the Present Day*, both London, 1961.

2. An interesting aspect of the struggle between the Portuguese and the Dutch and the different influence of the two nations on the native population is given by M. Burrows in 'The Conquest of Ceylon' in *The Cambridge History of India*, vol. 5, Cambridge, 1929. The author points out on p. 402 that almost all Singhalese words connected with *building* are of Portuguese origin. The Dutch, on the other hand, are said to have influenced the terms dealing with town planning and sanitation.

i The Enclaves

1. Albuquerque's conquest in 1510 is usually referred to in Portuguese history as the 're-conquest of Goa'. The historical background of this event as well as of those referred to below is sketched in F. C. Danvers, *The Portuguese in India*, London, 1894, and C. R. Boxer, *The Portuguese in the East*, Oxford, 1953. As regards the construction of the fort in Cochin, see António Bocarro, *Livro das plantas de tôdas as fortalezas, citades e povoações do Estado da India Oriental*, 1635, published in *Arquivo Português Oriental*, Tomo IV, vol. 2, Bastorá-Goa, 1935, p. 338.

2. Gritli von Mitterwallner has recently presented a monograph on the town of *Chaul*, Berlin, 1964. This treatise deals in great detail and with competence with the matters which my survey could only touch upon. The book presents on the whole a good introduction to a study of Portuguese architecture in the East. The quotation from Gaspar Correia is given in this book on page 39. Cf. ibid. note 16.

3. Carlos de Azevedo, *Arte Cristã na India Portuguesa*, Lisbon, 1959, p. 86 and figures 12 and 13. The fort in Daman mentioned below originally belonged to the king of Cambay which explains its 'medieval' appearance. Cf. G. von Mitterwallner, op. cit., pp. 46 f. and pp. 53 ff.

4. W. Foster, *The English factories in India 1618–23*, Oxford, 1906, and H. G. Rawlinson, *British Beginnings in Western India 1579–1657*, Oxford, 1920. In the latter publication there is much information about the competing nations and a number of photographs of Surat. The factory was fortified in 1642.

5. The enclosed lay-out, function and environment of the factories invite a comparison with the Indian *caravanserais*.

6. The engraving from Pieter van Broecke, *Korte Historiael ende Journaelsche Aenteyckeninghe*, Haarlem, 1634.

7. 'Afteekening van 's Comp. Logie in Atchin', tinted pen and ink drawing, Algemeen Rijksarchief, 's Gravenhage, reproduced in *Wonen in de Wijde Wereld*, catalogue of an exhibition in the Tropenmuseum, Amsterdam, December 1963 to March 1964, No. 49. Subsequently

established Dutch colonies were often designed in accordance with models of towns in the mother-country. Thus, for example, Negapatnam on the Coromandel Coast was 'neatly laid out with squares and characteristic canals', P. Spear, *The Nabobs*, 1st ed. 1932, London, 1963, p. 43. The main model for this planning in South-East Asia was, of course, Batavia, cf. J. J. Ebert, *Beschreibung und Geschichte der Hauptstadt in den Holländischen Ostindien, Batavia*. Leipzig, 1785.

8. Danmarksnagore was founded in 1698 and destroyed in 1714. The plan is clearly a reconstruction of the factory as it looked immediately before the destruction. It is to be found in Ostindisk Kompagnis arkiv, No. 2186b, National Archives, Copenhagen, and is reproduced in *Vore Gamle Tropekolonier*, Copenhagen, 1952, vol. 1, p. 127. When J. T. Wheeler in *Early Records of British India*, London, 1878, pp. 195 f., reproduces a story of Alexander Hamilton and says that the Danish in Bengal abandoned their colony 'after having robbed the Mogul's subjects of their shipping to keep themselves from starving,' he is referring to Danmarksnagore and not to Serampore. Cf. above, page 70.

9. This charter is mentioned in the current historical handbooks.

10. In L. Langlès, *Monuments anciens . . . de l'Hindoustan*, Paris, 1821, vol. 1, facing p. 113. The earlier development of the town is sketched clearly in a series of maps in D. M. Reid, *The Story of Fort St. George*, Madras, 1945. See also W. Foster, *The founding of Fort St. George, Madras*, London, 1902.

11. G. W. Forrest, *Cities of India*, Westminster, 1903, p. 306, relates that Indians sought protection from the English and that they formed a colony outside 'White Town'. *Hobson-Jobson* says that 'Black Town' in Madras was 'inhabited by Gentoos' (i.e. Hindus) 'Mahometans and Indian Christians'.

12. 'Black Town', later called 'George Town' after George V, has, like Fort St. George, kept part of its original character. The railroad has been laid outside the old walls; a couple of bastions are still preserved; the English Garden and part of the western Esplanade have been turned into the 'People's Park'. Concerning earlier plans to regulate the streets in these parts of the town, see H. D. Love, *Vestiges of Old Madras*, London, 1913, vol. 3, p. 299 and passim.

13. L. Langlès op. cit., vol. 1, facing p. 105.

14. See P. Lavedan, *Histoire de l'Urbanisme, Renaissance et Temps Modernes*, Paris, 1941 pp. 86 f.

15. The division of Indians into occupational groups would seem to follow the Hindu caste system, resulting in streets of the homogeneous character which can still be observed in some of India's old towns. The Danes applied the same methods in their planning of the towns of Tranquebar and Serampore. See above, pp. 48 and 71. Cf. B. B. Dutt, *Town planning in ancient India*, Calcutta, 1925.

16. According to a 'reconstruction' of R. P. Fancheux, reproduced in P. Lavedan op. cit., p. 490. The general background of the development of Pondicherry is sketched in S. P. Sen, *The French in India*, Calcutta, 1948. The plans of the engineers for new constructions and alterations are preserved in the Dépôt des Fortifications des Colonies (D.F.C.) in the Bibliothèque de la Section Outre-Mer des Archives Nationales, Paris; see there Inventaire des Archives, Registre Définitif, Pondichéry. Cf. below, pp. 94–98.

17. P. Lavedan, op. cit., p. 491.

18. L. Langlès op. cit., vol. 1, plates after p. 44. The official year of the settlement of the

French in Chandernagore is 1690. S. P. Sen, *Farmans and Parawanas for the Establishment of the French in Bengal*, Indian Historical Record Commission Proceedings, 1946.

19. This use of warlike elements is not unique. The city of Copenhagen also had a gate with flanking gun barrels in the 17th century; cf. below, p. 162.

20. The plan and map in D.F.C., Chandernagore, Cart. 1, No. 1, 2 in the Bibliothèque de la Section Outre-Mer des Archives Nationales, Paris.

21. W. H. Carey has described the destruction of Chandernagore in *The Good Old Days of Hon'ble John Company*, Simla, 1882, p. 53. In The King's Topographical Collection CXV 46-i in the British Museum a map and a detailed report on the condition of Chandernagore in 1769 are kept, 'corresponding with the Report given to the Board by Lieu^t. Col. Arch^d. Campbell, Engineer in Chief'. See also S. P. Sen, *The French in India*, p. 83.

22. C. R. Wilson, *Old Fort William in Bengal*, Indian Record Series, London 1906, vol 1, p. 7, Wilson points out, ibid., p. 191 that Fort William was not the first construction of the English in Bengal. As early as 1640 they built a factory called Hooghly: 'the Mogul Empire jealously prevented anything like a bastion being erected about it'.

23. A. Hamilton, *A New Account of the East Indies*, Edinburgh, 1727, vol 2, p. 11, quoted in G. W. Forrest, op. cit. pp. 279 f.

24. A plan of Fort William is reproduced in G. N. Curzon, Marquis Curzon of Kedleston, *British Government in India*, London, 1925, vol. 1, facing p. 4. Cf. H. D. Love, *Descriptive List of Pictures in Government House and the Banqueting Hall, Madras*, Madras, 1903, p. 35. The plan reproduced there by Love dates from 1825, but the colonnade facing the sea replaces the older one, ibid., p. 45. Cf. below, p. 108.

25. A. Hamilton, op. cit. vol. 2, p. 9, quoted by H. G. Rawlinson, *The British Achievements in India*, London, 1948, p. 12.

26. The results of the attack of Siraj-ud-daulah and the later development of the town are described below in the section 'The Growing Towns: Calcutta', pp. 63–70. Cf. Ram Gopal, *How the British occupied Bengal*, London, 1963.

ii The Growing Towns: Tranquebar

1. The sources concerning Denmark's trade in India and the history of the town of Tranquebar are largely unpublished and distributed over a number of archives; the greater part is, however, in the National Archives in Copenhagen. These have previously been used to some considerable extent in two works mainly, Kay Larsen, *De Dansk-Ostindiske Kompagniers historie*, part 1, Copenhagen, 1907, and the authoritative work, *Vore Gamle Tropekolonier*, part 1, Copenhagen, 1952, where G. Olsen, K. Struwe, AA. Rasch and G. Nørregaard dealt with various periods and aspects of the colonial events. The latter book also touched upon the architectural history of Tranquebar, not so much in its text as through its numerous illustrations. The pictorial material largely consists of illustrations inserted rather at random, showing old maps, engravings, drawings and, more rarely, also structural drawings. To this material must be added the architectural pictures and the scaled drawings made by Ib Andersen, Fredensborg, from 1948–49, which continue this investigation in a much more purposeful manner. The material mentioned forms the main basis for a serious investigation of Denmark's tropical architecture in India.

When referring in the following to the sources used, this will be done if possible with reference to the above *printed* works, Kay Larsen's book being abbreviated as *D.O.K.* and *Vore Gamle Tropekolonier* as *V.G.T.* As regards reference to unpublished material I should like to mention particularly some important sources: Inventarielister og regnskaber, 1782–1820; Ingeniørens regnskaber, 1785/86–1818/19; Regnskaber for bygnings-og vejvœsendet, 1821–48, to be found in Det Kongl. Ostindiske guvernements Arkiv, Nos. 1762, 1764 and 1765, in the National Archives, Copenhagen. Another important source of reference is Kay Larsen's likewise unpublished Dansk Ostindiske Personalia og Data, 1–3, Royal Library, Copenhagen. See also the notes below and *V.G.T.*, pp. 623 ff.

2. *V.G.T.*, p. 42 f.

3. The manuscript of the description which comprises *all* the months of the year, Rostg. 40 Fol., in the Royal Library, Copenhagen; *V.G.T.*, p. 39.

4. *D.O.K.*, p. 20; *V.G.T.*, p. 44 and illustration, p. 91; J. Olafsson, *Oplevelser som Ostin-diefarer . . .*, Copenhagen, 1907. The plan of the fortress and the main building itself, or the 'palace', recall the Danish fortress Christiansborg near Accra in Guinea. See, for example, *V.G.T.*, pp. 481 and 592 and A. W. Lawrence, *Trade Castles and Forts of West Africa*, London, 1963.

5. When the area outside was later fortified it was called 'The fortress of Tranquebar with the Fort of Dansborg'.

6. *D.O.K.*, p. 39.

7. Reproduced in *V.G.T.*, p. 106. The drawing is kept in Ingeniørskorpsets Samling, XVIII: 3, No. 8, Billedsamlingen, Royal Library, Copenhagen.

8. Cf. Vilh. Lorenzen et al., *Christian IV's Byanlaeg*, Copenhagen, 1937.

9. *D.O.K.*, p. 38; *V.G.T.*, p. 101.

10. *D.O.K.*, p. 43.

11. *D.O.K.*, pp. 51 f.

12. *D.O.K.*, p. 59; ibid. p. 57 a picture is reproduced showing the Tranquebar fortifications *with* the ravelin; the plan was originally carved out on an ostrich's egg!

13. *V.G.T.*, p. 114.

14. Even smaller structures in the fort and the town mosque have this shape of roof.

15. *D.O.K.*, p. 52.

16. *Hallische Missionsberichte*, Halle, 1710 ff; I. F. Fenger, *Den Tranquebarske Missions Historie*, Copenhagen, 1843; W. Germann, *Ziegenbalg und Plütschau. Die Gründungsjahre des Trankebarschen Mission*, Erlangen, 1868. Cf. *V.G.T.*, pp. 126 ff.

17. B. Ziegenbalg and J. E. Gründler, *Grundlegung, Bau und Einweihung der neuen Missions-kirche in Tranquebar, genannt Neu-Jerusalem*, Tranquebar, 1719; it contains a plan of the church. Claus Krøckel came to Tranquebar in 1704 and died in 1721 on the journey back to Copenhagen. He is mentioned as a good drawer. K. Larsen, Dansk Ostindiske Personalia og Data, Royal Library, Copenhagen.

18. For this information I am indebted to Dean B. Tiliander, Madura.

19. Map reproduced in *V.G.T.*, p. 145, No. 253; 49, in the Commercial and Maritime Museum in Kronborg Castle, Elsinore. A similar copy is kept in Ingeniørskorpsets samling, XVIII: 3, No. 7, Billedsamlingen, Royal Library, Copenhagen.

20. Immediately behind the wall a number of large 'guard-houses' lie at intervals.

21. *V.G.T.*, p. 144.

22. *V.G.T.*, pp. 148 ff.

23. *V.G.T.*, p. 153.

24. Reproduced in *V.G.T.*, p. 155, after an engraving of L. de Thurah, *Hafnia Hodierna*, Copenhagen, 1748. Tab. L., see Chr. Elling, *Arkitekten Philip de Lange*, Copenhagen, 1931.

25. Reproduced in *V.G.T.*, p. 267.

26. Frederiksstaden with its octagonal square is one of the most distinguished architectural ensembles in Europe. The central buildings now serve as a permanent residence for the Royal Family. Several of Denmark's architectural historians have dealt with this construction. H. Langberg gives a useful summary of its origin in *Arkitekturens oprindelse og andre perspektiver*, Copenhagen, 1963, pp. 17–34.

27. *V.G.T.*, p. 153; cf. above, p. 50.

28. Cf. *V.G.T.*, pp. 154 f.

29. See below, p. 94.

30. *D.O.K.*, p. 131.

31. *V.G.T.*, pp. 159, 164, 165, 217. Det Kongl. Ostindiske guvernements arkiv, No. 199, in the National Archives, Copenhagen, contain information on the work carried out by Kyhn, the military engineer, in strengthening the foundation.

32. *V.G.T.*, pp. 165, 223 f.

33. 'Plan og Profil-Teginger over det udi Droningens Jade lige for Tijer-Gaden beliggende Pack-Hüüs'; measurement drawing dated 24 March, 1755 by C. A. von Passow; pen and water-colour, 1370 × 530 mm., in Samlingen af Land-og Søkort, G. K. Mappe, 8, No. 15 in H.M. the King's Private Library, Christiansborg, Copenhagen.

34. *V.G.T.*, pp. 204 f. The buildings are arranged around a large courtyard. The one described here has the date 1741 on the gable.

35. *D.O.K.*, p. 77. The gable ornamented with volutes almost gives the impression of Iberian Baroque.

36. *D.O.K.*, p. 80. See also A. Hennings, *Gegenwärtiger Zustand der Besitzungen der Europäer in Ostindien*, 1–3, Copenhagen, Hamburg & Kiel, 1784–86.

37. *V.G.T.*, p. 161.

38. *V.G.T.*, pp. 217 ff. Cf. above, p. 70.

39. *V.G.T.*, pp. 261–65 and 375–80.

40. *V.G.T.*, pp. 275 ff.

41. A. A. Rasch and P. P. Sveistrup, *Asiatisk Kompagni i den florissante periode, 1772–1792*, Copenhagen, 1948.

42. Det Kongl. Ostindiske guvernements arkiv, No. 1510, in the National Archives, Copenhagen. See also Kommerce kollegiets Ostindiske Kongl. Resolutioner, dated 22 May and 24 September, 1777, and Kommerce kollegiets Ostindiske Journal, sager, 1777, No. 15; ibid.

43. Sales Contract in Det Kongl. Ostindiske guvernments arkiv, No. 1510, in the Danish National Archives, Copenhagen. The term 'godown' which is used several times in the following is derived according to *Hobson-Jobson* from the Malayan *gadong* and is so written in earlier Danish documents. It denominates a store-house or an outbuilding used for stores.

44. 'Mandtals Rulle over Byen Tranquebar. April 1790.' Det Kongl. Ostindiske guvernements arkiv, No. 1447 a, in the National Archives, Copenhagen.

45. *V.G.T.*, pp. 184 f.

46. *V.G.T.*, p. 247; According to *Hobson-Jobson*, 'Pintado' is the name for patterned chintz. The dissention between the various castes is described in ibid. pp. 248 and 339 ff.

47. Kommerce kollegiets Kongl. Expeditioner, Ostindiske Forestillninger, 17 November, 1777, in the National Archives, Copenhagen.

48. *V.G.T.*, pp. 319 and 342 f.

49. *V.G.T.*, p. 368.

50. Det Kongl. Ostindiske guvernements arkiv, No. 1378 d, in the National Archives, Copenhagen. It contains correspondence with British and French government officials.

51. Ingeniørens regnskaber, October 1788. Det Kongl. Ostindiske guvernements arkiv, No. 1764, in the National Archives, Copenhagen.

52. Drawing in Peter Ankers samling, No. 4416, Ethnographical Museum, Oslo. Reproduced in *V.G.T.*, p. 422. Other drawings and water-colours by Anker are reproduced in ibid. passim.

53. *V.G.T.*, pp. 333 f; in October 1777, Mühldorff had been appointed engineer of the fortress of Tranquebar and soon afterwards made an application for an advance payment to obtain books and instruments according to K. Larsen, Dansk Ostindiske Personalia og Data, Royal Library, Copenhagen, Cf. note 56 below.

54. This gateway was measured by Ib Andersen. The drawing in water-colour is kept by its owner in Fredensborg, but is reproduced in *V.G.T.*, p. 415. Cf. ibid. p. 323. A couple of simple original drawings by M. Mühldorff are included in Kommerce kollegiets Ostindiske Sager, B.2b, 'Trankebars Befaestning angaaende,' in the National Archives, Copenhagen.

55. Ingeniørens regnskaber, September 1791. Det Kongl. Ostindiske guvernements arkiv, No. 1764, in the National Archives, Copenhagen. The 'plan' is included in Ankers samling, Nos. 4531 and 4532, in the Ethnographical Museum, Oslo. Reproduced in *V.G.T.*, p. 296. A similar drawing, with the measurements of 355×285 mm., is contained in Kortsamlingen, 337a, icke Vestindiske tegninger, No. 1, in the National Archives, Copenhagen.

56. Ingeniørens regnskaber, 1785/86, contained in Det Kongl. Ostindiske guvernements arkiv, in the National Archives, Copenhagen. Cf. the section on 'The Training of the Architect', below, p. 157.

57. The inland duty was not abolished until 1832. *V.G.T.*, p. 383. The Gates of Pondicherry, below, p. 97.

58. F. Weilbach, *Arkitekten Lauritz de Thurah*, Copenhagen, 1924.

59. Det Kongl. Ostindiske guvernements arkiv, No. 1510, in the National Archives, Copenhagen.

60. I have only had the opportunity to study a photograph of the drawing in Kortsamlingen, Tranquebar, 1943, No. 70 in the Royal Library, Copenhagen.

61. The drawing in Ankers samling, the Ethnographical Museum Oslo, reproduced in *V.G.T.*, p. 351, but has been wrongly dated 1790; it should be *1793*.

62. Ingeniørens regnskaber, 1793/4, May 1794.

63. Reconstructions are recorded in the accounts of the engineer for the following years, and the same is true of the inventories.

64. A few of Ib Andersen's wash drawings of King Street convey an idea of this. They are reproduced in *V.G.T.*, p. 307 and 371. See also the map drawn about 1800 which is reproduced ibid., p. 335.

65. The Danes encouraged foreign merchants to settle in Tranquebar. *V.G.T.*, p. 281. The

large houses on New Street as well as the other private buildings cannot be studied in the archives and thus are only dealt with briefly in this chapter. At the time of my visit to Tranquebar in February 1965 they had completely disappeared, but at the end of the 1940's, they stood as ruins and were then drawn by Ib Andersen. See the reproductions in *V.G.T.*, pp. 289, 315 and 353.

66. *V.G.T.*, p. 322.

67. One example is Mr. Jørgensen's House. See also below and the chapter on 'The Forms of Architecture as determined by the Climate'. Government House, on the other hand, had a thatched 'bungalow' on the roof according to a water-colour, No. 2111:49 in the Commercial and Maritime Museum in Kronborg Castle, Elsinore. Reproduced in *V.G.T.*, p. 420, but there wrongly called 'Mr. Jørgensen's House'.

68. These drawings are kept by the architect in Fredensborg, Denmark. In the following a description of the houses is made in accordance with these drawings and the structures themselves which are often greatly changed.

69. Violations of style of this kind are not uncommon in Euro-Indian architecture. Cf. below, p. 108.

70. Cf. below, p. 104. I show there how a British military engineer, Charles Wyatt, changed an older pattern by similar means.

71. The back of the Convent and John's tower have been drawn by Ib Andersen. *V.G.T.*, pp. 171, 393, 395, 425. Part of C. S. John's title-deed to the house No. 22, King Street, has been preserved, see the *Catalogue of Danish Records*, Madras, 1952, gen. No. 1168, ser. No. 220 (86).

72. This drawing is reproduced as a large colour illustration, *V.G.T.*, facing p. 355. An early water-colour dated 1835 of the same house, No. 2110:49 is kept in the Commercial and Maritime Museum in Kronborg Castle, Elsinore.

73. The gateway is included in the reconstruction mentioned in the previous note. *V.G.T.*, facing p. 355. The portal of the fort has also had crowning urns. It is still possible to see the broken-off bases by going up on the battlements.

74. A group of teachers and architects of the Danish Royal Academy of Fine Arts has studied the architecture on the formerly Danish islands in the Caribbean. A considerable number of measured drawings from this journey are kept in the School of Architecture of the Academy and also by Ib Andersen, Fredensborg. Thus the study started almost fifty years ago by Tyge Hvass, *Dansk Vestindien, AEldre Nordisk Architektur*, vol. IV, Copenhagen, 1925, has been followed up. See I. Mejer Antonsen, 'Researches on the Domestic Culture of the Danish West Indies', *Dansk Folkemuseum & Frilandsmuseet, History and Activities*, 1966.

75. See J. Humlum, 'St. Croix, St. Thomas og St. Jan', in *Kulturgeografi*, October 1964, and O. Svensson, ed., *Three Towns, Conservation and Renewal of Charlotte Amalia, Christiansted and Frederiksted of the U.S. Virgin Islands*, Copenhagen, 1964.

76. Regarding agriculture in Tranquebar, see *V.G.T.*, pp. 282 ff.

77. See the map from about 1830 which is reproduced in *V.G.T.*, p. 280.

78. Cf. below, p. 125.

79. *V.G.T.*, p. 354.

80. See, for example, Chr. Elling, *Klassicisme i Fyn*, Copenhagen, 1939, and the same author, *Danske Herregaarde*, Copenhagen, 1942, p. 38 and photos, pp. 187–89.

81. Cf. below, p. 162.

82. J. Johnson, *The Oriental Voyager*, London, 1807, p. 306.

83. *V.G.T.*, p. 356.

84. *V.G.T.*, pp. 381 ff.

85. Regnskaber for bygnings-og vejæsendet, 1821–45, Det Kongl. Ostindiske guvernements arkiv, No. 1765, in the National Archives, Copenhagen. See also a memo about repairs and reconstruction for the year of 1839, No. 1391a, ibid.

86. Kommerce kollegiets Ostindiske Journal, Sager, 1845, No. 209 in the National Archives, Copenhagen.

87. *D.O.K.*, pp. 146 f. *V.G.T.*, pp. 383 ff.

88. Cf. above, p. 29.

89. *V.G.T.*, pp. 406 ff.

90. G. Nørregaard, 'The English purchase of the Danish possessions in the East Indies and Africa 1845 and 1850', *Revue d'Histoire des Colonies*, No. 3, 1933, p. 58.

91. *Ibid.*, p. 62.

92. S. Andersen Bille, *Beretning om Corvetten Galathea's Reise omkring Jorden, 1845, 46 og 47*, Copenhagen, 1849–51, p. 136. Cf. above, p. 29. A. Ihle gives an elegaic description of Tranquebar's decay and past in *Under Sydkorset*, Copenhagen, 1894, p. 73.

iii The Growing Towns: Calcutta

1. The best idea of these events and their scene of action is given by C. R. Wilson, *Old Fort William in Bengal*, Indian Record Series, London, 1906, vol. 2, pp. 50 ff. Here we find many maps including one by Wm. Wells from 1753, plate VIII. See also J. T. Wheeler, *Early Records of British India*, London, 1878, p. 212.

2. C. R. Wilson, op. cit., loc. cit.

3. Ibid., pp. 40, 104, 140.

4. On the old fort being changed into a customs house, ibid. p. 180. On the new fort, ibid., pp. 114 ff.

5. The old fort was built according to the Indian bricklaying technique, cf. below, p. 170. Military security regulations have prevented me from studying the inside of the present Fort William. For the sake of comparison I should like to refer to Fort St. George, Madras, where the buildings inside the walls are arranged in small blocks consisting mainly of barracks. Ward's 'Views in the Fort' give us an idea of its appearance in the 1780's; these form part of F. W. Blagdon's, *A Brief History of Ancient and Modern India*, London, 1805. An anonymous traveller describes the buildings within Fort St. George and emphasizes the peculiar mixture of military and commercial life: 'Here you may contrast, at every step, the man of war with the man of traffic, the muster-roll with the ledger, the bayonet with the pen, the sentry-box with the desk and counter'; *A Visit to Madras*, London, 1821.

6. The clearing of the Maidan, C. R. Wilson, op. cit., vol. 1, p. 132. The maps comprise 'Survey of the Country and the Banks of the Hughley River Extending from the Town of Calcutta to the Village of Ooloobareah', 1780–84, dedicated to George III by Mark Wood, King's Topographical Collection CXV 37, British Museum, and the same collection CXV 39, and A. Upjohn's map of 1794, Maps Collection K. 115. 43.2 TAB. T, British Museum, and W. Daniell, *Oriental Scenery, Twenty-four Views in Hindoostan*, London, 1797.

7. G. N. Curzon, Marquis Curzon of Kedleston, *British Government in India*, London, 1925,

vol. 1, p. 139. W. H. Carey, *The Good Old Days of Hon'ble John Company*, Simla, 1882–87, vol. 1, p. 58, describes the Calcutta Maidan as 'laid out with fine broad macadamized roads, bordered with trees'. Otherwise the area consists of 'plain turf'.

8. See below, pp. 101, 116.

9. See above, p. 26. Three fine pictures of Calcutta from 1833 show the completely built-up 'city of palaces'. These pictures were painted by W. Wood jr., pen and sepia wash, No. 615. Victoria Memorial Hall, Calcutta.

10. Madras' waterfront, the line of light buildings painted by John Gantz and which formed a screen in front of Black Town, must have been built during the first decades of the 19th century. 'All the offices of Government as well as the counting houses, stores, ware houses, etc., of the European merchants were in the Fort' quotes H. D. Love in accordance with T. Twining's description of 1793; *Descriptive List of Pictures in Government House and the Banqueting Hall, Madras*, Madras, 1903, p. 33. Cf. W. B. Cramp, *Narrative of a Voyage to India*, London, 1823, p. 6, 'from the deck the view of the land has a magnificent appearance; the different offices have, to the beholder, the appearance of stone, and they are formed along the beach in a beautiful manner.' The illustrated map of Madras, printed in 1866 by Higginbotham, shows the waterfront both in view and section. Private mercantile houses interchange with official buildings, the largest being the High Court and the Customs House. Map Collection 54570 (5), British Museum. Tranquebar's parade is described above, pp. 58 f. and Serampore's above, pp. 73 f. Bombay developed on different lines from the above towns, but around its Maidan or 'The Green', a number of public buildings were erected. See R. M. Grindlay, *Scenery, Costumes and Architecture*, London, 1826–30, part 1, plate 1 and caption, and J. Douglas, *Bombay and Western India*, London, 1903, with maps.

11. The way of building is verified, for example, by Upjohn's map from 1794. 'There is little evidence that houses were built in rows, except in Portuguese Church Street', says M. Martyn in 'Georgian Architecture in Calcutta', *Country Life*, 3 December, 1948.

12. See K. Blechynden, *Calcutta, Past and Present*, London, 1906, p. 83.

13. W. Hodges, *Travels in India during the years 1780, 1781, 1782 & 1783*, London, 1793, p. 15.

14. The lay-out of the roads is described according to the maps mentioned above, note 6. Writers' Buildings is dealt with below in a special chapter, pp. 100 ff.

15. 'Map of the City and Environs of Calcutta' published in 1832, Maps Collection 53725 (2), British Museum.

16. St. Andrew's Church is described below on page 128. As regards the perspectives and their focal points, it may be worth recalling the drawings of Indian monuments analysed by M. Archer, 'Company Architects and their influence in India', *R.I.B.A. Journal*, Aug. 1963, pp. 317–21.

17. Strand Road is mentioned by W. H. Carey, op. cit., vol. 1, p. 57. Concerning the Mint which was built by N. W. Forbes from 1824–31, see below, p. 117.

18. J. T. Wheeler, op. cit., p. 213. Cf. W. H. Carey, op. cit., vol. 1, p. 46.

19. J. T. Wheeler, op. cit., loc. cit.

20. From a letter dated 15th December 1832, Calcutta. R. Heber, *Narrative of a Journey from Calcutta to the Upper Provinces of India; from Calcutta to Bombay 1824–25*, London, 1828, vol 2, p. 296.

21. C. R. Wilson, op. cit., vol. 2, p. 132.

22. The information is quoted by *Hobson-Jobson* under the heading 'Calcutta'.

23. W. H. Carey, op. cit., vol. 1, p. 46.

24. *Bengal, Past and Present*, vol. 15, July–December, 1917, pp. 82 ff.

25. J. Tyrwhitt, *Patrick Geddes in India* with a preface by H. V. Lanchester, London, 1947, p. 19. Cf. the following extracts from a Committee report of 1840; the improvements proposed are: *1st*. A new and complete system of drainage. *2nd*. A more perfect ventilation of the city by the construction of new open streets and roads, and the removal of old buildings and walls. *3rd*. The cleansing, clearing jungle, and levelling of ground in and about the city. *4th*. Construction of large new tanks, and the supply of water for all purposes. *6th*. Improved construction of the native habitations. . . . *7th*. Widening, paving and making streets and roads. See James R. Martin, 'Official Report on the Medical Topography and Climate of Calcutta', *The Medico-Chirurgical Review*, No. LXVII, Westminster, 1840.

26. L. von Orlich, *Travels in India*, London, 1845, vol. 2, p. 177.

27. The climatic aspects of the architecture are dealt with in a special chapter, below pp. 176–186.

28. 'As the limits of the city are not marked by walls or ditches, an uninterrupted series of suburbs and villages are attached to it i.e. Calcutta on every side'; L. von Orlich, op. cit., vol. 2, pp. 176 f. The urbanization problems in Calcutta and of other rapidly growing towns in Asia have been studied during the past few years. See P. M. Hauser, editor, *Urbanization in Asia and the Far East, proceedings of the joint U.N./Unesco Seminar*, Calcutta, 1957, *Regional Seminar on Public Administration Problems of New and Rapidly Growing Towns in Asia*, New Delhi 1960, New York, 1962, R. Turner, editor, *India's urban future*, Berkeley, 1962, J. F. Bulsara, *Problems of rapid urbanization in India*, Bombay, 1964, and N. V. Sovani, *Urbanization and Urban India*, London, 1966.

29. From an extract from Bengal Public Consultations, 5 January, 1761, quoted by C. R. Wilson, op. cit., vol. 2, p. 160.

30. Chowringhi as being 'out of town' and consisting of only twenty-four houses. See W. H. Carey, op. cit. vol. 1, pp. 58 f.

31. T. and W. Daniell, op. cit. text to plate 6.

32. Cf. below the chapter on 'Heroes' Tombs and Monuments', pp. 136 f.

33. Re. Dum Dum, Baraset, Ballyganj etc. see J. Long, *Peeps into social life of Calcutta a century ago*, Calcutta, 1868. Concerning Dum Dum as the headquarters of the Bengal Artillery and Ballyganj, see also above, p. 77. Hastings' House in Alipur is described in the chapter 'Country Residences near Calcutta, Madras and Delhi', below, p. 122.

34. See 'Suburban changes: the Cantonments', above, p. 76.

35. G. N. Curzon, op. cit., vol. 2, p. 13.

36. W. H. Carey, op. cit., vol. 1, p. 57. In Kidderpur docks and wharves were erected.

37. Concerning Hooghly, the first British colony in Bengal, see above the chapter entitled 'The Enclaves', note 22. A naïve and rather fantastic water-colour, signed J. Hammer 1810, shows European houses in Hooghly surrounded by tropical vegetation, S.R. No. 1176: 52, Commerical and Maritime Museum in Kronborg Castle, Elsinore. The history of Serampore is described in detail above, pp. 70–76.

38. 'Topographical survey of the river Hooghly from Bandel to Garden Reach', Calcutta,

1841. One copy in the Commercial and Maritime Museum in Kronborg Castle, Elsinore.

39. L. von Orlich, op. cit., vol 2, p. 194, described Garden Reach, and so does C. A. Bluhme in 'Af en Ostindiefarers Breve', issued by H. Müller, *Tilskueren*, Sept. 1934 p. 204. Cf. above p. 27.

40. E. Buck, *Simla, Past and Present*, Calcutta, 1904.

41. Government House, Ootacamund, was built during the governorship of the Duke of Buckingham and Chandos, 1880, but long before that the place was used for recreation. D. H. Love, *Descriptive List of Pictures* etc., p. 35. See also below the chapter 'Country Residences near Calcutta, Madras and Delhi'. Regarding Bombay's hill resort, see D. B. Parasnis, *Mahabaleshwar*, Bombay, 1916.

iv Suburban Changes: Serampore

1. For Serampore the same holds good as for Tranquebar, the other Danish town in India. See above, p. 81. The material can be found mainly in the Danish National Archives, Copenhagen. It has been treated especially by Kay Larsen, *De Dansk-Ostindiske Koloniers Historie*, vol. 2, Copenhagen, 1908, as well as by the authors of the large work, *Vore Gamle Tropekolonier*, vol. 1, Copenhagen, 1952. In the following I again refer whenever possible to these printed works, which are abbreviated as *D.O.K.* for the former, and *V.G.T.* for the latter. Regarding unpublished sources I should also like to mention here a few special documents, 'Diverse regnskaber', 1781–1833, Det Kongl. Ostindiske guvernements arkiv, No. 2050, in the National Archives, Copenhagen, as well as 'Etablissementet i Bengalen', Kommercekollegiets Ostindiske Journal, Sager, 1837, ad. No. 175, to be found amongst Sager, 1845, in the National Archives, Copenhagen. In Serampore also Ib Andersen has made measurements and wash drawings with architectural motifs.

With reference to the negotiations with the Nawab of Murshidabad, and 'Serampore' which originally was the name of only one of the acquired villages, see *V.G.T.*, pp. 230 f., as well as the above mentioned, 'Etablissementet i Bengalen'.

2. *V.G.T.*, pp. 125 ff. Cf. above, p. 42.

3. *V.G.T.*, p. 241.

4. Cf. above, p. 63.

5. *V.G.T.*, p. 232.

6. *D.K.O.*, p. 33.

7. 'Plan over Fredericksnagore den 30 januar 1762', signed by Windekilde and Knudsen, Samlingen af Land-og Søkort, G. K. Mappe, 8, 249 No. 8, H.M. the King's Private Library, Christiansborg, Copenhagen.

8. *D.O.K.*, p. 40.

9. *D.O.K.*, pp. 42 f.

10. Cf. the above-mentioned 'Etablissementet i Bengalen' and *List of Ancient Monuments in Bengal*, Calcutta, 1896, p. 44. Cf. *D.O.K.*, pp. 36 and 45.

11. Det Kongl. Ostindiske guvernements arkiv, No. 1510, National Archives, Copenhagen.

12. Cf. above, p. 74.

13. *V.G.T.*, p. 358.

14. Kommerce kollegiets Ostindiske Journal, 1780, No. 190, National Archives, Copenhagen.

15. I am thinking primarily of Wellesley in Calcutta, the second Lord Clive in Madras and the British Resident in Hyderabad. See below, pp. 104 f., 107 and 115.

16. *D.O.K.*, p. 47.

17. *V.G.T.*, p. 359.

18. Diverse regnskaber, 1781–1833, Det Kongl. Ostindiske guvernements arkiv, No. 2050, National Archives, Copenhagen. Cf. the chapter on 'The Forms of Architecture as determined by the Climate', below, p. 179.

19. 'Etablissementet i Bengalen', Kommerce kollegiets Ostindiske Journal, Sager, 1837, ad. No. 175, National Archives, Copenhagen.

20. Ibid., Kommerce kollegiets Ostindiske Journal, 1806, No. 370, and Kongl. Ostindiske resolutioner, 2 May 1798, both in the National Archives, Copenhagen, Cf. *V.G.T.*, p. 362.

21. See below, p. 123.

22. 'Plan af Catcherrie Bygningen i Frideriksnagore, 1803', pen and water-colour, 400 × 525 mm., signed by B. Wickede, with a memo on the building. Kommerce kollegiets Ostindiske Journal, Sager, 1804, No. 110.

23. *V.G.T.*, pp. 322 ff.

24. The drawing is in the possession of the architect himself, in Fredensborg. The plan of the house is reproduced in a map of Serampore which was drawn in 1827 by J. Thompson, Samlingen af Land-og Søkort, G. K., Mappe 8, 249, No. 8a, H.M. the King's Private Library, Christiansborg, Copenhagen.

25. When I photographed the house in January 1965 it was very decayed and quite uninhabited except for a monkey chained in the entrance near the courtyard.

26. Cf. above, p. 87, note 10.

27. The water-colour in Ankers samling, No. 4416, Ethnographical Museum, Oslo. Reproduced in *V.G.T.*, p. 238.

28. 'Panorama of the City of Dacca', lithographed and published by Messrs. Dickinson, etc., with a list of 43 houses. Victoria Memorial Hall, Calcutta. Cf. a picture by an Indian artist, No. 257: 49, Commercial and Maritime Museum in Kronborg Castle, Elsinore.

29. G. Annesley, Viscount Valentia, *Voyages and Travels to India, Ceylon, the Red Sea . . . in the years 1802, 1803, 1804, 1805 and 1806*, London, 1809, vol. 1, p. 68.

30. *V.G.T.*, p. 381.

31. *D.O.K.*, p. 60.

32. The portal has been preserved, but has lost part of its original decoration. The monogram has disappeared and likewise the capitals of the pilasters and the rustic work, which should be studied on older photographs. See *D.O.K.*, p. 63.

33. J. C. Marshman, *The Lifes and Times of Carey, Marshman and Ward*, London, 1859. C. Rendtorff, *William Carey, Pionermissionaeren under dansk Flag*, Copenhagen, 1943. Cf. G. D. Bearce, *British Attitudes towards India, 1784–1858*, Oxford, 1961, pp. 78 ff., and *V.G.T.*, pp. 401 ff.

34. Kommerce kollegiets Ostindiske Journal, Sager, 1819, No. 130. *College for the Instruction of Asiatic Christian and Other Youth in Eastern Literature and European Science*, Serampore 1818, p. 11, National Archives, Copenhagen.

35. W. K. Firminger, *Thacker's Guide to Calcutta*, Calcutta 1906, p. 223. Re Middleton's College and its style, 'Gothic of Queen Elizabeth's time', see R. Heber, *Narrative of a Journey*

from Calcutta to the Upper Provinces of India; from Calcutta to Bombay 1824–25, London 1828, vol. I, p. 43.

36. 'Plans of Serampore College', pen and wash, 485 × 328 mm; 'Transverse Section of Serampore College', pen and wash, 342 × 485 mm; 'Elevation of Serampore College', pen and water-colour, 368 × 743 mm. Samlingen af Land-og Søkort, Mappe 8, 249, No. 9, H.M. the King's Private Library, Christiansborg, Copenhagen.

37. See below, pp. 110–111.

38. W. K. Firminger, op. cit., loc. cit.

39. The main building is now terminated by a straight wall instead of the original apse which was destroyed in an earthquake.

40. Bernhard Aug. Wickede came to Tranqeubar in 1793 and died in Serampore in 1822. In June 1804 he was appointed supervisor of public buildings in Serampore. See further K. Larsen, Dansk Ostindiske Personalia og Data. Royal Library, Copenhagen.

41. The drawing in Kortsamlingen, 337a, Icke Vestindiske Tegninger, No. 2a, pen and water-colour, 1115 × 760 mm., National Archives, Copenhagen. A further drawing, 'Altar of Corinthian Order', signed Lt. Armstrong 1806, pen and water-colour, 600 × 800 mm., ibid., No. 2b. The architect is probably Alexander Armstrong (1782–1817), who arrived in India in 1800 and was appointed lieutenant in 1802.

42. St. John's church was built in the middle of the 1780's after the model of St. Martin-in-the-Fields. Cf. below, p. 127.

43. H. Langberg, *Danmarks Bygningskultur*, Copenhagen, 1955, vol. I, p. 289. Vor Frelsers kirke in Copenhagen is also reproduced in L. de Thurah, *Den Danske Vitruvius*, Copenhagen, 1746, Tab. LXXXIII, with a spire which must have been drawn with a knowledge of Gibbs's models, therefore after 1728, when *A Book of Architecture* was published.

44. This sea front was painted in 1810 by J. Hammer, 'Frederiksnagor: eller Sirampur: en Dansk Plads i Bengalen', pen and water-colour drawing, No. 246:49, Commercial and Maritime Museum in Kronborg Castle, Elsinore, reproduced in *V.G.T.*, p. 363. Strangely enough on this drawing the church spire can be seen protruding above the roofs already, but we must assume that it was *added* with knowledge of the existing plan of 1806.

45. *D.O.K.*, p. 61.

46. Samlingen af Land-og Søkort, Mappe 8, 249, No. 8a. H.M. the King's Private Library, Christiansborg, Copenhagen, C. A. Bluhme, 'Af en Ostindiefarers Breve', issued by H. Müller, *Tilskueren*, Sept. 1934, describes in detail Serampore at that time. He emphasizes the strong English influence, p. 200.

47. A building in Serampore in which the British showed an early interest was an inn which was established in 1786 in a house near the flagstaff; It is often mentioned in press notices. See W. S. S. Karr, *Selections from the Calcutta Gazettes*, Calcutta, 1864, vol. 2, pp. 168, 283.

48. Kommerce kollegiets Ostindiske Journal, 1806, No. 370, National Archives, Copenhagen, Cf. below, p. 123.

49. *V.G.T.*, p. 403.

50. *V.G.T.*, p. 384. Bishop Heber observed in December 1823 a vessel flying the Danish flag; the captain on his own boat stated that he had never seen any vessel of that nationality in the harbour of Calcutta. R. Heber, *Narrative of a Journey from Calcutta to the Upper*

Provinces of India; from Calcutta to Bombay, 1824–25, London, 1828, vol. 1, p. XXV. Heber also described the decline and fall of Serampore. Ibid., pp. 50 f.

51. Cf. above, p. 62.

52. *V.G.T.*, pp. 406–9.

v Suburban Changes: The Cantonments

1. Winston S. Churchill, *My Early Life*, London, 1930, pp. 118 f.

2. Ibid., p. 117.

3. K. A. Nilikanta Sastri, *A History of South India*, Madras, 1955, p. 296.

4. See above, p. 69.

5. The painting is reproduced in G. N. Curzon, Marquis Curzon of Kedleston, *British Government in India*, London, 1925, vol. I, facing p. 244. The Calcutta Maidan was earlier used as a place for the encampment of troops. Th. Daniell's engravings from the end of the 1780's show a number of tents erected in front of the Esplanade Row.

6. This special type of building is dealt with in the chapter on 'The Origin of the Dwelling-House', see below, p. 187.

7. G. N. Curzon, op. cit., vol. II, p. 3. The map of Barrackpore surveyed in 1851, published in 1862. British Museum's map collection I.S.

8. 'The Cantonments and Civil Station of Berhampoor, surveyed in 1851–52, and showing improvements to May 1859'. British Museum's map collection I.S. See M. & W. G. Archer, *Indian painting for the British 1770–1880*, Oxford, 1955, pp. 22 ff. Thomas Lyon, who originally came out to India to assist in the building of the new Fort William in Calcutta, was active in Berhampur in the 1780's. Cf. below, p. 100. See also *Bengal, Past and Present*, vol. 2, Jan.–July 1908, pp. 216 f. and ibid., vol. 30, July–September 1925, plates facing p. 131.

9. See, for example, M. Edwardes, *Battles of the Indian Mutiny*, London, 1963.

10. R. C. Majumdar, *History of the Freedom Movement in India*, Calcutta, 1962, and S. N. Sen, *Eighteen Fifty-Seven*, New Delhi, 1957.

2 · Individual Patterns

THERE is no great difference between the urban patterns which we have studied and the individual models which we shall now study. Even separate structures reflect political relations, social contradictions and functions of an official nature. But I think that in order to understand how intimately they are connected with their background, we must examine certain buildings in greater detail.

The architectural works and plans which are to be dealt with were all erected or projected after 1750 and built by the French or British, i.e., the nations which were then politically dominant. They are available for a closer examination in drawings that have been preserved or buildings that still exist and can therefore be studied (sometimes both). We shall make the acquaintance of a number of types of buildings: churches, town halls, residences in town and country, as well as tombs and monuments fulfilled very important functions in the lives of the colonists. Other structures have a function of a more specialized official or private nature, such as the Palais de Justice in Pondicherry, Writers' Buildings, The Mint in Calcutta and Bombay.

If we concentrate our attention on the architectural work, we find that this mainly had the character of variations on a given theme: a prototype or model of European origin. The architect's contribution was to adapt the building to the climate or other rather impersonal factors. The architect himself was, in fact, anonymous, although we may know his name. It is very seldom that we find originality in the forms or 'temperament' that can be read into the structures, and when we do so, as in the godown for grain at Bankipur or General Martin's Palace-Tomb in Lucknow we are more or less confused.

Thus when we talk of individual patterns, we think of the structures as being individual rather than of the architect. It is difficult to arrange India's European buildings according to models normally used by architectural historians. I think that only in one section can I establish with certainty a connection that fulfils the general requirements of 'causality'. It is, to be sure, an important connection, as it includes large buildings: Government House, Calcutta, plans for a palace at Murshidabad, the British Residency in Hyderabad and the College of Serampore. Otherwise the architecture must be regarded in very general terms if we are to find anything meaningful in the various stylistic characteristics.

It might be said then, that the baroque character disappeared about 1780 (e.g. Writers' Buildings), and that alterations in the neo-Classical architecture appear as a

93

divergence between architects such as Garstin and Wyatt (Town Hall and Government House, Calcutta) and Cowper and Forbes (Town Hall, Bombay and the Mint, Calcutta).[1] While the former still follow Palladian models, the latter represent the pure Greek Revival. This change took place about 1820 and it can be simultaneously observed in Europe — even in England, despite the fact that there Palladio's dogmas were adhered to for a very long time.[2]

i French Government Houses in Pondicherry

In the middle of the 18th century Dupleix had a government house built in Pondicherry. Its design possessed a military weight and a magnificence that corresponded well with Dupleix's politics in other spheres.[1]

The plan for the new building is attributed in the inventory to an engineer, Dumont. His plans do not seem to have been preserved; those now existing were made later, probably to be sent home to France.[2] They represent a very large building. The façade is dominated by a two-storey loggia; the Tuscan–Doric arcade of the ground floor supports an Ionic order. Masks and festoons can be seen between the columns, and the central pediment of the centre part, like those above the side projections is crowded with coats of arms and trophies.

The impression made by the richness of detail and magnificence in this Franco-Italian formation has been heightened by the effect of contrast: the loggia is placed in front of a building which has been designed very simply. But it is also disturbed by two staircase towers and the upper storey of the central part which projects above the horizontal roofline. The integration of the parts of the building therefore seems to be very much a matter of chance, and the exterior — particularly the rear, which resembles a fort — suggests that the architect had been a builder of fortifications and not used to civil constructions of this kind. The planning and interior treatment are, however, carried out with great consistency.

The loggia forms a screen in front of the south façade; inside it lie the most important rooms with a corridor on the other side. Two short wings have been extended at right angles to the main building. The corridors run into the wings, and smaller staircases have been placed in the angles thus formed and lead up to the roof terrace. Between these staircases lies a rectangular staircase, which is actually one of the largest components of the whole building. Thus much space has been taken up to form an impressive entrance. If we are impressed, as the architect hoped, and go through the building once more, we proceed as follows: flight of steps, loggia, entrance hall, corridor, grand staircase up to the second storey, and open corridor. Finally we stand in the large drawing-room, a high-ceilinged room which gets its light from an upper gallery. All the rooms are decorated in a magnificent Rococo style. The entrance hall has niches holding allegorical sculptures and a fountain;[3] wall panels, friezes, mirrors, lintels, lattice-work and other details correspond very closely to the models elaborated by Jacques François

94

Blondel and other French interior decorators. Thus they have been transferred, quite unaltered, from their European environment. But on the whole the building is excellently suited to its tropical setting. This is specially the case with the upper storey, where the row of rooms for banquets, council meetings and for the governor's private use have been placed between well-ventilated galleries which provide coolness and fresh air.

Pondicherrry was destroyed by British troops in 1761,[4] Dupleix's Government House demolished with other buildings. It had been completed in 1752 and thus was scarcely ten years old. Dupleix had the opportunity of living there for only two years, before being called home, in 1754, to a life which did not require such a grand setting.

Bourçet, the engineer, was responsible for the reconstruction of Government House.[5] It was situated in the same place as before; part of the old foundations could be used, and the site was arranged on the whole after the pattern of the *maisons de plaisance* then fashionable in the homeland. In an edition of *Architecture Moderne*, a book written by C. E. Briseux, and published by C. A. Jombert in 1764, we find several models which resemble Bourçet's plans,[6] which were approved in October, 1766. The architect designed separate parts for the use of the governor and his family and for the kitchen quarters and offices. Walls and large courtyards divide the various units.

Bourçet's main construction is considerably more modest than the one designed by Dumont. It consists of one storey and has on the south side a complete small loggia with six columns supporting the roof. No longer do groups of trophies or allegorical figures bear witness to the dignity of the house. The column order is undecorated Tuscan, and the walls, including those outside, are arranged in simple panels.

Two years later another storey was added, also by Bourçet.[7] He reverted to the old design with a combination of Tuscan–Doric and Ionic columns in the loggia, while the side walls with simple window surrounds and quoins also recall the back of Dupleix's Government House. Thus the whole structure is not impressive, but it seems that the interior gradually acquired a more splendid character. The traveller Grandpré says in 1789 that the building was more magnificent as a residence than that of the British governor in Calcutta, which at that time was certainly true.[8] We know how the upper storey was arranged through a later architectural drawing signed by the engineer, Spinasse, in 1821.[9] In the centre lies a large square drawing-room surrounded by corridors, the gallery of the south side, bedrooms and the governor's office. Between the corner rooms of the house runs an open loggia along the south façade. A detail added later was a spiral staircase leading up to the flat roof. Its upper part protrudes above the roof-line with its balustrade and urns, which again recall Dupleix's Government House. Thus it can be said that the latter was of significance as a prototype for many decades. What were copied were mainly the functional elements, while the brilliant elements became weaker. Baroque-Classicism changed into neo-Classicism.

One element in Dupleix's Government House which I have not yet mentioned is formed by the two outer rooms of the wings, which cannot be included in the official or residential suites. They were certainly used as storerooms which explains the enormously thick walls. Such an arrangement of the bottom or basement storey of the house was very usual in India. In the British area it is often called a 'godown'.[10] A plan of Government House in Cuddalore, drawn in 1789 by an engineer, Malavois, indicates just such a function. Thus the whole basement-storey consists of vaulted storerooms, and in addition storage space was even made in the ramps leading up to the first floor.[11] The actual residence lies like a small hump on this foundation which was put to a definite commercial use.

ii The Palais de Justice in Pondicherry

The existence of architecture in Pondicherry always seemed to be threatened. We have seen the influence of the destructive forces through the history of Government House. Repeated wars with England end unfortunately and building activity follows in the backwash of political changes.

In 1778, as a result of the development of events in the American War of Independence, Pondicherry was taken by the English and its fortifications were destroyed. The town was restored to the French in 1783; peace was made in 1785, and towards the beginning of the 1790's some building activity started in spite of the fact that the place was no longer the centre of the French colonies in the East. The governor-general then had his seat of government on the Île de France.

In 1788 the engineer La Lustière signed the drawings for a Palais de Justice du Conseil Supérieur which was placed in 'White Town', a little way north-east of Government House.[1] The building has one storey and was constructed on an almost square ground plan. Towards the street the façade is dominated by an Ionic gallery with a slightly projecting entrance. In the pediment over the latter is an allegory of Justice. For the rest the structure is topped only by a panelled parapet. The openings in the façade towards the garden form an arcade; Ionic columns in couples lend distinction to this part of the building, while the offices are much more simply designed.

Even if the treatment of the façade is conventional, the terrace roof and the galleries as well as the height of the rooms show the adaptation to the tropical climate which is an outstanding feature of the plan.[2]

The gallery has a counterpart inside the building. The space between these two parallel corridors is arranged symmetrically. Round a large central hall lie audience rooms, offices and archive rooms. On the other side of the inner corridor is a semicircular courtyard, and round this, the offices. A staircase in the background leads up to the roof terrace which was certainly used in the same way as in dwelling-houses.

Thus the plan adopted shows that, like the façade, it has a double function. While it takes the climate into account, it keeps the beautifully laid out administration rooms apart from the simpler offices. The same division is to be found in the front towards the sea. The ornamental garden with its oval pond and strict parterres is enclosed by a wall; on the other side lies the kitchen garden.

This is how the Palais de Justice probably appeared until 1821, when Spinasse, the engineer, who made changes in Government House, also made certain additions to the former.[3] The garden was treated as a more organic composition. The baroque scheme was softened by pergolas and large, freely growing trees. And the building itself received an addition which may seem insignificant but which altered both the exterior and the central room. The addition was an octagonal lantern which gave a vertical effect to the long façade and which at the same time illuminated *la grande salle*.

iii The Gates of Pondicherry

The work of the French engineers in Pondicherry covered the entire range of building activity. As we have seen, they even constructed a palace in a somewhat heavy style following the pattern in France, but had an eye to the requirements of the situation and the climate. The pattern becomes even more conventional in their natural field of activity, i.e. the construction of fortifications. In this field they followed Bélidor in particular. His book, *La Science des Ingénieurs* (Paris 1719) was used in Pondicherry, as well as in other European colonies, far into the 19th century.[1]

The builder of the Palais de Justice, La Lustière, also designed a couple of gates in 1788 which were to guard the most important access roads to the rown.[2] The models on which he based his designs were Bélidor's.[3] Similar structures had already been erected in the English forts in Calcutta and Madras, and some years later the Danes in nearby Tranquebar were to adopt the same pattern.[4]

La Lustière did not copy the models slavishly, but the alterations he made were small. He simplified the model by taking away the groups of trophies and the coats of arms and gave the superstructure a clearly neo-Classic effect. The consoles of the sides disappeared and what remained was a strict attic storey above the cornice. The foundations, the system of pilasters against their background of rustic work, the composition of the centre section and the mouldings of the entablature, on the other hand, correspond with the prototype. In the Porte Villenour the order remained Tuscan; in the Porte Madras the Doric order was adopted with more richly worked details.

This was the façade which the visitor saw first. The inside was not so elaborately designed. In the middle, the Porte Villenour has an arcade divided into three sections with pilasters on both sides. This is an example of pure engineering architecture of which we shall find more in the next chapter. The heaviness of the wall overpowers the elements of style. The function of the construction is, so to speak, obvious through its composition, without its being emphasized. The long building on the inside of the wall was erected to serve as a passage and patrol post. On both sides of the three dark tunnels there were guard-rooms and on the short sides straight stairs lead up to the top of the wall where there is a possibility for a look-out and for defence.

iv Godowns for Opium and Grain

Patna, together with Ghazipur, was the centre of the opium trade in North India. All three Companies, Dutch, Danes and English, had 'factories' there.[1] A set of architectural drawings, possibly dating from the 1780's, shows a proposed rebuilding of the English 'factory' which was located in Gulzarbagh, somewhat to the west of the town of Patna.[2]

The plan includes some stores in the immediate vicinity of the river (the Ganges) and a main building composed of three equally long units which form an open square. The elevation reveals a very simple type of architecture. On the north as well as on the south side, the centre is emphasized by a portico with heavy arcades which are almost completely without decoration. The walls are enlivened only by window openings which succeed each other in an irregular rhythm. Everything points to the fact that the building was designed to serve its function and nothing else. The conformity with recognized architectural models is quite accidental.[3]

Some miles west of Gulzarbagh lies Bankipur. The place is known as an early English military centre, but the name has chiefly been connected with a monument erected there at the end of the 18th century: the Bankipur Gola. Following disastrous experience of crop-failure and famine during the 1770's and during several years in the beginning of the next decade, it was urged in Calcutta to erect *golas* which should contain grain stores, reserves which could be used in times of crisis.[4] The driving force behind this project was J. P. Auriol, agent for supplies to the Presidencies other than Bengal. A general plan issued in January 1784 decreed, amongst other things, that such a granary should be built in Bankipur.[5] Already in December of the previous year, John Garstin, who was then a captain, had been recommended for this work; later on he was to be responsible for several architectural works: in 1788 he constructed the Futwa bridge, and in the beginning of the 19th century he was active in Calcutta.[6]

The drawings for the gola in Bankipur have been preserved; they are not signed, but it is possible to ascribe them to Garstin even though it has been maintained that Lt.-Col. Henry Watson, who was chief engineer for Bengal and approved the suggestion, was also partly responsible for the design of this gola.[7]

The plan is simple enough: a collection of concentric circles indicate thick walls and an opening in the middle. The largest radius amounts to about 120 ft. Two staircases have been indicated. On the side elevation they prove to be symmetrical spiral ramps which run on the outside up to the opening at the top of the gola. The actual wall shell is formed like a gigantic globe. The idea was to carry the corn up the stairs and throw it into the opening. The gola should then be emptied through two doors at ground level.

The building was finished in 1786 and Garstin made a completion report as follows: 'The Dome was closed in the month of December last, and from the uncommon Heat of the Season, it is much drier than would be expected, and will I think be sufficiently

98

so to receive the grain after the hot winds of the next year have blown through it.' The architect was satisfied with his work, although the dome of the building was not exactly as he intended. The inconsiderable deviation he attributes to the expansion of the chain which was used in the construction.[8] But Garstin was also the only one who was satisfied with the building which was quite unsuitable for its purpose. Why this was so, it is difficult to say. Possibly it was filled with grain once, but immediately changes in the walls were noted and it was feared that they would burst, or, perhaps, they never dried as was expected. Thus the fame of the godown is not connected with its intended function. Mrs. Sherwood, who visited it in March 1806, used it as a whispering gallery: 'It has so good an echo that it repeats 32 times.'[9] And William Parry Okeden, who came here some years later, merely stated that it was the most ridiculous thing he had ever seen. In spite of its size it could not contain more than a day's ration for the inhabitants of the town and the surrounding province. He also pointed out that the walls were badly constructed and had started to give way.[10]

Nevertheless, in spite of the criticism of Okeden and others, the gola still stands like a colossus on the bank of the Ganges. By its shape and its size it forces itself upon our notice and invites attempts at interpretation: Why does it have that shape?

When comparing the gola with contemporary monuments, one spontaneously recalls the projects of the French architects of the Revolution. They include without exception simple stereometric shapes, pyramids, cones and spheres which are often of gigantic size. Ramps and stairs run up their sides; but they convey the impression of being impossible to mount: superhuman in scale, heroic and *mysterious*. Nevertheless, many of them indicate their function in a very direct manner. Jean Jacques Lequeu's Temple de la Terre is shaped like a terrestrial globe, and the house which Nicolas Ledoux conceived for the river warden in Chaux simply consists of a gigantic water pipe.[11]

Can we regard Garstin's gola as an analogous example of *architecture parlante*? It is shaped like a beehive and in it the products of the fields should be collected in the same way as the bees collect their store of honey. Such an interpretation would be feasible, but not very probable; it presupposes a spiritual conception which cannot so easily be ascribed to a military engineer like Garstin. The other buildings constructed by him do not display any imagination or daring. It is also rather difficult to assume that he had the possibility of picking up the new ideas which were then in vogue in Europe.

The explanation is considerably simpler and can be found near at hand in the Indian environment where circular houses were erected for storing grain.[12] These buildings could be made fairly large; 'Their round granaries are all raised considerably above other buildings,' reports Bishop Heber from Futwa very near Patna.[13] The buildings with which he compares it are, however, small and it is quite impossible that there existed an Indian granary that could be compared in size to Garstin's gigantic creation which, incidentally, is reproduced as a veritable Tower of Babel in Heber's account of his travels. It is unique in its dimensions and its use.

Is it possible to trace any deeper meaning in Garstin's adaptation of the Indian prototype? Probably not, although we know that Garstin was interested in old Indian architecture, which he sketched.[14] The godown in Bankipur must be regarded as an experiment for purely practical purposes.[15] It is tragic that the attempt failed. The central store which was to provide grain for the starving multitudes was changed into a mere curiosity.

v Writers' Buildings

In 1780, a building of considerable length was erected at Large Tank in Calcutta, intended to accommodate the junior staff of civil servants of the East India Company. It contained nineteen sets of apartments and in the centre some rooms which, from the beginning of the 19th century, were used as class-rooms for the newly started College of Fort William. Young clerks received their first training in this institute after their arrival in India.[1]

The architect of Writers' Buildings was most probably Thomas Lyon, a carpenter who was summoned from England in the 1760's to assist with the construction of the new Fort. In time he advanced to the position of superintendent of the works at Dinapur and Berhampur and he also took part in the erection of several buildings in Calcutta.[2] It is, however, doubtful whether he personally had any influence on the design of the buildings or whether his work only covered directing and superintending the actual construction work, while the plans were obtained elsewhere. The hotel-like lay-out of Writers' Buildings was not unique; it was more or less a product of its time. In the same year as these enormous quarters were erected in Calcutta, in far-away Sweden a wing with similarly arranged small apartments for the ladies and gentlemen-in-waiting was annexed to one of the Royal pleasure-palaces. Each apartment had exactly the same furniture and equipment.[3] The origin of this type of building would seem to lie in an attempt at standardization according to the military pattern.

This impression is recalled when looking at the façade of the building. The outside as well as the inside show a symmetrical composition which is almost dull.[4] The windows succeed one another in monotonous repetition. There are fifty-seven sets of them in all, distributed over two corner projections, flat sections in between, and a central projection articulated by Ionic columns. Only the attic over the latter rises above the long straight roofline. Everything conveys the impression of civil barracks.

Mrs. Graham called Writers' Buildings 'a shabby hospital', and probably meant it partly morally.[5] Others agreed as to the frequently extravagant mode of living within its walls and talked naïvely of champagne suppers and 'the joyous songs and loud rehearsing tally-hoes of the many generations of writers.'[6]

Later on, attempts were made to enliven the aesthetic appearance of the building: the façade was given low pediments, as can be seen from photographs dating from the middle of the 19th century.[7] The construction was completely rebuilt in 1880, and was turned into the Bengal Secretariat.

vi British Government Houses in Calcutta and Madras

In his book, *British Government in India*, Lord Curzon has described in detail the fairly itinerant existence of the governors and (after 1774) the governor-generals in 18th-century Calcutta. Their residence was originally inside Fort William, and was described by Alexander Hamilton as 'a most regular piece of architecture', but was later moved into the city. Lord Curzon was able to mention a number of such places; the last of these, called Government House V, was used by, among others, Warren Hastings, Cornwallis and John Shore and lay on Esplanade Row, with the Council House as its nearest neighbour.[1] Both these buildings had to make way for the Marquis of Wellesley's new building in 1798.

Wellesley had come to Calcutta in May of that year and immediately found the existing buildings insignificant and unsuited to their high purpose. By June he was said to have already decided on the erection of a new residence.

The Company's architect, Edward Tiretta, and Lieutenant Charles Wyatt of the Bengal Engineers, each presented a plan for the new residence. Wyatt's plans were preferred. The reason for the choice is not known, but Wyatt's project was undeniably striking. The dimensions of the proposed building were considerable; by stretching out in all four directions, the plan gave an impression of expansion and power, and by its provenance was reminiscent of the lordly country seats of the homeland. The prototype was Kedleston Hall in Derbyshire, which was built in the middle of the 18th century for the first Lord Scarsdale. Much has already been said about the resemblance between the two buildings; Lord Curzon, who undoubtedly had the greatest possibility of being informed, provides the best information. He knew Government House in Calcutta as Viceroy, while Kedleston was his own home. Others have not been so well acquainted with these places. Elsewhere it is stated, for instance, that Government House in Calcutta is a copy of Robert Adam's Kedleston Hall.[2] That is very misleading.

It is true that Robert Adam had a part in building Kedleston. His greatest contribution to the exterior was the grandiose triumphal arch on the south façade. But Adam was engaged in the work at a late stage. His predecessor was James Paine, and it was the latter's drawings that Charles Wyatt used; they had been reproduced in Paine's own survey of his work, *Plans, elevations, and sections of Noblemen's and Gentlemen's houses*.[3] Thus when Wyatt saw the publication it was not more than fifteen years old, as it was issued in 1783, but it reproduced designs that were considerably older. The plan of Kedleston was dated 1761. Wyatt must have been aware of this, and he did not copy the prototype, but altered and integrated it into the aesthetic scheme of the 1790's. The final result bears a certain resemblance to Nash, not to Paine — or Adam. But the changes were not made only for aesthetic reasons.

The plans for both buildings have the same basic structure, which is very characteristic.[4] The houses consist of a centre part which has an apsidal arrangement on the south, a staircase in the north and large state apartments. From the corners the corridors branch

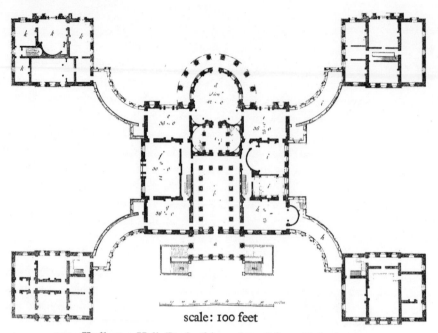

scale: 100 feet

11a. Kedleston Hall, Derbyshire; plan of the principal storey.

off, four winding passages connecting the main building with four wings. There the resemblance ceases. Paine's design is characterized by bold forms. The walls are thick and here and there niches are cut into them. In some of the rooms the architect has placed segmental walls which repeat the windings of the corridors and interlock almost like the wheels of a clock in the apsidal part and the staircase attached to this.

In Wyatt's drawing the rhythm has slackened off: the contours are thinner; small pieces of wall are arranged in rows around large empty surfaces. If we look at the principal storey, the large hall is intersected by two rows of columns and is situated between transverse halls. One of these serves as an entrance hall, while the other is connected to the apse. There is no longer any staircase in the centre; the stairs have been placed in the corners, where the corridors join the main building. The ceremonial elements thus have been renounced. The magnificent succession in the centre part of Kedleston has been broken. That is to say, the ceremonial staircase has been moved to the exterior. Here there is a tremendous flight of steps for ceremonial purposes quite different in formation from that of Kedleston. It forms a gently rising processional way with space for a large number of soldiers presenting arms at the sides. I believe that this change, like several of the others, has climatic causes. On account of the heat, a plan with almost independent wings which would get cooling winds from all quarters was desirable. For purposes of ventilation the walls were broken through at short intervals, the openings all being placed opposite each other. And for climatic reasons the flight

102

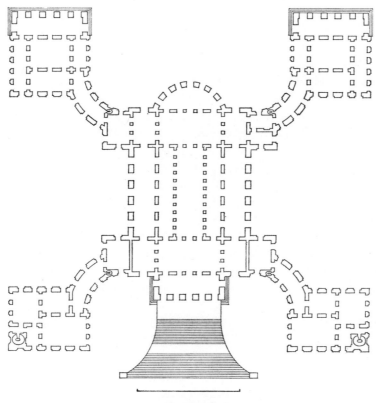

scale: 100 feet

11b. Government House, Calcutta; plan of the basement storey.

of steps faced north, where it was 'least unsuitable', and could be used at any rate in winter.[5] A special hall for 'dining in the hot season' was situated on the ground floor.

The greatest change in the horizontal elevation was that the Indian residence had three storeys instead of Kedleston's two. The ground floors can be said to correspond; they are low and dark. In Calcutta one enters the ground floor through a porch concealed under the large flight of steps. Above this plinth Kedleston has its fine state apartments with high-ceilinged rooms which continue through the attic into arched roofs and domes over both the staircase and the round salon on the south side. The state apartments in Calcutta are on *two* floors. The large halls lie uniformly above one-another. The lower one is called 'the principal dining room' and the upper 'the Levée and Ball room'. These receive their light from the side through Venetian windows, while Kedleston's salons, which have adjoining rooms at the sides, are lit from above. These differences have naturally left clear traces on the exterior.

In its façade effect Paine's building is based on a repetition of the whole complex of forms. This can be seen most clearly on the north side, where the wings reproduce on a

103

small scale what is 'happening' at the same time in the middle: the rusticated plinth supports a high storey and an attic and the latter a sloping roof; the columns of the centre part bear a pediment etc. In this way an effect is achieved which is simultaneous, directed from the centre and baroque in character. Wyatt on the other hand has placed the whole complex under *one* straight roof ridge. Thus the wings and the centre part of the structure are connected by the corridors being carried up to the same height, and the wings run uniformly through the façades; that is the most important alteration. Further, the centre part, which no longer dominates by its size, alone retained the row of columns, the pediment and the large Venetian windows. The flight of steps of course, also draws attention to the centre, where it widens out like a peacock's trailing tail.

The treatment of detail is finally what definitely breaks the baroque scheme and gives Government House in Calcutta traits of John Nash's London architecture. The material is brick and plaster, not stone, and the finish or 'make-up' of the façade, as Sir John Summerson would call it, gives homogeneity to all the different elements. The rusticated work, the inlaid ornamental panels with their festoons, even the pilasters and pediments have an effect of blind-tooling in the plastering. This effect is, of course, clearer now, when the whole building has the same creamy white colour, but it also appears on the drawing, where the ground colour is a light ochre.

In February, 1799, the foundation stone of Government House was laid. About four years later the building itself was reported to be finished. Then an iron fence was still being erected, and the clearing of the large area round the house had not yet been carried out. The open space aimed at was specially important for giving the gates their proper effect. These had been erected outside each wing in order to guard the entrances from Old Court Street and Council House Street. There were four of them, in themselves considerable structures which dominate the foreground on most early drawings of Government House, especially those made by James B. Fraser.[6] The plan for the gates was borrowed partly from Robert Adam's Syon House, where a walking lion crowns the arch of the gate and adjoining colonnades mark the boundary between park and street, and partly from William Chambers's arch at Wilton. But even here Wyatt altered the prototype. Instead of the ornamental pilasters and lightly handled details, he used a Tuscan–Doric order with bucranes and shields in the metopes and flanking sphinxes on the colonnade.[7] These sphinxes were originally made of teak, but cracked and were replaced by cement bodies.

When completed, Government House occupied an ostentatious place on the Esplanade and, as no trees concealed it, it could be seen at a distance over the flat Maidan. As an architectural manifestation, Wellesley's building was magnificent and even a challenge — the latter being particularly the opinion of the Court of Directors of the East India Company in London. They had not seen the building: in fact, they had hardly received any information about its erection. But they were informed of the cost, which was tremendous. Wellesley's architectural policy, in which the beginning of a considerable country residence at Barrackpore should also be included, led, in fact, to prolonged proceedings with his superiors in England and was one of the reasons why he was recalled from his post as Governor-General.

Among those who defended Wellesley was Lord Valentia and, later, Lord Ellenborough, who both regarded the new building from a very special point of view. They saw it as a symbol of political expansion and imperial power. They certainly shared this notion with Wellesley who, in June 1803, called Calcutta the 'Capital of the British Empire in India, and the seat of supreme authority'.[8] Lord Valentia wrote:

'The Esplanade leaves a grand opening, on the edge of which is placed the new Government House erected by Lord Wellesley, a noble structure, although not without faults in the architecture; and, upon the whole, not unworthy of its destination. The sums expended upon it have been considered as extravagant by those who carry European ideas and European economy into Asia, but they ought to remember that India is a country of splendour, of extravagance and of outward appearances; that the Head of a mighty Empire ought to conform himself to the prejudices of the country he rules over; and that the British, in particular, ought to emulate the splendid works of the Princes of the House of Timour, lest it should be supposed that we merit the reproach which our great rivals, the French, have ever cast upon us, of being alone influenced by a sordid mercantile spirit. In short, I wish India to be ruled from a palace, not from a counting-house; with the ideas of a Prince, not with those of a retail-dealer in muslins and indigo.'[9]

Lord Valentia's self-confident words about princely power and English suzerainty speak for themselves; I would only draw attention to the conflict between military and political interests on the one hand and commercial ones on the other hand which he finally formulates in the opposites *palace* and *counting-house*. The same gulf shows itself almost at the same time in Madras, where, however, the argument is the reverse. The traders feel that their commerce is threatened by the too challenging gestures of the ruling power.[10]

Valentia's way of regarding Government House from the point of view of the ruling caste did not make possible any detailed criticism. He overlooked the structure itself in considering its significance. Other travellers, on the other hand, liked to dwell upon details, among them the Dane, C. A. Bluhme, a member of the Government Council at Tranquebar, who came to Calcutta in 1824. He admired the outside, but was disappointed with the interior of the building. The ceilings were low and decorated without taste and were also in great need of repair, as they had been destroyed by termites.[11] This was clearly a recurrent problem. The same thing had happened to the first fabric ceiling — painted by one Greuze — and it had to be repaired only a few years after being completed. The traveller Steen Bille was still more critical. He considered that the exterior was too compressed to produce a fine architectural effect. He also described the flocks of large birds — adjutant cranes — which alighted every evening on the balustrades of Government House, where they settled themselves to sleep like queer-shaped urns.[12] Such 'fixed' elements now form interruptions in the roof ridge. They are not in Wyatt's original drawings, but were set up a hundred years later by Lord Curzon, after the model of Kedleston.

Far more important than marginal notes of itinerant Scandinavians, however, is a report by an Oriental, the son of a Malayan merchant, who visited Government House soon after it was finished. He came to attend the Governor-General's levée, was carried to the palace in a palanquin and then taken up through the state apartments to go through all the ceremonial. Thus what he describes is the building's highest function. Everything made a vivid impression on him, and one would like to say that he was overwhelmed in exactly the way Wellesley had intended. After seeing the magnificence around the European Resident and realizing the political strength behind the façades and uniforms, he could tell his countrymen about the journey on his return home, 'that Malays may no longer be ignorant of this great country'.

But it is not certain that his report can be interpreted in this direct way. Maria Graham, who reproduced the description as an appendix to her *Journal of a Residence in India*, points out that it has also the form of a caricature, and in that case the satire is serious, because it is more or less unconscious.[13] This scepticism is an interesting fact, whether it arises from Maria Graham herself or from her witness, Ibrahim, son of Candu the merchant:

'It was in this country, in this country of Bengal, which is in this place called Calcutta, — how many months journey from Penang! — on the fifteenth day of the month of Shaaban, in the year of the Hegyra one thousand two hundred and twenty-five, at the hour of ten in the morning, when all Malays remained in the same state of ignorance as when I left them, that I, Ibrahim, the son of Candu the merchant, went to the palace of the Rajah, with all the great men of the Rajah's court, and was admitted even to the second story, (or rather second heaven).

'How beautiful is this palace, and great its extent — who can describe it! Who can relate the riches of this country, and, above, all, the beauty of the palace! When I entered the great gates, and looked around from my palankeen (for in this country even I, Ibrahim, the son of Candu the merchant, had my palankeen) and when I beheld the beauty and extent of the compound, the workmanship of the gates, of which there are five, and on the tops of which lions, carved out of stones, as large as life, seem small, and as if they were running without fearing to fall.[14] I thought that I was no longer in the world I had left in the east . . .

'The floors of the great hall are of black stone, polished and shining like a mirror, so that I feared to walk on them; and all around, how many transparent lustres and branches for lights were suspended, dazzling and glistening so that I could not look for long upon them!'[15]

'Until I arrived at the second story, the stairs were all of stone, which formed part of the wall, and had no support. I then entered the great hall where all the Tuans were assembled, . . .

'The floor of this great room is not of stone, because it is of dark-coloured wood beautyfully polished . . .

'At the end of the hall is a throne, superlatively beautiful, supported by four pillars of gold, and having hangings of the colour of blood, enriched with golden fringe; it is beautiful in the extreme, and the elegance of the drapery is surprising. Within this throne there is a golden chair, with hangings and fringe of gold, in which the Rajah sits when he receives other Rajahs and Vakeels. . . .

'It was three days after before I could think of, and recollect all I had seen on this great day. I write this history, that men may not be ignorant of Bengal, and of the manners and customs of the great Rajah of the English;'

Wellesley's active architectural policy in Calcutta was to a large extent repeated by Lord Clive in Madras.[16] He came out to India in 1798. Like Wellesley, he regarded the existing buildings as unsatisfactory for ceremonial purposes, and therefore carried out a programme of rearrangement and new construction. And, like Wellesley, he was finally recalled from his post, partly because the Court of Directors in London considered that his building activity had been far too expensive.

The situation regarding the government buildings in Madras was very complicated. At the close of the 18th century a number of premises inside and outside the fort were at the disposal of the governor. H. D. Love has given a detailed account of their location and at what times they were used. Clive tried to sort out this confusion, in the first place by converting one of them into his permanent residence.[17]

The house he chose lay outside the fort, on the other side of the Island. It therefore already had a name, Triplicane Garden House, and an interesting history. During the struggles with the French it had been damaged by Count Lally's troops, was repaired in 1762 and considerably improved during the governorship of Archibald Campbell. It was with this improved building that Clive started. Love states that it had an extent of 130 ft. Clive increased it to 205 ft. What does the change involve? It probably means that the entrance was moved from the west side to the east. If we study the new plan, we see two rooms, in the one case a room with a staircase that protrudes into the long corridor on the west side of the house.[18] The outer walls on this room may have been the outer walls of Campbell's residence; the distance between them is 130 ft, symmetrically divided on each side of the axis. Thus Clive enlarged the house, and it was certainly he who had the enormous verandas constructed. If we see them in elevation, they give the impression of a pleated coat round three sides of the house. The intercolumniations vary, but in the portico they are as large as ten diameters! Thus the colonnades look like a wide and airy latticework.[19] Along both storeys and terraces run balustrades, and over the roof three 'attics' rise which recall Dupleix's Government House at Pondicherry and give top light to the large rooms in the upper storey. Here the governor had state apartments and his private suite (the levées were still held in the fort). It should be noted that the house lies on a low basement which does not leave space for godowns or sunken offices; in this way the building shows its pronounced character of a country residence. The ground floor was used for living in. The household department is beside the house.

The architect whom Clive used for these structural alterations was John Goldingham.

He is said to have been Danish, but neither the name nor anything else would suggest that this was the case. It is possible that he may have become a Danish citizen during a short residence at Tranquebar. It is, however, known that he was active as a mathematician and astronomer and that in 1799 he designed and built Kerr's Chapel in Black Town, and that in March, 1800, he was appointed Civil Engineer, as Clive was dissatisfied with the man who had held the post before.[20]

Goldingham did his utmost to be worthy of the Governor's confidence. Government House was only a detail in his building activity — and in a considerably greater compositional context. Goldingham utilized the location of the house to make a large English park around it. Details in the landscape were accentuated and improved: the plan contains both artificial mounds and a sunken garden. A proposed bridge leads across from the Island; actually, the road comes all the way from Fort St. George and continues its winding way to the Residence. But that is not what first catches the eye. The road passes the main building in the complex — the Banqueting Hall.

There was an earlier banqueting hall inside the fort, a basilican construction for which the black granite columns were used which had been lost to and re-captured from the French at Pondicherry.[21] The Triplicane Banqueting Hall was a new construction and completely the work of John Goldingham. The external columns continue through two storeys; the order is Tuscan–Doric, and the longish hall rests on a high podium, which on three sides was turned into a terrace over rustic arcades. Sphinxes guard the entrance by the large flight of steps on the fourth side. In the frieze can be seen metopes with spoils of war and in the pediment a large group of trophies where the name Seringapatam was inserted among the arms. On the opposite side could be read: Plassey.

An aquatint, published by Edward Orme, shows us how we should interpret the building: as a marshal setting, an antique hall with columns beside the façade of Government House and a centre for brilliant receptions.[22] But let us regard it for a moment as a concrete structure and observe a few details of the exterior. The columns are a quarter sunk into the wall. Between them is a lower row of door openings and niches and an upper row of square openings, lighting a mezzanine. These openings, especially the doors with their cornices, are wedged in between the columns. Such an arrangement of colonnade and wall motif belongs to the architecture of Mannerism; it is full of contradictions and very sensitive to alterations in the structure.

Even the column order is borrowed from 16th-century Italy, not directly, but probably through William Chambers. He used it for his Temple of Bellona in Kew Gardens, both as to the columns and the metope motif: urns set against shields.[23] In this connection, Goldingham's elimination of the mutules is rather surprising. The upper part of the cornice lies directly on the frieze.

Thus the façade shows a somewhat old-fashioned and free treatment of the classical elements. This is not unusual amongst architects in India, and one could perhaps say that they allow themselves breaches of doctrine because they attach importance to the effect and the function of the *building*, not the style. Another clear example of this are the urns which are now in the niches, but which were not included in the design. They are large in order that they may be visible, and if one sees them from directly in front, they also easily fill the concave profile in which they are placed. But from the side it is seen that they have no more volume than a flat fish. As they cannot stand sufficiently steady on their narrow bases, they have been chained to the wall!

The function of the Banqueting Hall, both outside and inside, was for official entertainments. The interior was to form a magnificent framework for the public receptions held there, and it also shows the same attempts at effect as the exterior. It is formed as a large hall; columns in two tiers support the ceiling and have a gallery between them; this gallery is lit by the attic windows, though the latter are not visible from the floor. This upper light emphasizes the ornaments on the ceiling, which are made in relief. The frieze and cornice of the first floor are also extremely ornamental. The general colouring of the large room is now white and gold, but Lord Valentia, who saw the buildings in 1803, tells of a bolder colour scheme:

'the floors, the walls, and the pillars are of the most beautiful chunam, of different colours, almost equal in splendour to marble itself.'[24]

In its alternation between pink, white and yellow, the frieze of the outside of the Banqueting Hall is the only part which now follows this colour scheme.

The Banqueting Hall was open to the public on 7 October, 1802,[25] on which occasion the Peace of Amiens was celebrated; this amongst other things fixed the relations between the English and French colonies. But one should not be misled on that account into believing that the building was a sort of temple to peace. Its deeper symbolism rather indicates the contrary; it points to victories which had been won by force of arms and had resulted in territorial gains and great prestige. I have mentioned that the names of Plassey and Seringapatam are to be found on the pediment. After the latter name stands, significantly enough, not the year of the treaty, 1792, but '1799', the year of the fourth war against Mysore which finished with the death of Tipu and the conquest of the province.

The symbolism of the building is well suited to the military atmosphere of the time of Napoleon. The groups of trophies on the pediment, the war trophies of the metopes and the decoration of the large ceiling form a complete arsenal with inserted banners, fasces and eagles. The martial decoration was a perfect frame for the portraits which were set up in the hall: Eyre Coote, Cornwallis, Medows and a long succession of other famous military men were commemorated in this way. Thus the Banqueting Hall functioned very like a *Heroum*, a neo-Classical temple for hero-worship.

Not everyone joined the group of admirers. The peace-loving Heber was opposed both to the building and to the portraits.[26] And, as I mentioned, the Court of Directors in London was strongly critical. The Court's statement possibly indicates that Clive had excused himself by a reference to the neighbouring magnificent residence of the Nawab of Arcot:

'It by no means appears to us essential to the well-being of our Government in India that the pomp, magnificence and ostentation of the Native Governments should be adopted by the former; the expense to which such a system would naturally lead must prove highly injurious to our commercial interests.'[27]

That is to say, the conflict is exactly the same as in Calcutta, and the antithesis formulated by Valentia is just as applicable to the situation in Madras.

vii Plans for a Palace at Murshidabad

The new Government House in Calcutta was of some significance as a model for other structures in India. The merchant's son from Malaya was not the only Oriental to be impressed. The Nawab of Bengal gave concrete proof of his appreciation by ordering from the European architects plans for his own residence at Murshidabad. Two such drawings have been preserved.[1]

One of the plans is dated 16 February, 1804, but is not signed. The very limited drawing material makes all comparisons and attributions difficult, but one can possibly point to three presumptive designers: Blechynden, who succeeded Tiretta in 1803 as civil architect of the Company, Anbury, who at that time was working in Barrackpore on behalf of Wellesley, and finally Wyatt, who left India in the beginning of March 1804.[2]

The plans have several features in common with Government House in Calcutta. This is especially true of the central building which has a portico towards the north, a rectangular vestibule, a large hall with two colonnades and an adjoining absidial extension towards the south. These are characteristic resemblances, but they do not go further. The palace intended for the Nawab is constructed around a long lateral axis. The constant component used by the architect is a square of about 70 ft. per side. Corridors which are cross-vaulted in the middle form a connection between the buildings. The distribution of stairs has been effected with a certain precision. On most sides, the building is protected by verandas and the wall openings face each other. So much can be seen from the actual drawings which show the ground floor. We learn more about the whole structure from some notes on the drawing. Thus we can read amongst other things:

'The whole of the basement to be as plain as possible, to serve as Godowns, Closets etc. The wings are proposed to be plain throughout with common simple Cornices — Of the Centre the whole of the first floor to be of the Dorick Order, the Centre Hall complete with Frieze exposing Metopes & Triglyphs — the rest of the Rooms with the Dorick Cornice only. The Dimentions for the Columns of the Centre Hall in the first floor are as follows — f 20.6 in height with Entablature 3.6 equal to 24 feet under the beams, diameter of the Columns encreased from f 2.7 to 2.8. The Upper Story of the Centre to be of the Corinthian Order Complete the whole 27 feet under the beams, the Centre Hall, the Two Side Rooms, the Vestibule to be decorated with Friezes enriched either with relief Arabesques or painted as at Chumperpoka; The dimensions for the

Columns of the Centre Hall on the Upper Story are as follows: 23 f in height with Entablature 4 ft equal to 27 ft under the beams diameter of the Column 24/2-q. The whole of the floors to be laid with Chunar Stone on tiles without Burgahs — except in the upper Story of the Centre which the Nawab has expressed a desire should be boarded, & of 3 or 4 Inch plank to prevent too great a Sound when the Carpets are taken up in the hot Season. The whole of the Exterior of the building of the Jonic Order of Michael Angelo or that in the Ruins of Palmira & Belbec, of 9/2 diameter.'

No doubt, all this conveys the impression of an architect's trading in Classicism. The direct reference to the ruined Roman towns in Syria is of great interest; their monuments had been described by, amongst others, Wood and Dawkins. Here the attempt was made to teach an Oriental prince an architectural language, or rather a dialect, which already had a colonial and eastern touch. Perhaps the change in the functions as indicated in the plan was more radical. By tradition, the Indian palaces were divided into various units, each of which served a special purpose. There was a *Diwan-i Amm* or Hall of General Audience, a *Diwan-i Khass*, or Hall of Special Audience, etc. Now the state rooms were placed in *one* building together with the private apartments of the Nawab.

The other palace plan is signed by a famous name: Edward Tiretta. Here he calls himself 'Civil Architect to the Honbl. Company', which would indicate that the drawing was made before 1803. In that year he was succeeded in his post by Blechynden. The drawing could even be identical with the one he prepared for Government House in Calcutta and which was rejected.

In Tiretta's plan the wings are arranged linearly with the northern façade of the main building. The large rectangular hall contains an inner uniform frame of columns. The southern walls are protected by verandas with an intercolumniation of one diameter. The portico has also been designed differently, but on the whole his suggestions correspond to those of the first plan.

The plans did not give any quick result. It was not until a few decades later that a palace was erected in Murshidabad by Duncan Macleod, who during 1825–26 was the superintendent of Nizamat buildings and as from 1836 chief engineer for Bengal. His building shows that Government House in Calcutta was still used as a model.[3]

In the meantime, the motif of the two plans had been used in other places. The college in Serampore is the most obvious example, but the British Residency in Hyderabad could also be included in this series of large ensembles.[4]

viii British Residencies in Lucknow and Hyderabad

As do government houses, so British Residencies in the various Indian principalities display growing power. They do this quite obviously through their geographical location; they can be regarded as greatly advanced chessmen whose position is strengthened, without any actual change in their situation, as the political game advances. The Resident, who originally acted more like an ambassador to the foreign court, finally becomes the person who represents the real power when the British take over the control of the foreign policy of these principalities. In home affairs, the princes act, however, mainly in accordance with traditional Indian forms and remain almost unaffected by Western influence. The British Residency looks like an isolated phenomenon, an island in the Oriental environment.

In 1775, the capital of the province of Oudh during the reign of Asaf-ud-daulah was transferred from Fyzabad to Lucknow which became the centre of a hectic commercial activity and on the whole presented an over-heated milieu where practically everything was allowed and possible. We shall meet one of the European adventurers, Claude Martin, who was attracted there, made his fortune and built for himself a large palace.[1]

The Nawab himself invested fabulous sums of money in construction work; one item in his vast architectural programme was the erection of an official building for the British Resident.[2] Already in 1763 the old Nawab had signed a treaty in which he committed himself to accept a permanent Resident at his court.[3]

The Residency was placed high up on the green hill which is to-day encircled by the Buland Bagh Road and Old Kanpur Road. The construction work commenced in 1780, but the building was not completed until a few decades later under the Nawab Sa'adat Ali Khan.[4] As a result the composition became very irregular and contradictory. The actual ambassador's house was to be found in the north-eastern part of the construction equipped with a portico and a large veranda. These structural elements were placed against heavy walls and towers. The main storey in the south comprised a large hall in the centre and long and narrow galleries adjoined. To-day there is still beneath these rooms a suite of *tykhanas* which were used during the hot season. A spiral staircase leads to these rooms; the walls are very thick and, as is often the case in India, niches have been built into them for cupboards.

Several other buildings were added in the course of time to the ambassador's house; they served different purposes and were scattered all over the hill and surrounded by simple defences; these buildings were entered through a guard-house and a large gate which were both named after Major John Baillie, Resident from 1811–15. The composition included a banqueting hall and council chamber. The latter was erected immediately east of the Residency and would seem to have been added in the beginning of the 19th century under Sa'adat Ali Khan or Ghazi-ud-din Haidar.[5] In this case it would be of a later date than its counterpart in Madras. On the slope beneath the new building was the treasury.

The ground-plan of the banqueting hall is rectangular and clearly arranged with a large staircase in the west and two similar state apartments facing each other in the centre of the main storey. The exterior is dominated by a motif of coupled columns and by the Venetian windows through which light falls onto the staircases. Both these motifs occur on a plinth storey of normal height, the load-bearing sides of which have been emphasized by rusticated work. The veranda on the east is similar to the one of the Residency. These features were probably made at the same time.

As the buildings are now, it is very difficult to make any distinction between the inside and the outside, as they have been shot to pieces, destroyed, turned into ruins; when walking around in them one gets the impression of a rocky landscape.[6] The roofs and floors have fallen in. In this way very high open rooms are formed which extend through several storeys. When looking up from the arcades on the ground floor we see the fireplaces of the state apartments and the capitals of the columns protruding from the walls high above. One stands in the shadow and the upper portion of the wall is bathed in sunlight. In this way we experience in a concrete manner the way in which many of the buildings of Classicism were composed: darkness is opposed to light, heavy to light, raw material to sculptured forms. However, the idea of such contrasts is shown very *superficially* in the banqueting hall as well as in other neo-Classical constructions; it lies in the layer of plaster which covers a homogeneous structure.

The buildings in Lucknow are constructed of a kind of thin brick showing a very characteristic pattern in those places where the yellow and white plaster has fallen off. The technique reveals Indian workmanship, and thus the body of the buildings was Indian, while the outer shell was European and decidedly neo-Classical. It would seem as if the English had endeavoured to keep the style *pure* in order to emphasize the distance from the hybrid structures which were erected elsewhere in the town.[7] As usual, the designer of the banqueting hall would seem to have been a European military engineer. We can possibly guess at William Tricket, who at the beginning of the 1820's was referred to as 'architect and engineer to the King of Oudh'.[8]

In 1779, Henry Holland was appointed to the court of the Nizam of Hyderabad. It is held that he was the first real Resident. Holland as well as his immediate successor and assistants were stationed in a place north of the river Musi.[9] They lived in smallish houses, some of which were known as 'bungalows', scattered over a rather large area. The main feature of the Residency was a large Indian building of which we know something owing to the negative commentaries of Major J. A. Kirkpatrick when he wished to make certain improvements in 1800.

'The Musulman building which has always been used as a dining hall and place of public entertainment is both uncomfortable and inconvenient in a very great degree, from its being open and exposed to the south and from its roof being supported on very large Gothic pillars which fill so considerable a space in the middle of the room.'[10]

However, no alterations would seem to have been made in this building. Instead, in 1803 the construction of a proper Residency, containing official suites as well as living quarters for the Resident, was begun. The new building was of large dimensions and its appearance was completely European. Obviously, the time for such an alteration had come. As late as in the beginning of the 19th century, the French had had a representative in Hyderabad. He was, however, recalled. In 1802, on the basis of the Treaty of Bassein, the English had obtained the supremacy of the Deccan and the following year continued with new successful wars against the Mahrattas.[11] Wellesley's policy of expansion was about to succeed and it is certainly not by accident that the Residency in Hyderabad both in detail and in its general architectural features recalled his newly completed Government House in Calcutta.

The drawings for the new Residency were prepared by the military engineer, S. Russell, who borrowed his ideas from Palladian models. He presented a construction consisting of a villa with two flanking wings[12] and a lower system of arcades, stables and colonnades which line a broad ascent and a large courtyard. The longitudinal axis is the more pronounced: it runs from the approach on the south to the main building on the north. A transverse axis cuts the courtyard and is emphasized by two small gates.

Russell himself has mentioned the functions of the various structural parts. As mentioned above, the main building was intended for the Resident and his family and for official purposes, the east wing served as a kitchen and in the western wing, the butlers, tailors, washermen and assistants lived. Then stables for the horses, camels and elephants as well as smaller annexes were added. The comments of the architect also give an idea of the forms and the abstract space conditions he employed. As an example he describes the main building as follows:

'On the north front to this house you ascend to the first floor by a large flight of steps into a portico of the Corinthian order 60 feet long, 34 in width and 40 in height. From this you enter a great hall, which includes in its height the apartments of the second floor, on the right hand and left hand of the hall you pass into large oval rooms each having in front some circular porticos of the Ionic order. These rooms communicate with four others, forming a complete suite of apartments and having without private staircases leading to the second or chamber floor and one to the top of the house.'[13]

The use of 'circular' motifs is striking. Russell concentrated them around large simple room units. They particularly dominate the staircase which lies immediately behind the large hall in an apse. The stairs divide in the middle and continue in two serpentine sweeps. The arrangement displays a great likeness to the staircase in the house at No. 20 Portman Square, London. This building, which is now used by the Courtauld Institute, was erected between 1773 and 1777 for Elizabeth, Countess of Home. The architect was Robert Adam, and the staircase can be said to be the most dramatically designed part of the excellently treated interior. The staircase is illuminated from above by means of a glass dome, thus forming an upright cylinder in which the stairs rise boldly from a lower shadowy region to an upper part which is bathed in light. The architect in Hyderabad did not fulfil his task with the same elegance. Here the staircase is broader and the walls seem bare. The greatest difference lies in the distribution of light. Russell has, so to speak, broken up Robert Adam's blind motif and let the light fall through three windows in the actual barrel, while the dome consists of a shallow vault in heavy material intersected by ornamental bands. The central niche in Adam's composition is preserved in Russell's version, but above it a balcony protrudes.

In spite of all, the differences are distinct. On the whole, the interiors in Hyderabad are of larger dimension and more simply designed, but not without an elegant touch. Marble floors alternate with ornate parquets, mirrors create imaginary galleries in the large hall, and ochre-coloured wall panels show up against minutely sculptured door mouldings and cornices. The ornaments continue in the large portico of the north side where dentils, enrichments and elaborate modillions are crowded together in the ceiling. Otherwise the exterior is strict and recalls Government House in Calcutta. This similarity becomes especially clear in the large entrance portal in the south which Russell, so to speak, borrowed from Wyatt's construction. The only features in which the structures differ are the heraldic emblems over the portals: in Calcutta there is a lion and in Hyderabad the British coat of arms with beasts supporting the shield.[14]

As in the case of Government House in Calcutta, the Residency in Hyderabad is also intended for extravagant state occasions. The gate, the ascent, the large courtyard, the south façade of the main building and the two wings rise like a pageant in front of the visitor, who actually should make his entry on an elephant! In one of his aquatints, R. M. Grindlay has shown such an 'ideal' situation with a party riding on elephants, camels and horses between the colonnades.[15] An elephant is just passing under the gate; others are on their way surrounded by a gay crowd; a group of lancers water their horses in the foreground, everything giving the impression of an operetta parade. And what we see is also a piece of idealized reality. The artist has altered the milieu in order to increase the effect. Some pencil drawings which may be regarded as models for the aquatint are more exact and 'plain' in their reproduction.[16] However, even the final picture can be said to comply with the intentions of the architect: the classicists of Romanticism aimed at an ideal, a visionary reality.

This attempt to get away from the rational can be illuminated from another angle with the help of another early picture of the Residency in Hyderabad and a complementary text. The picture is a large oil-painting of the Resident (possibly Henry Russell, Resident 1811–20) and his escort on their way to call upon the Nizam.[17] A long line of horsemen and soldiers winds like a colourful ribbon through the landscape, and behind them, the European buildings form another light-coloured procession. The text can be taken from a letter dated 1811, commenting on a proposal to cut down the formal grandeur around the Resident. The proposal is rejected with the following motivation: 'Among people whose opinions are built upon a rational ground the existence of real power and authority ought to make all external marks of it in a great degree unnecessary. But this is by no means the case with either the Court or the people at Hyderabad. Their opinions are seldom or never rational. They can judge of power and authority by no other standard than the external marks of it; and if they saw a Resident with less state than his predecessor nothing would convince them but that he had less power too. The keeping up of an outward appearance of power will in many instances save the necessity of resort into the actual exercise of it. The Resident's authority must be either seen or it must be felt.'[18]

Thus the outer grandeur around the Resident was considered necessary in the political game. It was actually regarded as an *alternative* to the practical wielding of power. We are again reminded of Lord Valentia's argument when defending Wellesley's architectural programme in Calcutta.[19]

ix Town Halls and Mints in Calcutta and Bombay

John Garstin, who was responsible for the construction of the gola in Bankipur during the 1780's, worked as an architect in Calcutta some ten years later. At that time he was chief engineer for Bengal and erected on the Esplanade, beside Wellesley's Government House, a Town Hall of considerable size. The necessary funds were collected from the public with the help of lotteries. In 1807 the plans and cost estimate were approved and construction work was commenced in December of the same year. In 1813 the town hall was finished. The following year certain annexes were built and an iron fence was erected on the south side facing the Esplanade.[1]

Regarding its use, the Governor General in Council ruled as follows on March 22, 1814:

'The Town Hall . . . shall be reserved for authorized general meetings of the inhabitants of Calcutta, or for meetings of merchants or other classes of society, for the transaction of mercantile affairs or other business, and for public entertainments on great occasions . . .'

Usually the inhabitants of the town were only admitted to the 'marble hall' which was situated immediately behind the main entrance and where statues of famous men were placed, amongst them, John Bacon Jr's great allegorical representation of Cornwallis.[2]

Garstin's town hall had certain weak points,[3] only a few years later it became necessary to make repairs and to strengthen it, although nothing of this seems to have been obvious from the outside, as it was much admired by the travellers of that time. The Dane, Steen Bille, wrote in 1845:[4]

'With its exterior as well as its stylish decoration of the large well-proportioned hall with the adjoining galleries and rooms, it is truly worthy of its function.'

The building had two storeys shaped like a solid block with protruding porticos, the one to the north serving as a gateway for carriages. The elegant façade facing the Maidan consists, when analysed, of a double substructure: a low plinth supports the arcade of the ground floor and the latter in its turn supports the *piano nobile*. Through the corners of both storeys run high pilasters and above the centre section is a standard Palladian hexastyle portico. The order is Tuscan–Doric and the entablature is continued to form a heavy horizontal throughout the entire structure.

The Town Hall in Bombay was built according to the same principles, i.e. the necessary capital was collected by lotteries and the construction work in this case was also carried out by military architects. Colonel Thomas Cowper prepared the drawings and commenced construction work; after his death in 1825, the building was completed (in 1833), by other officers of the Bombay Engineers, one of them being Charles Waddington.[5]

Compared with Garstin's town hall, Cowper's structure would seem to be strikingly neo-Classical. Palladian features are entirely lacking; the order is likewise Doric, but now Greek–Doric with sturdy fluted columns and a solid entablature. On the whole,

Cowper's building conveys an impression of might and *mass*. The plinth is of normal height and its arcades indicate a considerable wall thickness. The steps in the centre are divided into such broad platforms that one is almost tempted to call them cataracts, and the long façade has room for three porticos. The one in the middle, above the flight of steps and the main entrance, is like the whole Doric order borrowed from the Parthenon in Athens. In Stuart and Revett, or some other books of engravings, Cowper had studied the Greek pattern and then applied it both strictly and freely. Characteristic details are the palmettes which fill the space between the mutules at the angles of the cornice and the lions' masks of the gargoyles.[6] More important for the overall impression is, of course, the system of proportion.

Cowper placed the Greek frontages high up and against heavy walls. Between the columns, tall windows are inserted. The cornices above these project considerably, but not enough to protect against the sun which shines on the façade in the afternoon. An attempt has been made to overcome this by means of wooden shades, so-called *jhilmils*. Such additions were unknown in antique architecture, but Cowper or his co-operators integrated them in the building by means of supplying them with neo-Classic decoration: a fine row of palmettes.[7]

The Town Hall in Bombay also has porticos on its return walls. Originally, these were the less significant entrances. Through the portico on the north side we come into a vestibule and, by a winding staircase, to the room above which is shaped with a view to producing dramatic effects. The staircases which form a large ellipse in the floor are illuminated from above by a skylight. The corners of the room lie in semi-darkness and here we find in niches commemorative statues of civil servants.[8] The entrance into an adjoining room is flanked by columns, and here again the light is thrown down in a white cone from a skylight. In the centre stands a statue of John Malcolm. In the world of shadows which is formed by the contrast of light, in the outer parts of the room we also discern white marble heads and dark window and door mouldings. Adjoining these impressive rooms is a large hall with columns of the Corinthian order. (This hall comes immediately behind the central portico).

As regards the function of the building, we know that it was to house the Asiatic Society and its fine library and that, in addition, the Bombay Legislative Council met there. The Governor and the Commander-in-Chief also had some rooms there for official purposes.[9]

During the 1820's, large constructions for currency production were built in various parts of India. In 1821, a Mint was erected in Benares, and two others in Bombay and Calcutta. The building in Bombay was completed in 1829; it was a rectangular structure of two storeys, equipped with a Ionic portico. As usual, an officer of the engineers, John Hawkins, was the architect.[10] On 31 March, 1824, the architect W. N. Forbes laid the foundation stone of the Mint in Calcutta. Six years later it was completed and was inaugurated in 1831.[11] On the plan, the building is square with a courtyard in the centre. The main façade reflects the same ideals of style as the Town Hall in Bombay. The centre section, however, which again imitates the Parthenon, is in this case not placed against solid walls but instead against new *colonnades*. The entire façade is composed of three successively broader rows of columns giving an extremely heavy impression.

The Mint is placed on a high foundation like a temple and flights of steps lead up to the portico in the middle. At the sides, the three steps at the top continue and thus form a regular stylobate. Below the building, there are rooms which go down as deep as 26 ft. The details are not worked out as well as in Bombay. The masks are considerably smaller and are placed between the mutules; the frieze is compressed; the abacus is unusually thick and is cut into by the architrave.

The site for the Mint was in Strand Road. In the quarter around this site, several smaller buildings were erected, some of them even having the Doric order in two storeys and their triglyph friezes which run right through the structure give an impression of uniformity to the whole of this considerable and heavy complex of buildings.[12]

Together with the Mint in Calcutta, the Town Hall in Bombay is the most striking exponent of the Greek Revival in India. There are several other buildings related to these as regards style, among them being the Calcutta Madrasha which was completed in 1824, and Tara Wala Kothi in Lucknow which was erected during the reign of Nasir-ud-din Haidar.[13] Thus all these structures were built during the 1820's, the decade when the war of independence was fought in Greece. It is, however, difficult to see a direct connection between this far-away romantic setting and the Euro-Indian architecture.

As parallels on a different, purely stylistic level, I would mention Strickland's Second Bank of the U.S. in Philadelphia and Thomas Hamilton's High School in Edinburgh which were completed in 1824 and 1825 respectively. Thus at that time the engineers in India had caught up with their colleagues in Europe and in the former 'Western Colonies'. They worked after the same clear-cut Antique ideals.[14]

x Town Residences and Clubs in Calcutta

England made important contributions to domestic architecture in the 18th century, especially to urban structures. The shortage of sites in the quickly expanding towns was utilized with great virtuosity by building contractors and architects. People with a great knowledge of London's architecture, such as Steen Eiler Rasmussen and John Summerson, have described these town-houses and their functions.[1] Their small, sometimes even diminutive, size and simple exterior design were characteristic. Not even did the rich Londoners spend money on façades. On the contrary, we can discern a desire to get away from outer splendour, a phenomenon which Steen Eiler Rasmussen connects with the Puritan tradition.[2]

At the same time, the architecture of the British in Indian towns follows quite different patterns. The houses are arranged freely to form irregular streets and in most cases their individuality is maintained.[3] They are frequently situated on their own in large compounds which offer unlimited possibilities in lay-out and effect.

If these houses recall any London architecture at all, it would be Nash's *villas* in Regent's Park, but here the dimensions of the houses are considerably larger. As a matter of fact, these town houses in India have more in common with country seats than with any urban pattern.

From around 1780, the pattern was most distinctly developed in Calcutta in the Chowringhi area.[4] The prerequisites for these buildings were special and quite different from those in contemporary London and other English towns. It was easy and cheap to buy sites, and the same was true of material and labour costs. The houses could well be designed with large dimensions, as there were always numerous servants available for the necessary communication between the different parts of the building.[5]

Thus the houses were large and of an external design remote from the Puritan ideal, in spite of the fact that they were built for families without any great social prestige. They were mostly merchants and civil servants of the East India Company. This fact has been used as an argument when criticising the houses. They were considered to be upstart villas, extravagant creations of men with quickly acquired fortunes and rather uncertain taste.[6] Seen from the social point of view, this might perhaps be correct so long as these people are regarded against the background of a strict class system and the relatively slow mixing of different social classes in England. As regards 'taste' the matter is different.

The houses in Chowringhi were built in the shape of solid blocks with added porticos, staircase towers and verandas. The façades display the same features as the public buildings: tall colonnades rise on a plinth usually executed in rusticated work, and the pediments and mouldings of the windows stand out against the smooth walls. The order is usually an undecorated Tuscan or a more richly designed Ionic. A little later in the 19th century purely Greek elements of style can also be observed. The models for the walls dividing the compounds from the street have been taken from the customary sources of the 18th century. The pillars of the portico may be a variation of a motif by Batty Langley, and the rustic work and the niches of the walls may have come from Palladio either directly or through the intermediary of an English pattern book.[7]

The combination of all these heavy forms appears exaggerated when applied to the house of a simple civil servant. There appears to be no relation between the representative character of the elements and what they actually are to represent. However, this is an incongruity which only occurs when an attempt is made to fit the buildings into a traditional background, where they do not belong.

The houses in Chowringhi are an extravagant type. They resulted from an economic upheaval which recalls the same phenomenon which was to take place some decades later in Europe during the time of the Industrial Revolution and which resulted in corresponding architectural features.[8] Thus these houses have more in common with the pseudo-palaces of the 19th century than with the simple private houses of the 18th century.

Another important prerequisite for the design of the Calcutta residences was the climate. Adjustment to it requires large dimensions, space and high ceilings and may also result in the colonnades not getting the correct proportions or intercolumniation. The buildings had to afford shade and ventilation, even if these had to be obtained at the expense of the accepted rules of classicism.[9]

W. H. Carey, the temperamental author of *The Good Old Days of Hon'ble John Company* regarded the houses in Chowringhi with a certain contempt. He remarked, amongst other things, that the columns 'are some ridiculous number of diameters apart . . . only in a solitary example or two are they correctly proportioned and spaced.' He capitulated in the case of one house, No. 9 Russell Street, 'a bit of perfect Astylar work'.[10] This house still exists to-day and is one of the finest and best preserved examples of the original buildings in this area. It is used as premises for the Calcutta Turf Club which at the beginning of this century took over the house from the Apcar family, a shipping house which played a certain part in the commercial life of the town.[11] The year of its construction is not known, but should lie around 1820. The house stands on a large compound and beside it are other buildings which had been erected during the last decades of the 18th century.

The house consists of two storeys with a broad veranda on the south. This front recalls many Palladian inspired façades in Europe; West Wycombe Park in England can be mentioned, although there the loggia has two storeys and closely arranged columns. The corresponding elements in the building of the Calcutta Turf Club are coupled and the distance between them is considerably larger than laid down by any architectural rules (in spite of Carey's conception of 'a perfect Astylar work'). On the north front there is a long protruding portico where vehicles can drive in and the passengers get out comfortably protected against wind and rain; the inner part of the portico has a marble floor. The teak doors are crowned by a Doric over-lintel and on the sides pilasters, niches with sculptures and a meander pattern give relief to the white plaster of the walls. Everything is architectonically worked out with a strong feeling for quality and exactness. The same spirit is displayed in the interior.

From the portico we enter a vestibule of the type which was found in the elegant houses in London and which extends through two storeys.[12] White architraves are supported by columns which, like the staircase and the panelling, are executed in Oriental wood of a warm reddish-brown. The open fire-places in the large rooms are also of wood and would hardly have been for use, but rather served as a homely background. They are shaped like small aedicules with straight entablatures.

The original distribution of the rooms is unknown. However, to judge from the arrangement today, they seem to have all been used by the European family, while the servants' quarters were in out-offices. In 1845, Leopold von Orlich described another of the large houses in Chowringhi:

120

'the dining room and drawing-rooms are on the ground floor; the middle storey contains the sitting rooms of the family, and the upper stories the bed chambers. Bath rooms are universally introduced . . .'[13]

The house described by von Orlich has three storeys, and the one under discussion only two. We may thus presume that the upper storey of the two contained both a drawing-room and bed-chambers. Naturally, also the large veranda on the south façade was used as a drawing-room in the evening when it was cool and perhaps also as an extra room for sleeping during the hot season.[14] Without any large alterations, 9 Russell Street could be changed from a private residence into a club house. All rooms were spacious and elegantly designed. Several houses in Chowringhi changed function in the same way.

Not far from the Turf Club, with a gate onto the Chowringhi Road, the Bengal Club is situated. This club was founded in 1827, and first had its premises in various places in the centre of the city, in Dalhousie Square. In 1845, however, it moved to Chowringhi, where it took over two private residences, Nos. 1 and 1/1 Russell Street.[15] In photographs taken in the middle of the 19th century we see servants in light-coloured robes swarming around the large blocks of houses which form various parts of the Club.[16]

The Bengal Club was not the first club in Calcutta, but it was the one which bore the greatest resemblance to the great clubs of London. Notorious gamblers met at Selby's at the end of the 1770's; this club was housed in a large building near Tank Square, which had been erected by Charles Child in 1775 and was later used as a private residence.[17] The members of the Asiatic Society had quite different common interests. In 1805, the Asiatic Society got its permanent premises in Park Street. The house had been designed by Captain Lock of the Bengal Engineers and was completed by a French architect, Jean Jacques Pichon.[18] When I saw this building in January 1965, the portico on the west façade had been pulled down, while the actual house with its row of pilasters of the Ionic Order facing the street was still there. It has now been replaced by a nine-storey concrete structure, a manifestation of the transformation which is taking place in the centre of Calcutta.

xi Country Residences near Calcutta, Madras and Delhi

The study of urban patterns and of town residences has shown that it is often difficult to draw definite lines between rural and urban structures: the town residence has borrowed the characteristics of the country seat. Nevertheless, such lines were drawn, and in this connection the climatic and functional aspects were decisive. When the Governor of Madras moved to Triplicane, which to us appears quite rural, his *country* seat was established in Guindy, even a few miles further outside Fort St. George, and in the course of time it was moved as far out as Ootacamund.[1]

It appears as if the governors of the colonies were the first to move into the country. They felt the need for recreation and social life under less strict forms. As we have seen, the British Governor of Calcutta, Robert Clive, acquired one of the first houses in Chowringhi for the above reasons[2].

The house of the French Governor outside Chandernagore, known as Ghiretty House, is another early example of this type of residence. The latter is said to have been erected on the ruins of a palace from the time of Dupleix. Around 1780 it was owned by Sir Eyre Coote and from that time, more exactly from 1782, there is a water-colour showing what it looked like.[3] In the water-colour we see the garden front, a one-storey loggia over a high arcade. Curved flights of steps lead up to the centre part which protrudes in the form of a half octagon. The hall in the middle obviously has this shape and would seem to have a very high ceiling to judge by the superstructure which projects above the balustrade. To the right and left are two smaller, symmetrically built annexes with loggias and flat roofs. They appear to have been designed in quite a different scale from the main building. In the background we can discern even more buildings belonging to this country seat. A detailed description of Ghiretty House is given by the Frenchman Grandpré in 1801:

'le palais de Garati, seul reste de l'ancienne grandeur française, et qui peut servir à prouver sur quelle proportion on avait dessiné les premiers plans de cette nation en Asie. Garati est la plus belle maison de l'Inde. La façade vers le jardin est dans le goût que les Européens ont adopté en Asie, c'est-à-dire, décorée d'un péristile d'architecture grecque, d'ordre ionique. L'intérieur du palais est somptueux, la grande salle est du grand genre, le plafond et la corniche sont peints de main de maître. La façade verse la cour est toute à la française, sans péristile. Elle représente trois corps de bâtiment, chacun décoré d'un fronton dans lequel sont les cartouches pour des basreliefs qui d'ont pas été sculptés. La cour est circulaire e d'un bon goût, précédée d'une avenue qui annonce très-majesteusement ce bel édifice. Garati est la demeure ordinaire du gouverneur français au Bengale.'[4]

When Grandpré came to Chandernagore, the town lay in ruins and what he described were the last remains of French splendour. To-day not even these are left. Only a few decades later, Bishop Heber was able to meditate upon the ruins of Ghiretty House which had then been almost engulfed by the jungle.[5]

At the end of the 1770's, Warren Hastings moved to his country residence in Alipur south of the city of Calcutta. The building was erected at the time of his marriage to Mariana Imhoff. It does not matter whether this was before or after his wedding day, said Lord Curzon. It is, however, interesting that the new house can be seen in Zoffany's portrait of the Hastings couple and that in this painting it has its original appearance, i.e. a two-storeyed white cube. In 1778 it was described by Mackrabie, private secretary to Philip Francis as milky white and dazzling.[6]

Soon other buildings were erected on the estate. Before Hastings left Calcutta in February 1785, he offered for sale, amongst other things:

'An upper-roomed house consisting of a hall and rooms on each floor, a handsome stone staircase and a back staircase all highly finished with Madras chunam and the very best materials. A lower-roomed house containing a large hall and four good bed-

122

chambers; a complete bathing house containing 2 rooms finished with Madras chunam; a convenient bungalow containing two rooms and a verandah all round; a large range of pukka buildings containing stabling for 14 horses and four coach houses . . . .'[7]

Thus the country seat had been considerably enlarged during the few years that had passed, but the main building had not yet acquired its present appearance. The wings and the protruding portico on the north front are later additions. It is noticeable that the living quarters were on the ground floor at that early stage.[8]

Lord Curzon, who gave such a well-informed report of Hastings' house, has also commented on the country residences of the later governor-generals in Barrackpore and so thoroughly that my comments will be almost a summary only of his descriptions. However, I should like briefly to emphasize some specifically architectural aspects; Curzon's interest was more directed towards personal history.[9]

The establishment of a country residence in Barrackpore is connected with the history of the cantonment. One of the first bungalows which was built there for officers was for Captain Mackintyre, and when he sold his property in 1785 it was turned into the residence of the commander-in-chief. The first governor-general who at the same time was commander-in-chief and thus was entitled to the house was Cornwallis. And in December 1800 Wellesley came upon the scene with some proposals for alterations which soon changed the status of the house and finally also its appearance. Wellesley was very eager to move there, as the hot season was approaching and he required time to prepare the structure more effectively against the heat. His wish was fulfilled. The commander at that time, Sir A. Clarke, left and on 1 February, 1801, the use of the bungalow was granted to the Governor-General in Council.

The building which Wellesley took over was in poor condition, and Charles Wyatt was appointed to supervise the repair work. The reconstructed house has been described by Lord Valentia and Henry Salt, the artist who accompanied the former on his journey. Salt's engraving shows a light-coloured villa with an Ionic portico, around which several smaller buildings are arranged. Valentia writes:

'Several of the bungalows belonging to the lines have been taken into the Park and are fitted up for the reception of Secretaries, Aides-de-Camp, and visitors.'

All buildings were erected in a spacious park. In the same way as Clive had ordered the ground around Triplicane Garden House to be altered, Wellesley had the ground on the banks of the river changed into a slightly undulating landscape with long, narrow ponds, open vistas and a variety of vegetation. The finished project was thus half English and half exotic, a picturesque hybrid of the type which at that time was frequently designed in Europe, but which in India must be considered from the opposite point of view, as an expression of *occidentalism*. Wellesley also missed 'the distant view of a steeple', a feature with very strong associations with his mother country. The scene was, in fact, complemented in this way when the church in Serampore on the opposite bank of the Hooghly got its tall steeple in 1821.[10] Later a Gothic aviary and a menagerie with a pilaster arrangement recalling the architecture of John Soane were added.

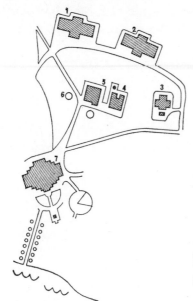

12. Country Residence of the Governor-General at Barrackpore. Plan showing: 1–3, staff bungalows; 4, guard-room; 5, kitchen; 6, meat-store; 7, the residence proper.

In spite of the repairs and rebuilding, Wellesley did not approve of the bungalow as it was, and it was pulled down in 1804 to make room for a big house, a rural counterpart of Government House which had just been completed in Calcutta. The architect of this building was probably Thomas Anbury, who succeeded Wyatt as superintendent of public works. Of the actual structure we do not know much more than that it was to lie on the bank of the river and to be of large dimensions; perhaps it had some resemblance to the plans for the palace in Murshidabad which were made at the same time. Its history was very short. When Wellesley left India in August 1805, the plinth had been constructed and then all work stopped. The material which had been brought there was taken to Calcutta, where part of it was destroyed in a fire and the remainder was sold by the first Lord Minto. A last glimpse of the building was given by Maria Graham, who came to Barrackpore in 1810 and saw its 'unfinished arcades'. The moonlight over the heaps of stone gave a romantic touch to the lines she wrote, which I have already mentioned in connection with other projections of this kind.[11]

However, a country residence was erected in Barrackpore. It was completed during the time of Governor-General Hastings in 1815 or somewhat later. A beginning had been made by Wellesley in the form of a bungalow which was meant to serve temporarily while the large house was being built. Lord Minto had used it and referred to it as a cottage, 'but a very considerable building compared with the European scale.' Hastings or his architect — who was in all probability Thomas Anbury who had become superintendent of Buildings at Barrackpore — enlarged and improved it considerably. Later, during the time of Lord Auckland, a veranda was added to the west façade. The total effect was impressive. There were façades on the south and north fronts where windows,

124

niches and blind wall panels give a strict pattern to the walls. The house has only one storey over an arcade, and to improve ventilation, there is an attic. The verandas are not completely integrated in the structure; their order is Tuscan and one would have expected a more splendid Ionic or Corinthian order. However, the simplest possible decoration was chosen, perhaps in opposition to Wellesley's extravagance or perhaps consciously in accordance with the heavy style of the 1820's.[12]

As before, bungalows for kitchen quarters and servants, aides-de-camp and guests were erected in the park around the main building. Some of these are really 'primitive' with thatched roofs, while others are more in style with the house of the Governor-General. One bungalow, a small flat-roofed building, has at the angles and around the windows, rustications recalling Gibbs's architecture.

The private residences which were built in Bengal during the last decades of the 18th century largely follow the pattern of Barrackpore, which does not imply that they merely imitate the residence of the governor-general. It was possible to group around a large European building a number of out-offices based on Indian models. 'Comillah', the residence of John Buller, is arranged in this way with a large bungalow and smaller *curvilinear huts* on both sides of the main building.

'Felicity Hall', which was owned by the Hon. David Anstruther, on the other hand, lies in splendid isolation on a large open space without a trace of rustic additions. The servants obviously lived in the basement of the building which is tall and spacious.[13] In front of the latter a flight of steps leads up to a broad veranda which is set back in the building. On one side, a number of tall arched windows suggest a large hall inside. The appearance of 'Comillah' and 'Felicity Hall' is known from engravings published by Edward Orme in 1805.[14]

Leaving Bengal and continuing further south to Madras, we find that the country residences become larger and more elegant. Many of them were erected at an early stage. When Lally approached the town from St. Thomas Mount in 1758, he found the plain 'thinly scattered with garden houses'.[15] After the Government had been granted special permission in 1772 to let sites for the erection of new houses, their number increased considerably.[16] H. D. Love, who supplied the last information, emphasizes the unfortunate fact that there are no maps on which we may follow the development of the built-up areas.

The pictures we have of the country seats around Madras are, in fact, of a late date. They were made during the 1820's and later. However, these are excellent pictures which were made by two artists with a special feeling for the delicate and etherial character of the structures, the two water-colourists John and Justinian Gantz.[17]

Here the houses are not block-shaped as in Bengal. The façades are interrupted by curved verandas and protruding porticos and the central part of the structure continues into corridors or long wall sections with adjoining wings. The living quarters are on the ground floor and the dominating horizontals of the houses fit smoothly into the flat landscape. The orders generally used are Ionic or Corinthian, and together with the light-coloured plaster they convey a festive and attractive impression.

Unfortunately, John and Justinian Gantz do not mention the names of the buildings they painted. All we know is that they were situated near Madras. Many could probably be found on the large map of Madras of 1866, where 'black spots' along the Adyar River and Poonamalee Road are especially frequent.[18] Some of these buildings still stand to-day, among them the Adyar Club, which was originally owned by Robert Monbray (1771), and which on the map of 1866 is ascribed to Sir C. Scotland.

We know also a few country residences in Delhi situated north of Kashmir Gate near the old cantonment, Hindu Rao's and Metcalfe's houses. The former was built in 1830 by William Fraser, an agent to the governor-general, posted in Delhi.[19] It became famous during the events of the Mutiny in 1857, and some of the first photographs which were taken in India show the greatly battered structure. The plaster has fallen in great patches from the walls, and the brick core of the columns are perforated by bullets.[20] Nevertheless, it is possible to discern the basic features of the building. Cube-shaped living quarters are supported by a tall plinth and on one side there is a veranda. Metcalfe's house, which was built in 1835, has been described in great detail by Lady Clive Bayley, the daughter of the owner, Thomas Metcalfe. I shall quote her description below in connection with a survey of the climatic aspects of the buildings.[21]

As we know, the country residences were in the first place meant for recreation and as complements to the town-houses. In this they correspond with their counterparts in Europe. However, the tropical or sub-tropical climate gave them a new function, a greater necessity. The first Lord Minto said that 'Barrackpore is delicious and takes the sting out of India.'[22]

The extreme conditions also demanded unconventional solutions. The 'primitive' architecture of the Indians, both in its original and later forms, was used by the Europeans. The bungalow was created and here became a functional type of building and not merely a fashionable phenomenon as in Europe in the period of Romanticism. However, I shall deal with this in another chapter.[23]

xii Christian Churches

Many of the churches built by the British in India had one and the same prototype: James Gibbs's St. Martin-in-the-Fields. This is scarcely surprising, as conditions were the same all over the English-speaking parts of the world. In the homeland the prototype is found again and again, especially from the 1740's to the 1760's, and somewhat later in North America.[1] The last church to be built after this model was, perhaps, the Dutch Reformed Church at Cradock, South Africa, which was erected in 1867.[2]

The explanations of this phenomenon are many. In the first place, St. Martin's lies in a very prominent place in the heart of London, beside what is now called Trafalgar Square. Secondly, the architect himself ensured that the church should become famous by reproducing it in 1728 — two years after its completion — in his *Book of Architecture*. Those who had not had the chance to see it on the spot or who needed to study it more in detail could use this set of engravings which show the building in perspective, section and in plan, and in addition there is a series of designs for steeples not carried out. Another important fact was that here Gibbs had found an archetype for Anglican churches: a long nave of three bays with the altar in a simply-shaped chancel at the east end.

If the structure is regarded from the point of view of style, it can also be understood to a certain extent why neo-Classicism adopted this type of church. With the portico on the short side and rows of high pilasters and columns on the long sides, it looked extremely like a Roman temple. The weak spot was the tower which projected above the roof and by its strongly vertical effect distracted attention from the building beneath. The tower was no more classical than it was neo-Classical. With its different elements one above another and its complicated composition, it constituted a Baroque element that, as the 18th century proceeded, became more and more preposterous in its prominent position. Sir John Summerson has called it an anomaly, and from a neo-Classical point of view it was one, in fact.[3]

The problem does not, however, seem to have arisen in India, where Gibbs's prototype was accepted in its entirety. The slight deviations to which it was subjected did not change the main features of the structure.

Like other buildings, the old St. Anne's Church in Calcutta was destroyed during the conquest of the city by Siraj-ud-daulah in 1756.[4] It was a long time before a new building was erected. A mission church called Beth Tephillah was consecrated in 1770 and it was not until 1787 that St. John's, the new presidency church, was completed.

The mission church is thought to have come into existence through Scandinavian collaboration. The architect, M. B. de Melvell, is said to have been Danish, and it would seem that he had the same right to this nationality or lack of it as John Goldingham in Madras had later.[5] It is easier to trace the extraction of the person who ordered the church. He was a Swedish missionary who had come to India (Cuddalore) in 1739 and who in 1758 had started the mission in Bengal. He therefore had this church erected for his congregation. The outside recalls St. Martin's, but the proportions between the tower and the nave have been changed; it is a one-storey structure and ends in an apse; Ionic columns have replaced the Corinthian and along with the windows give a very Rococo impression. Instead of Gibbs's rusticated surrounds, the windows have softly curved profiles finishing in an ornament at the top (cherubs?).[6] From the start the church was partly faced with red brick, for which reason it was called, the 'Red Church.'

One of the first references to St. John's is to be found in a notice in the Calcutta Gazette on 1 April, 1784, when it was stated that the foundation stone was to be laid 'next Tuesday'.[7] We have a letter from the church building committee at the end of the year, asking for the grant of a piece of land and a sum of money.[8] The site lay in the centre of Calcutta, at the crossing of Hastings Street and Council House Street. Here the church was erected and was finished in 1787; on the 28th of June that year it was consecrated.[9] The architect was James Agg, a young engineer officer who had come to India in 1779 with William Hickey on the *Sea Horse*.[10] He copied St. Martin-in-the-Fields, but with certain alterations; the most important was perhaps that the portico was eliminated. Instead, the entrance was placed at the back and designed as a veranda set back in the building. Here therefore there is no pediment; the columns support an isolated projecting part of the roof. The tower on the opposite side is the only vertical accent above the roof parapet.

So far the description of the building is made after an engraving which was published in 1787 and which probably goes back to Agg's original drawing — and after one of Thomas Daniell's Calcutta pictures.[11] They reproduce the original appearance of the church, but in a somewhat idealized way. The actual structure was more clumsy. The steeple did not get the proportions intended, but was more compressed and gives an impression of great heaviness, as it was built of large square blocks of stone which were not plastered. The anomaly was still more evident!

James Agg returned to England as a captain and with a fine fortune, it is said.[12] His church was altered several times, first by Edward Tiretta in 1797 and then again in 1811.[13] The entrance was moved to the west side, an apse was constructed at the east, and on the long side a pair of galleries was added. The changes were made for liturgical and climatic reasons. An attempt was also made to enrich the effect by placing between the triglyphs of the frieze an ornament which had probably never been used in that position before; it normally belongs to the soffit of the cornice where it is placed between the mutules. Similar liberties were taken with the interior, where the Doric columns were changed to Corinthian — through changing the capitals! Nevertheless, Agg's original church was much admired. Grandpré, for instance, wrote in 1790:

'On compte à Calcutta deux paroisses anglicanes, l'une desquelle est un superbe bâtiment d'architecture régulière, précédé d'un péristile dorique d'une belle proportion: la corniche et l'architrave simple décoré de ses triglyphes sont d'un très-bon gout. En un mot, l'édifice est dans sa totalité un modèle de grâces et d'élégance.'[14]

The admiration for St. John's left clear traces. The church at Serampore, the building of which was started in 1800, follows the same pattern,[15] and St. Andrew's, which was erected at Tank Square in Calcutta in 1815 also does so, to a still greater degree.[16] It was very like St. John's; among other things, the Doric order was repeated here and the original frieze with its succession of triglyphs and acanthus motifs. At the same time a return was made to the English prototype in the entrance. The portico protrudes on the south side, and if one studies James B. Fraser's engraving of 1824 it stands out very effectively against the monotonous façade of Writers' Buildings which is the nearest neighbour.[17]

The use of the Doric order is clearly symptomatic of Calcutta at that time. The Catholic church at Dum Dum, the foundation stone of which was laid in February, 1822, shows even heavier forms.[18]

In Madras, St. Mary's Church in the Fort was already old. It had been built in the

17th century, but in 1795 a steeple of the type we now know was added.[19] When the town gradually grew outside the original walls, new churches sprang up in various parts. The most distant was built at St. Thomas Mount, which was a place long associated with Christian worship. Two of the largest were erected on roads leading from the town: St. George's on Mount Road and St. Andrew's on Poonamalee Road.

St. George's was designed by the then Captain James Caldwell. Thomas De Havilland was responsible for the actual erection and the church was consecrated on 8 June, 1816.[20] Here, as in Calcutta, Gibbs's prototypes were used, but the pattern was complicated by Ionic portals and aedicules on the long sides and numerous columns in the main portico on the west side. The steeple was an exact copy of the one designed by Gibbs for 'a circular church'. Owing to its size, its chunam-white façade and elegant ornamentation in the interior St. George's was a splendid gathering-point for the English colonists. In the semi-darkness along the walls there was gradually added a long row of monuments to deceased military men and civil servants.

With this building, Thomas De Havilland distinguished himself as an architect designing in the manner of James Gibbs. A few years later he erected St. Andrew's Presbyterian Church, but by this time he had evolved a style more of his own.[21]

The building was set in a large compound surrounded by a wall, but with its façades visible from various directions. The architect took this into account and used a ground plan which is no longer rectangular; the walls curve outwards and enclose a large circular hall. The façade on the chancel side has striking ornamentation; on the pediment two enormous lions flank national emblems, and beneath them the writing on the frieze reads: AUSPICIO REGIS ET SENATUS ANGLIAE. The order is Ionic, after a Roman pattern with elaborate ornamentation. Details such as the coffered ceiling in the portico, the acanthus fillings in the capitals and the fret ornaments on the frieze are particularly striking. The interior is also magnificent. The columns supporting the dome stand on a chequered black and white marble floor.

From an artistic point of view, St. Andrew's is undoubtedly the best designed church in Madras. In spite of the obvious relationship with both St. Martin-in-the-Fields (the choir wall, the steeple) and the design for a 'circular church' (the ground plan), it stands out as an individually designed building with great expressiveness. In the same way as the large Doric structures which were being erected simultaneously in Calcutta and Bombay, it represents the feeling of growing political power of the English.

The themes from Gibbs's book on architecture were varied in many places in India, amongst others St. Mary's in Poona, consecrated in 1825, and in Bombay, where St. Andrew's Church was built in 1818 not far from the Fort.[22]

Others churches followed other patterns. The Catholic Church in Patna (1772-1779) has no tower, but, like its counterpart in Serampore, with which it is almost contemporary, has a characteristic motif above the entrance; here it is a powerful Ionic portico with high columns placed on plinths, and niches on both sides of the door. Tiretta has been mentioned as the architect of this building. In that case it would be one of his first works in India, but it seems impossible to prove this.[23] The fact that the façade has an appearance which is in general Italian does not necessarily indicate that the architect was an Italian. This classical style was common to all.

While the Anglican church interiors were arranged simply, we read of more involved arrangements in the Dutch Church at Chinsura:

'at the present altar-end a railed-in space was raised above the floor of the church on three steps and entrance to it was made by means of a door from the back, the pulpit was here. At the opposite end, under the tower was another raised space also railed in, in which were the seats of the "consistory" (or "vestry") of the church, and the official seat of the Director of the Settlement.'[24]

When Chinsura became English in 1824, the church was changed to suit the Anglican liturgy; the altar was then placed by the north wall inside the railed-in space and the pulpit and the reading desk were placed in front.

In Delhi, just inside the Kashmir Gate, Colonel James Skinner built a central church in the 1830's, a very unusual building in Indian territory.[25] It was formed like a Greek cross; the dome, which was supported by an octagonal drum, recalls late-Baroque Italy. But the three Tuscan porticos are neo-Classical, and the fourth arm of the cross has been turned into the choir. Thus the inside of the church has a striking length in spite of the ground plan. A low clock tower has been placed between two of the porticos. On the walls pilasters alternate with arched window frames and blind sections. The colours are yellow ochre and white, and the whole is particularly effective against the surrounding greenery and the blue sky.

The elements of classical architecture, whether taken from Gibbs or some other European designer, seem to have coalesced to form a Christian church in India. The variations are numerous and considerably more than I have been able to indicate, ranging from the Serlian Bom Jesus built by the Portuguese in Goa to Skinner's church in Delhi;[26] but the theme remains the same. A classical portico marks the entrance to spacious places of worship dominated by white colonnades; and a high steeple rises towards the heavens providing a new feature beside the vimanas, gopurams and minarets. The neo-Gothic, which made many important contributions to the European Romantic architecture for ecclesiastical purposes, only appears occasionally, as in St. Paul's Cathedral in Calcutta (1829–47).[27]

xiii General Martin's Palace-Tomb in Lucknow

On the eastern outskirts of Lucknow stands the structure called 'La Martinière', after the builder, the French-born general, Claude Martin. It is almost always described as 'strange' or 'fantastic', and it undeniably differs from most other monuments in its function, size and composition of disparate architectural elements. The premises consist of a large park, a T-shaped lake reflecting a tall column and a four-storey main building with low, outward curving wings. It is this building that puzzled its beholders most.

Seen from the front, from the lake, it rests on an enormous podium. The ground floor is the widest and the first floor considerably wider than the two above, which rise from the main building like a tower and are themselves a combination of octagonal tower forms connected by 'bridges'. Thus the silhouette is stepped; on each step there are striking features, at the bottom massive bastions and higher up small open pavilions with sculptures on the roofs. In its silhouette and in certain details La Martinière recalls Mughal architecture, but it is, in fact, a *hybrid* like many other buildings in Lucknow and is largely composed of European style elements. In the horizontal direction arcades and parapets of various shapes predominate; strong vertical lines run through pilasters and columns, and continue where possible, in pedestals and statues. The series of orders is extremely unconventional: three Composites above a Tuscan. And in the central tower single pilasters support half-columns in pairs with heavy cornices; this arrangement is contrary to all classicist functional theory. In addition to statues we find among the architectural details large, heraldic lions supporting the bastions, and sphinxes that seem to be mere ornaments.

The conception of the enormous building has been ascribed to General Martin himself. No drawings are known; possible models for such may have disappeared on the General's death in the year 1800, when his large collection of books and a great deal of furniture were sold by auction. It is known, however, that at the time the building was unfinished, and that the parts which were missing were later erected according to instructions in his will.[1]

Travellers have written about La Martinière at various times. Thomas Twining visited it in January, 1794, when the building was still uninhabited. He traced in the structure 'the singularity of the Colonel's taste' and pointed out that below the ground floor there were underground rooms intended for the hot season. Among these catacombs for the living the future proprietor had arranged his own sepulchral chamber, where oil lamps were already lit to burn 'for ever'.[2] Regarded from this angle, the building could be seen to have a double function as palace and mausoleum.

In February, 1797, Lord Teignmouth dined with General Martin in the main building, which was then finished. Six years later Lord Valentia was there,[3] by when the dead general was in his burial chamber. As already stated, the furniture had been scattered and some of the sculptures destroyed in an earthquake, but there was still much to admire and marvel at. The large lions on the outside were red with shining lamps instead of eyes and the stucco had been painted yellow to imitate gilding.

The Earl of Moira (later the Marquis of Hastings) saw the building from another point of view when he visited it in 1814. He indicated that the terraces between the storeys were made for defence purposes, and other features in the structure point in the same direction.[4] In some places the parapets are shaped for rifle-fire. The question is whether these fortification details were really intended to be used against attack or siege. It is possible that they were merely intended to look menacing, strong and characteristic in the same way as the lions; they give the General's house a very belligerent appearance.

THE STRUCTURES

Leopold von Orlich mentioned the battlements when he saw La Martinière in 1845, but he was most interested in the interior. He found the rooms small and dark, 'ornamented with looking-glasses, shells, various kinds of Italian sculptures and basreliefs of plaster of Paris and marble'. This décor is still preserved and is most magnificently executed in the rooms immediately behind the front. Above the pilasters of the walls are arched ceilings with stucco ornaments: creepers and rosettes frame relief panels of a Wedgwood character.[5]

When von Orlich visited La Martinière, the whole structure was complete. The large column crowned with a pavilion now stood in the pond in front of the house and the heavy columns of the Tuscan order in the wings finished the building at the sides. In this way the instructions in the General's will had been carried out.

The final verdict on General Martin's house and grounds could easily be a negative one. It might simply be said that the building expresses an individuality that is not the artist's, and that the palace has become a parvenu's monument to himself. One could also call the construction a folly, thus implying that it belongs to a world that does not obey aesthetic or other laws, but is dominated by an imaginative self-assertion. All this would undoubtedly be true, but also rather futile. For La Martinière should actually be regarded in a certain context, in an economic and social condition that is somewhat outside what we regard as 'normal', but which existed and caused other such monuments to be created.[6]

Martin had served in several armies; he had received his high military rank for services to the Nawab of Oudh, while his fortune was the result of his trade in indigo. He was, in fact, a typical product of the military and commercial environment in 18th century India, an adventurer who knew how to make use of changes in the political scene and trade booms.

Thus he used his riches and his position to surround himself with splendour. He behaved in the same way as most Europeans in Bombay, Calcutta or Madras. But the extravagant milieu of the Indian princes in Lucknow gave him still greater possibilities of display. It would seem as if Martin had built his palace to rival Asaf-ud-daulah, who had a very great passion for architecture.

xiv Heroes' Tombs and Monuments

The Baroque architects often supplied a magnificent setting for the great events in the life of the Church, states and princes. By means of decorations they lent splendour to the events and interpreted them, so to speak, *through* the monuments with the help of the semantics of the time. The constructions were often numerous and of large size. They were not, of course, of durable material, but of wood and fabric, and therefore could grow and multiply like the scenes in a theatre, being removed when they had had their effect and the performance was over.

One is reminded of this tradition by a notice in the *Calcutta Gazette* about the opening ceremony at Wellesley's Government House in January, 1803. The new palace was opened with festivities that were enhanced by a great number of architectonic stage-properties. The scene around Government House had been enlarged and galleries of coupled Doric pilasters were constructed which led to two temples dedicated to the divinities of Fame and Valour. On the large banqueting table were decorations in the form of Egyptian obelisks covered with hieroglyphics and also a small temple, this time to Peace, made like a Corinthian construction with four pediments and a light dome.[1]

Who was responsible for the decorations is not told, but it is very likely that Tiretta and Wyatt were active here as in the design of Government House itself, and that Wellesley himself was responsible for the allegorical programme. For naturally the décor was in conformity with the actual structures which were then being erected in Calcutta as well as in other places in India. The architectural landscape of the celebrations is only a reflection of the reality outside, where the monuments are repeated on a larger scale and in heavier material. They often symbolized the same virtues, but Fame and Valour generally occupy a more central position than Peace.

The Banqueting Hall in Madras, as previously mentioned, was erected entirely as a *Heroum* and on its pediment stood the victorious names of Plassey and Seringapatam. The latter referred to the war against Tipu Sultan and the subjugation of his realm, Mysore.[2] The person who was most active in preparing the way for the final British dominion over this area was Cornwallis, who had made an important treaty with Tipu in 1792. During the following decade and after his death in 1805, Cornwallis was the object of ardent hero-worship. His portrait was, of course, included in the gallery of heroes in the Banqueting Hall and monuments were erected to him in Madras, Bombay and in several places in Bengal. Several of the monuments took the form of small temples erected over statues which were sent out from England. Such a Cornwallis statue was sent to Madras in 1800 and was erected on Fort Square in Fort St. George.[3] The most magnificent of them was made by John Bacon Jr.; this was finished in 1803 and placed in due course in the newly built city hall in Calcutta.[4] Cornwallis was represented here in antique costume, as a Roman pro-consul presenting Peace and Prosperity to his province. Below him on the pedestal sit Fortitude and Prudence personified, and between them lies the attribute of Hercules. Thus there was a desire to recall the military power behind the peaceful gesture.[5]

The fame of Cornwallis was further manifested in a cenotaph at Ghazipur. A set of drawings for this have been preserved; they were probably made in 1805, the year of Cornwallis's death, or shortly afterwards. The architect was Thomas Fraser.[6]

The building proposed is octagonal and raised on a podium. Tuscan-Doric columns support an outer circular arcade; inside is a cella with a sarcophagus, and over this central part rises a semi-spherical dome with a coffered ceiling. The detail treatment, like the whole structure, conveys an impression of heaviness and solidity. One of the water-colours in Fraser's series shows what effect the building was to produce on its surroundings: here slender palms and minarets are literally set aside to give preference to the

THE STRUCTURES

European structure which dominates the scene with almost brutal force. The outlines of the Indian landscape are drawn like a veil behind the arches.

The cenotaph at Ghazipur was not erected according to Fraser's plan — at any rate not completely. It seems likely that he or other architects made alternative proposals. The one selected is somewhat similar to Fraser's, but is more obviously connected with an earlier English prototype: Nicholas Hawksmoor's large mausoleum for Castle Howard, built in 1729. This also consists of a Tuscan-Doric tempietto raised on a high podium. There are no arcades, and here the columns form an unbroken peristyle around the centre of the structure. The similarity between the English and the Anglo-Indian building can be studied in more detail with the help of an engraving of J. Moffat. An inscription on the engraving says that the cenotaph was 'being erected,' but the picture shows the finished structure, and an elephant to the left of it.[7]

Bishop Heber visited Ghazipur during his journey through Bengal in the 1820's and recorded his impressions of the Cornwallis monument.[8] He compared it with the well-known Vesta temple at Tivoli, but this comparison was not particularly apt. He noted that the architect had 'replaced' the Corinthian order with a simple Doric, a change that he did not appreciate. On the whole he reacted negatively when faced with the austere soldier's grave, and one feels that he was criticizing more than the actual composition, as in the case of the parade of heroes in the Banqueting Hall in Madras.

Cornwallis seems to have been the hero who was worshipped in the greatest number of places, but he was by no means the only one. Public monuments were erected to other individuals who had shown power of action and bravery and who could serve as examples for new generations of administrators and soldiers. Two large obelisks were erected to Ranfurlie Knox and John Darby, the former in Patna, where Knox performed his heroic deed during the siege of 1760, and the latter at the British Residency in Hyderabad, where Darby was killed fighting rebels in 1815.[9] Perhaps the largest and most ostentatiously placed of these monuments is the tall column on the Maidan in Calcutta, erected as a memorial to Sir David Ochterlony, who had performed meritorious service in several Indian wars and crowned his career by the conquest of Nepal in 1816. The column was erected in 1828. The architect was J. P. Parker, who had also built the School Chapel of St. Thomas.[10] He produced a very daring composition with elements from different cultures. The column itself is Greek Doric. but drawn far outside the system of proportion prescribed by Vitruvius (1/7). It stands on a stylobate and this in turn on a pedestal which was called 'Egyptian'. It is almost cubic with outward curved corners and with a modillon cornice. The crown of the monument with its bulbiform cupola also recalls western monuments: minarets in the Near East have a similar termination.

It seems impossible to read any symbolical meaning into the combination of the different parts of the structure. In any case they do not allude to Ochterlony's record, but possibly to his private interests. His partiality to Islam is said to have contributed to the minaret-like design, but this is pure guesswork. It is, however, known that a lighthouse was erected in Madras in 1841 which was also shaped like a gigantic Doric column;[11]

134

the shaft of the column contained a spiral staircase in the same way as the Ochterlony monument, which can still be climbed by this means. This technique shows how similar antique forms could be used in widely different connections without any special reference to their significance.

The many wars which paved the way for the English dominion in India and in other colonies claimed a large tribute of dead — and numerous monuments.

After 1794 and the end of the second war against the Rohillas, a circular temple was erected at St. John's Church in Calcutta to the memory of the officers and men who had fallen in the battles.[12] It is a strong, beautiful structure in the form of an open Doric peristyle. The columns placed near together, with pairs of bucrania and shields supporting a dome are in the frieze. The name of the architect is not known.

About ten years later a young engineer officer, George Rodney Blane, designed another cenotaph to the memory of 'the brave', but usually called the Temple of Fame. It was erected at Barrackpore after 1815 and placed beside the governor-general's country residence facing the Hooghly river.[13] It was in the first place a memorial to the twenty-four officers who had fallen in the conquest of the Île de France and Java in 1810–11; later it also served to commemorate the battles of Maharajpur and Panniar in 1843.[14]

Blane's construction was rectangular in form. Corinthian columns surround a cella, a memorial chamber with a barrel vault and with four black inscription tablets and ornamental wall panels. From outside, the building gives a light, peaceful impression. In its green surroundings it looks more like an orangery than a soldier's grave.

In 1847 Henry Conybeare designed a church to the memory of those who fell in the occupation of Sind and in Afghanistan. It was erected on Colaba in Bombay and was consecrated in 1858.[15] It thus lies half outside the scope of this thesis, like the Dalhousie Institute, Calcutta, with its more heathen characters. The idea was that the latter, with its large sculpture gallery, should function as a kind of Valhalla.[16]

In addition to the public monuments erected in India during the period of the East India Company, a great many private memorial temples and tombstones were constructed. The number of graveyards and their precincts grew at the same pace as the European dominion. The towns of the living paid tribute to the cities of the dead. Many certainly died in battle, but considerably more fell victim to the climatic conditions and to epidemics. Child mortality was high. The foreign environment was in itself a threat to the men and women who had come from distant countries, and many died after all too short a time in the new country. In Bombay, which from the start was particularly unhealthy on account of its situation on marshy ground, it was finally considered that 'two monsoons are the life of a man'; this is often quoted, but deserves to be repeated in this connection.[17]

At the first English 'factory' at Surat a couple of enormous monuments of Islamic character were constructed in the middle of the 17th century.[18] As stylistic phenomena they scarcely served as models for later works; later on, purely European forms were used in other places. It is true that here and there a circular temple with an un-classically curved dome may be found, which indicates that the Indian craftsmen have used their own vault-making technique, but this is an exception.[19]

It is difficult to group the mausoleums in a historical way or according to their place in the history of art. For the purpose of dating we only have the year of the inscriptions, when these remain and are in the original position. The architects' names are unknown. It might perhaps be said very generally that older and provincial cemeteries such as that in the Danish settlement of Tranquebar have graves, tombs and burial mounds of definitely Baroque character until after the middle of the 18th century, and that these later disappear and are replaced by neo-Classical structures.[20] But the connection is far from clear. A pyramid-shaped sepulchral monument was erected in Madras as early as around 1680, another in Soranghar about a hundred years later and a vast number during the following decades.[21] Even the last of those erected may be Baroque hybrids, and one is often doubtful whether to describe them as pointed pyramids or obelisks with an unusually broad base. The neo-Classical alternative is, as we shall see, very distinct in form.

In spite of the above mentioned difficulties we shall, however, venture to make an analysis of the varieties of monuments in one of the best known English cemeteries in India, South Park in Calcutta.[22] The cemetery began to be used in August, 1767, when 'the sick season' was approaching.[23] In 1812 Mrs. Graham described the place as:

'many acres covered so thick with columns, urns and obelisks that there scarcely seems to be room for another . . . it is like a city of the dead.'[24]

The cemetery is intersected by a couple of straight roads. The monuments are rather arbitrarily arranged. Here and there groups of obelisks, temples and pyramids are formed. The largest pyramid is the one erected over the grave of Richard Barwell's wife, Eliza-beth, who died in 1778; she is perhaps better known by her maiden name, Miss Sander-son.[25] This is the most radically formed of the structures. The pyramid itself is completely smooth and is acute-angled at the apex. Thus the base is not broad, as in the case of the Egyptian pyramids, so that the structure rather resembles the sepulchral monument of Caius Cestius at Porta Paola in Rome. The Indian pyramid, however, does not lie directly on the ground, but stands on a podium from which on each side a low triangular pediment arises. If the pyramid was built about 1780, a year or two after Elizabeth Barwell's death, it is certainly early, even for European examples. At that time the European architects were beginning to work with the pyramid as an ideal form.[26] Again, if the monument is dated 1780, one might also possibly surmise that it was built by Thomas Lyon or Edward Tiretta, who in that year were in contact with Richard Barwell but this is extremely hypothetical.[27]

A tall obelisk in South Park Cemetery to the memory of William Jones is decorated with half-urns in relief; others have the top cut off to bear an urn. In a few cases these are still in place, in others they have fallen off.

Temples are a striking feature of the city of the dead. The form varies: a round temple (to the memory of Ann Chambers, died 1782) has simple column shafts of almost uniform thickness placed between cube-shaped plinths and capitals which might indicate the influence of Chinese architecture; in this case, however, the building does not have the strong colours that might be expected, but is finished in ochre and white. Another (a memorial to Captain N. Bacon, died 1799) is octagonal with Ionic columns. A circular temple (erected for Elisabeth Ricketts, died 1824) consists of a regular stylobate divided into three parts, supporting an Ionic order with graceful festoons on the frieze and a rather high arched dome. The last mentioned, like the others, is half closed and has an inscription tablet in black marble inserted in the wall. In general, the temples are made of brick and plaster; even the columns are composed of small bricks, but the architraves are of wood.

Although constructions rather similar to these temples exist in Europe, it is difficult to trace direct prototypes. On the whole, however, they call to mind the variations on classical temples designed by William Chambers and the brothers Adam.[28] This is also the case with a series of more complicated constructions. One of these is formed as a large triumphal arch with a marble slab inserted in place of the portal (the monument is to the memory of Edward Wheler, died 1781 and, in fact, recalls one of the gateways of Fort William). Others are shaped like large kiosks. The memorial to John Garstin (died 1820) might have been designed by the same person who erected the Catholic Church at Dum Dum at that time. The same type of heavy Doric architecture has been used. But in Garstin's monument it has been emphasized by ornamental additions: pateras and bucrania in the frieze, rustication and a scroll border on the structure itself.[29]

Where symbolic elements occur, they are of a conventional and easily interpreted kind, whether they allude to the status and occupation of the deceased or to all-conquering Death: crossed swords, gun-barrels, trumpets and banners, scythes, arrows, torches and hour-glasses. Original decoration can, however, be seen in the monument, adorned with spirals and roses, to Rose Aylmer, who died in 1800 (and who herself is well known through Walter Savage Landor's elegy for her); and in a small Tuscan temple, which, so far as can be ascertained, has a Meta in its pediment a symbol taken from the circuses of classical antiquity and representing the end of a journey, the goal of our life's course.[30]

I have mentioned the inscription tablets which are of marble; other details also occur in that material, including large sculptured slabs. One such remains, half destroyed, among the nameless monuments in South Park Cemetery. It shows a woman draped in the style of the Antique and beside her Thanatos, the genius of Death with his torch turned downwards.

A symbolic interpretation of the monuments in India's European graveyards, like the analysis of the form, discloses a world of ideas built around exalted and rigid conceptions of death and the memory of the dead. The enormous monuments with their wealth of 'eternal' elements from the architecture of the Antique seem doubly pathetic in India, where life is changing with such force and rapidity.

II THE STRUCTURES

2. *Individual Patterns:* Notes

1. John Garstin was born in 1756 and Charles Wyatt in 1758; William Nain Forbes was born in 1796 and Thomas A. Cowper *c.* 1780.

2. J. Summerson, *Georgian London*, 1st ed. 1945, Pelican Books 1962, p. 36.

i French Government Houses in Pondicherry

1. Re the historical background of the French architecture which is dealt with here and in the following chapters, see H. Dodwell, *Dupleix and Clive, the Beginning of Empire*, London, 1920. G. Hanotaux and A. Martineau, *Histoire des Colonies Françaises, vol. 5, l'Inde et l'Indochine*, Paris, 1932. S. P. Sen, *The French in India*, Calcutta, 1948, and R. Glachant, *Histoire de l'Inde Français*, Paris, 1966.

2. The drawings are kept in the Dépôt des Fortifications des Colonies (abbreviated below as *D.F.C.*), Pondichéry, Cart. 2, nos. 78–87, Bibliothèque de la Section Outre-Mer des Archives Nationales, Paris. The drawings I mainly use in my description are No. 78 called 'Façade du Gouvernement de Pondichéry, du côté de l'entrée' and signed 'fecit Champia de Sonbrun — sous lieutenant d'infanterie', pen and wash, 267 × 727 mm., and No. 85, 'Coupe et Arrière Facade du Gouvernement de Pondichéry', pen and water-colour, 580 × 940 mm. No. 80 is dated '1755'. Two of the drawings are kept in the Musée de la France Outre-Mer.

3. See Y. Robert-Gaebelé, *Créole et Grande Dame, Joanna Bégum, Marquise Dupleix*, Pondichéry, 1934, pp. 253 f. Here and there we can read that thirty-two black columns of granitic gneiss which had been captured by the French from Fort St. George in Madras were used in the construction of Dupleix's Government House. However, they cannot have formed part of the façade. The Tuscan–Doric order of the ground floor has different measurements and has more columns. Cf. above, p. 108 and p. 81, note 24.

4. The French scientist, Le Gentil, who was dogged by misfortune and who travelled to Pondicherry 'par ordre du Roi à l'occassion du passage de Vénus sur le disque du soleil, le 6 juin 1761'. also witnessed the destruction of the town and painted the houses which had been demolished. G. J. H. J. B. Le Gentil de la Galasière, *Voyage dans les mers de l'Inde*, Paris, 1779–1782, vol. 1, plate 5.

5. D. F. C. Pondichéry, Cart. 3, No. 152, 'Plan de l'hôtel du Gouvernement', signed Bourcet and dated 15th October 1766, pen and water-colour, 462 × 576 mm., No. 153 'Coupe et Elévation de l'hôtel du Gouvernement', signed and dated as the foregoing, pen and water-colour, 235 × 576 mm. Drawing No. 124 shows how parts of the demolished buildings were used in the new ones.

6. C. A. Jombert, *Architecture moderne ou l'Art de bien bâtir pour toutes des personnes*, Paris, 1764. See, for example, vol. 2, plate 92.

7. D. F. C., Cart. 4, No. 214, 'Façade du Gouvernement', signed by Bourcet and dated 28th February 1768, pen and wash, 345 × 544 mm.

8. L. O'Hier de Grandpré, *Voyage dans l'Inde et au Bengale . . . 1789 et 1790*, Paris, 1801. G. N. Curzon, Marquis Curzon of Kedleston, *British Government in India*, London, 1925, vol. 1, p. 18.

9. D. F. C., Cart. 9, No. 653, 'Plans, Elévation et Coupe de l'Hôtel du Gouvernement' signed and dated Spinasse 1821, pen and water-colour, 727 × 1044 mm.

10. See below, p. 178.

11. D. F. C., Cart. 8, No. 573, 'Bâtiments civils de Goudelour, Gouvernement', by Malavois, dated April, 1782, pen and water-colour, 440 × 260 mm.

ii The Palais de Justice in Pondicherry

1. The drawings are kept in the Dépôt des Fortifications des Colonies (abbreviated below as D.F.C.). Pondichéry, Cart. 8, No. 627, 'Plan du Palais de Justice du Conseil Supérieur,' signed La Lustière, pen and water-colour, 430 × 496 mm., and No. 628, 'Façade du Palais de Justice du Conseil Supèrieur', pen and wash, 443 × 560 mm. Bibliothèque de la Section Outre-Mer des Archives Nationales, Paris. The building is still preserved more or less unchanged.

2. The elongated plan with its inner courtyard recalls other European buildings which probably have been influenced by Indian architecture, e.g. Government House in Tranquebar, and the house of Sornay, the engineer, in Karikal. D.F.C. Chandernagore. See further the chapter on 'The Forms of Architecture as determined by the Climate', p. 182 below.

3. D.F.C., Pondichéry, Cart. 9, No. 654, 'Palais de Justice . . .', signed by Spinasse and dated 1821, pen and water-colour, 532 × 740 mm.

iii The Gates of Pondicherry

1. A copy of *La Science des Ingénieurs* is kept in the National Library, Calcutta. Two copies were included in the small library used by the Danish military engineers in Tranquebar. Cf. above, p. 56 and the chapter on 'The Training of the Architect'.

2. The drawings are kept in the Dépôt des Fortifications des Colonies. Pondichéry Cart. 8, No. 616, 'Elévation extérieure de la Porte Villenour', by La Lustière, 1788, pen and water-colour, 427 × 672 mm., and No. 631, 'Elévation extérieure de la Porte Madras', pen and wash, 418 × 387 mm. Bibliothèque de la Section Outre-Mer des Archives Nationales, Paris.

3. Cf. *La Science des Ingénieurs*, The Hague, 1734, Liv. IV, plate 17.

4. The gates in Calcutta and Madras are still in existence, although somewhat changed. An early reproduction of the 'Water Gate' of the Calcutta fort is to be found in 'View of Calcutta from Fort William', published by Edw. Orme, 1807. The King's Topographical Collection CXV 46-a, British Museum.

iv Godowns for Opium and Grain

1. In 1824, the Dutch factory was taken over by the British. It was reproduced that year by Sir Charles D'Oyly, 'View of the Ruins of the Dutch factory in the western suburbs of the City of Patna', No. 53, in a sketch-book, W. D. 2060, in the India Office Library, Commonwealth Office. The French factory is reproduced ibid., No. 56. Re the Danish factory see p. 70 above.

2. The drawings kept in The King's Topographical Collection CXV 48-b, 'General plan of the Opium Factory at Patna', 48-c, 'Plan of the Opium Godown', and 48-d, 'Elevation of the South Front of the Opium Godowns at Patna'. All drawings are unsigned, undated and measure 520 × 360 mm.; British Museum.

3. About 1860, the Patna artist Shiva Lal made sketches for a series of proposed mural paintings for the Gulzarbagh Opium Factory. See Mildred and W. G. Archer, *Indian paintings for the British*, Oxford, 1955, p. 37.

139

THE STRUCTURES

4. See W. W. Hunter, *Annals of Rural Bengal*, London, 1868, vol. 1, pp. 38 ff. and p. 49.

5. Letter from Mr. J. P. Auriol, Bengal Original Consultations, 25th April, 1782, No. 13, in the National Archives of India, New Delhi. For localizing, see the Presslist of ancient documents preserved in the Imperial Record Room of Govt. of India, 1780–84. In Bengal, *Past and Present*, vol. 2, July–October, 1908, pp. 388 f., the inscription on a marble slab above one of the doors is reproduced; this runs as follows: 'In part of a general plan ordered by the Governor-General in Council, 20th of January 1784, for the perpetual prevention of famine in these provinces, the granary was erected by Captain John Garstin, engineer'.

6. Garstin, who was born in 1756, was later appointed Surveyor General and Chief Engineer of Bengal. He died in 1820. Cf. above, p. 116 and p. 137.

7. *Bengal, Past and Present*, vol. 52, July–September, 1936, p. 48. The drawings are kept in The King's Topographical Collection CXV 48-e, 'Plan of the Granary at Patna', and 48-f, 'Section of the Granary at Patna', both pen and water-colour, 368 × 525 mm., British Museum.

8. R. H. Phillimore, *Historical Records of the Survey of India*, Dehra Dun, 1945 ff. vol. 2, p. 400.

9. Mrs. Sherwood's statement is reproduced in *Bengal, Past and Present*, vol. 30, July–September, 1925, p. 141.

10. *Bengal, Past and Present*, vol. 52, July–September, 1936, p. 47.

11. O. Reutersvärd has written about these projects in a not yet published paper on the architecture of neo-Classicism entitled 'Idealgestaltning, antikeklekticism och utopism'. MS in possession of the author, Lund, Sweden.

12. *Hobson-Jobson* says: *Golah* — Hind. golā (from *gol*, round), a storehouse for grain or salt, so called from the typical form of such storehouses in many parts of India, viz. a circular wall of mud with a conical roof. Cf. B. Ghose, *Primitive Indian Architecture*, Calcutta, 1953.

13. R. Heber, *Narrative of a Journey from Calcutta to the Upper Provinces of India, from Calcutta to Bombay 1824–25*, London, 1928, vol. 1, p. 236. The gola is reproduced ibid. p. 239. Heber also reflects on the function of the building and the reasons why it cannot be used.

14. Some engravings by T. Medland after drawings of J. Garstin are kept in the India Office Library, Commonwealth Office.

15. The godown in Bankipur somewhat recalls an ice-house which was erected in Bombay in 1834. Photo in the Victoria and Albert Museum, Bombay.

v Writers' Buildings

1. A letter to Warren Hastings sent from Calcutta and dated January 1780 from Joseph Cator, 'one of the Trustees', tells of the arrangements in Writers' Buildings, reproduced in *Bengal, Past and Present*, vol. 3, January–April, 1909, p. 142. Cf. M. Graham, *Journal of a Residence in India*, Edinburgh, 1812, p. 138.

2. Thomas Lyon arrived in India in March 1763 along with two colleagues. See E. W. Sandes, *The Military Engineer in India*, Chatham, 1933–35, vol. 1, p. 122. K. Blechynden, *Calcutta, Past and Present*, London, 1905, tells of Lyon's role in connection with the construction of Writers' Buildings. Cf. above, p. 136 and the chapter 'The Training of the Architect'. In *Bengal, Past and Present*, vol. 3, January–April 1909, pp. 139 f. Lyon is called 'a house builder' according to information of 11th January 1782. William Hickey, *Memoirs*, London, 1925, vol. 4, p. 117 mentions Lyon as the builder of the house of Chief Justice Sir Robert Chambers in Calcutta.

140

T. Williamson, *The East India Vade-Mecum*, London, 1810, vol. 2, p. 57, calls Lyon 'the Company's architect at Berhampore'. As early as 1788 he was active there and in Dinapur according to letters in the National Archives of India, New Delhi. For localization, see Presslist of ancient documents preserved in the Imperial Record Room of the Govt. of India, dated 11th March 1788.

3. This wing for ladies and gentlemen-in-waiting was erected in the 1770's at Gripsholm Castle after drawings by A. U. Cronstedt. The building is very well preserved and the fittings and all the furniture are unchanged.

4. The description is based on plate No. 4 in T. and W. Daniell, *Oriental Scenery. Twenty-four Views in Hindoostan*, London, 1797. The façade which dominates the long side of the square, naturally recalls the 'terraces' which were erected in London during the 1760's and 1770's by the brothers Adam and others. Cf. above, p. 66.

5. M. Graham, op. cit., p. 138.

6. K. Blechynden, op. cit., p. 199.

7. The photographs are kept by Bourne and Shepherd, Calcutta.

vi British Government Houses in Calcutta and Madras

1. G. N. Curzon, Marquis Curzon of Kedleston, *British Government in India*, London, 1925, vol. 1 pp. 19 and passim. In using information from this book below, I shall do so without special reference.

2. This information is found, for example, in *A Handbook for travellers in India, Pakistan, Burma and Ceylon*; 19th edition; London, 1962.

3. James Paine here writes of Kedleston, vol. II plates 50 ff.: 'The Author was employed to make the plans for this magnificent mansion in the year 1761 and the foundations were soon after accordingly laid . . . Messrs. Robert and James Adam . . . made several alterations in the Author's plans, as appears by those published in the fourth volume of the Vitruvius Britannicus.'

4. Charles Wyatt's drawings do not seem to have been preserved; I have studied the plan with the help of some copies, signed James Best: Plan of the basement storey of 'the new Government House', pen and wash, 685 × 750 mm.; plan of the principal storey, pen and wash, 724 × 807 mm.; plan of the attic storey, pen and wash, 655 × 743 mm.; elevation of the north-west front, pen and water-colour, 482 × 826 mm.; elevation of the south-east front, pen and water-colour, 470 × 762 mm. WD. 1003, 1004, 1005, 1319, 1320, India Office Library, Commonwealth Office, London.

5. Steen Bille remarked that the flight of steps was seldom used, as it was too much exposed to rain and sun; *Beretning om Corvetten Galathea's Reise omkring Jorden, 1845, 46 og 47*, Copenhagen, 1849–51, vol. 1, p. 188. However, the author points out that the flight of steps functioned as a covered passage to the vestibule of the ground floor. Cf. the chapter below on 'The Forms of Architecture as determined by the Climate'.

6. J. B. Fraser, *Scenery of Calcutta and its environs*, London, 1824–26.

7. The gateway of Syon House is reproduced in *The Works in Architecture of Robert and James Adam*, London 1778–1822, vol. I plate 1. The son of a merchant from Malaya has described the gates of Government House, see above, p. 106, and so has James Johnson in *The Oriental Voyager*, London, 1807, p. 100: 'Over the four colossal arches or gates that lead to it, there are placed sphinxes and various emblematic figures, that have a very good effect.' Emblematic

figures were also placed on Government House itself, amongst others a large Britannia on the south side; they can be studied in James B. Fraser's Calcutta pictures. The author is indebted to Sir John Summerson for the point about Sir William Chambers's influence. For an engraving of Chambers's arch, see *A Treatise on the Decorative Part of Civil Architecture*, London 1791.

8. Cf. *Bengal Past and Present* vol. 15, July–December, 1917, p. 82, and George D. Bearce, *British attitudes towards India*, Oxford, 1961, pp. 46 and 185, and below p. 163.

9. George Annesley, Viscount Valentia, *Voyages and Travels in India* etc., London, 1809, vol. 1, pp. 235 f.

10. Cf. above, p. 107.

11. 'Af en Ostindienfarers Breve', issued by Hakon Müller, *Tilskueren*, September, 1934, p. 203. The original letters in Bluhme's private records, National Archives, Copenhagen.

12. Steen Andersen Bille, op. cit., vol. 1, pp. 187 f. and 197.

13. There is, of course, also another possibility, that the story is fictitious and written as a parody by an Englishman in Calcutta.

14. Re the description of the gates, here mistakenly mentioned as being 'five,' cf. above, p. 104.

15. The floor of the lower hall was actually not black but dark grey, of marble which had been fetched from China; cf. Maria Graham, *Journal of a Residence in India*, Edinburgh, 1812, p. 137; some of the chandeliers had formed part of the original fittings of La Martinière, Lucknow, and had been bought at the auction in 1800; cf. above, p. 131.

16. Mildred Archer has described the Government Houses in Calcutta and Madras in three articles in *Country Life*, 'A Georgian palace in India', 9 April 1959; 'Georgian splendour in Madras', 26 March 1964; 'Aspects of Classicism in India: Georgian Buildings of Calcutta', 3 November, 1966.

17. H. D. Love, *Descriptive list of pictures in Government House and the Banqueting Hall, Madras*, Madras, 1903, pp. 31 ff; I also use information from this work in the following. It should be pointed out that Love states that the façade of Clive's Government House was 250 feet long, which is presumably a mistake for 205.

18. 'Plans, Elevations and Sections of the Buildings in the Government Gardens at Madras', pen and wash and water-colour, WD. 962, India Office Library, Commonwealth Office. There are sixteen drawings bound in one volume, size 515 × 724 mm. They are unsigned and probably copies which Lord Clive had taken home to England. The album was acquired by the India Office Library from his descendents.

19. This arrangement is regarded from purely climatic aspects below, p. 178.

20. Personal records of John Goldingham, V v. 839; XIII 69–90; XVII 135–147, India Office Library, Commonwealth Office; cf. op. cit. Mildred Archer and op. cit. H. D. Love. The information on Goldingham's Danish origin is to be found in the work of Mildred Archer and, before her, in R. M. Phillimore, *Historical Records of the Survey of India*, Dehra Dun, 1945 ff., vol. 1, p. 338. During the war between France and England at the end of the 18th century attempts were made to attract merchants to the Danish colonies, among other things by offering them neutral Danish citizenship; See *Vore gamle tropekolonier*; Copenhagen, 1952, vol. 1 pp. 281 f. On 2 September, 1793 a Governmental Decree was issued in Tranquebar, 'inviting all house owners and all His Majesty's Military Civil and Ecclesiastical officers to obtain certificates of Danish citizenship'; *Calendar of a Volume containing notifications (1779 to 1824); issued by the Danish Administration at Tranquebar*, Madras, 1908. Serampore was also a

place of transit for people of various nationalities, and thus it can be imagined that Goldingham had been transformed into a Dane through one of these channels. His name is not, however, included in Kay Larsen's carefully compiled Dansk Ostindisk Personalia, MS in three volumes, the Reference Library of the Royal Library, Copenhagen.

21. See H. D. Love, op. cit., p. 45 and above p., 108.

22. 'A view of the Government House and Council Chambers at Madras' (engraved by H. Merke, publ. by Edward Orme 1807); one copy in the British Museum, Dept. of Prints and Drawings, Topography, India.

23. The motif is actually taken from Vignola and is reproduced in William Chambers, *A Treatise on Civil Architecture*, London, 1759.

24. George Annesley, Viscount Valentia, op. cit., vol. I p. 390.

25. H. D. Love, op. cit., p. 52.

26. R. Heber, *An Account of a Journey to Madras and the Southern Provinces, 1826*; published together with *Narrative of a Journey from Calcutta to the Upper Provinces of India*, London, 1828, vol. 2.

27. Cf. Ibid. p. 51, Court's Despatch of 27 April, 1803.

vii Plans for a Palace at Murshidabad

1. Add. Ms 13. 904 a, unsigned, and b, signed: Tiretta; the measurements of the drawings are (a) 507 × 1402 mm. and (b) 608 × 870 mm, British Museum. It is stated that both drawings were presented to the Museum by Marquis Wellesley.

2. As regards Blechynden and Anbury, see G. N. Curzon, Marquis Curzon of Kedleston, *British Government in India*, London, 1925, vol. II. pp. 8 and 45.

3. Cf. *Bengal, Past and Present*, vol. 2, January–July, 1908, p. 207 and vol. 44, 1932, p. 57. Amongst other things, an engraving is here reproduced after a painting by F. C. Lewis Jr. It shows how the Nawab of Bengal was installed in Murshidabad on 21st May, 1847. The scene for the ceremony is the Pantheon-shaped durbar-room of the palace. A water-colour of William Clerihew, dated 1843, shows part of the building in Murshidabad; cc 4/2, the Drawings Collection of the R.I.B.A., London.

4. Cf. p. 74 and p. 113, above.

viii British Residencies in Lucknow and Hyderabad

1. Re Fyzabad and the environment in Lucknow, see *The Cambridge History of India*, Cambridge, 1929, vol. 5, pp. 239 and 349, also M. and W. G. Archer, *Indian Painting for the British*, Oxford, 1955, pp. 51–63. Re Claude Martin, see above, p. 132.

2. The information about the Residency and its annexes are also in the following taken from S. Hay, *Historic Lucknow*, Lucknow, 1939, pp. 59 ff. See also G. W. Forrest, *Cities of India*, Westminster, 1903, pp. 218 ff.

3. The treaty with the Nawab Shuja-ud-daulah was signed on 10 July, 1763. See the above-mentioned volume of *The Cambridge History of India*, p. 174.

4. The chronology of the various buildings and annexes given here in connection with S. Hay's information, see note 2 above, should be regarded as hypothetical.

5. The Banqueting Hall, Lucknow, was used as a hospital during the siege. Re the Banqueting Hall, Madras, see above, pp. 108 f.

6. Some of the first photos taken in India show the Residency in Lucknow after the siege. A good photo is kept in the India Office Library, Commonwealth Office, Photo 89. See also Nos. 468–83, *Catalogue of Pictures destined for the Victoria Memorial Hall and now exhibited in the Indian Museum*, Calcutta, 1908. The buildings were destroyed during the military operations in 1857. A great many books and articles deal with these events and are usually illustrated by sketch-maps of 'the entrenched position'. Cf. 'Sketch of the Residency and Palace at Lucknow', published by J. Wyld, January 13th, 1858, Maps Collection No. 57500 (5), British Museum.

7. The material of the buildings and the 'pure style' are dealt with below ,pp. 170, 164. Cf. also the chapter on 'General Martin's Palace-Tomb in Lucknow' p. 131 above.

8. *Bengal, Past and Present*, vol. 53, January–March 1937, p. 54.

9. The most important sources of information concerning the Residency in Hyderabad are *Some Notes on the Hyderabad Residency, collected from original records in the Residency office*, 1918. This book is abbreviated below as 'Notes'.

10. 'Notes,' p. 1.

11. See the above-mentioned volume of *The Cambridge History of India*, pp. 372 ff.

12. The general likeness of the plan with the project for a palace in Murshidabad, the Serampore College and as regards the main building with Government House, Calcutta, can be studied by comparison with pp. 110, 74, 101 f.

13. The letter was written in 1806. At that time the building was not finished. Russell is called 'Super Intendent for His Highness the Subehdar'. 'Notes,' p. 2.

14. Cf. above, p. 104.

15. R. M. Grindlay, *Scenery, Costumes and Architecture*, London, 1826.

16. 'The Residency of Hyderabad', pen drawing, No. F 3/21, the R.I.B.A. Drawings Collection, bought at Sotheby's together with a similar drawing, WD. 1712, in the India Office Library, Commonwealth Office. Both drawings are said to have belonged to Sir Henry Russell (1783–1852).

17. 'The British Resident and Staff going to visit the Nizam', oil-painting by an unknown artist, No. 982, Victoria Memorial Hall, Calcutta.

18. 'Notes,' p. 9.

19. Valentia's defence can be found above, p. 105. Both statements are given a wider meaning in the chapter on the 'Fundamental Principles of Architecture'. Below, p. 163.

ix Town Halls and Mints in Calcutta and Bombay

1. Bengal Past and Present, vol. 9, July–December, 1914, pp. 181 f. and W. H. Carey, *The Good Old Days of Hon'ble John Company*, Simla, 1882–87, vol. 2, p. 213.

2. W. S. S. Karr, *Selections from the Calcutta Gazettes*, Calcutta, 1864–1959. vol. 4, pp. 136 f.

3. R. H. Phillimore, *Historical Records of the Survey of India*, Dehra Dun, 1945 onw., vol. 2, p. 401.

4. Steen Andersen Bille, *Beretning om Corvetten Galathea's Reise omkring Jorden 1845, 46 og 47*, Copenhagen 1849–51, vol. 1, p. 190.

5. Cecil L. Burns, *Victoria and Albert Museum, Bombay*, Bombay, 1918, p. 15; E. W. Sandes, *The Military Engineer in India*, Chatham, 1933–38, vol. II, p. 91. The inscription tablet which was put up at the main entrance of the town hall mentions as architects Thomas Cowper and Charles Waddington.

6. Cf. Stuart and Revett, *The Antiquities of Athens,* London, 1762 etc., vol. 2, plates I–XXX.

7. The *jhilmils* and other sun-breaking elements are described below in the chapter 'The Forms of Architecture as determined by the Climate', p. 180.

8. Civil servants in memory of whom monuments were erected in this and in adjoining rooms are Stephen Babington (1790–1842), Montstuart Elphinstone, Charles Norris (1791–1842), William Erskine (1773–1852), John Malcolm and, on the stairs, Sir Jamsetjee Jeejeebhoy; cf. G. W. Forrest, *Cities of India,* Westminster, 1903, pp. 13 f. Several of these statues have been depicted in Roderick Cameron, *Shadows of India,* London, 1958, pp. 136, 152, 153 and 161.

9. Cecil L. Burns, op. cit., p. 15.

10. Ibid., p. 16.

11. E. W. Sandes, op. cit., vol. II, pp. 91 and 316; by the last reference a photo of the Mint is inserted which was taken from above and gives a good picture of the plan of the building and of its size. Cf. W. K. Firminger, *Thacker's guide to Calcutta,* Calcutta, 1906, p. 165.

12. On the position of the building in the Strand, cf. above, p. 66. Cf. Steen Bille's description of the Mint as being 'far too massive beneath the tropical sky'; above, p. 33.

13. On the Madrasha, see *Bengal, Past and Present,* vol. 8, January–June, 1914, p. 95; according to an inscription mentioned there, the building had been completed in 1824, 'planned and constructed by William Burns, James Mackintosh, and William Kemp.' An earlier building for the Islamic College had been erected in 1781–82. On Tara Wala Kothi, now the office of the State Bank of India, see Sidney Hay, *Historic Lucknow,* Lucknow, 1939, p. 223.

14. On the 'significance' of the use of the Doric order, see below, p. 162.

x Town Residences and Clubs in Calcutta

1. S. E. Rasmussen, *London, the unique city,* first published 1934, Pelican Books 1961, especially chapter 10, 'Domestic Architecture' and chapter 12, 'The London House'. J. Summerson, *Georgian London,* first published 1945, Pelican Books 1962, p. 239: 'The scale of London architecture, and indeed of English architecture as a whole, is small; it easily descends to meanness. Hawksmoor and Vanbrugh aimed at bigness of scale, but the middle and late Georgians — Chambers, Adam, Soane and Nash — designed small and even diminutive.'

2. S. E. Rasmussen, op. cit., p. 192.

3. The buildings in Fort St. George, Madras, are arranged with a certain regularity. See above, p. 86, note 5.

4. The origin and characteristic planning of the Chowringhi area have been dealt with above in the chapter on 'The Growing Towns: Calcutta'.

5. The social background has been sketched by D. Kincaid, *British social life in India,* London, 1938, and by P. Spear, *The Nabobs,* first ed. 1932, London, 1963. See particularly pp. 49 ff. All members of the domestic staff and their duties are described here.

6. E. Roberts, *Scenes and Characteristics of Hindostan,* London, 1835, vol. 1. p. 2. 'Even those residences intended for families of very moderate income cover a large extent of ground and afford architectural displays which would be vainly sought amid habitations belonging to the same class in England'. Cf. Ph. Woodruff, *The men who ruled India,* first published 1953, London, 1963, vol. 1, pp. 154 ff.

7. The wall of No. 4 Harrington Row obviously goes back to a Palladian rusticated motif

and the doorway of another structure reproduced in B. Langley, *The City and Country Builder's and Workman's Treasury of Designs* etc., London, 1745, plate XX.

8. P. Spear, op. cit., pp. 23 ff.

9. Cf. the chapter on 'The Forms of Architecture as determined by the Climate', p. 179 below.

10. W. H. Carey, *The Good Old Days of Hon'ble John Company*, Simla, 1882–87, vol. 2, pp. 154 f. One who strangely enough liked the residential architecture of Bengal, but only that, was J. Fergusson, *History of the modern styles of architecture*, London, 1862, pp. 416 f.

11. This information has kindly been provided by the secretary of the Calcutta Turf Club. The Apcar family is mentioned in M. Massey, *Recollections of Old Calcutta*, Calcutta, 1918.

12. For example the now demolished Montagu House, which was built by James Stuart 1777–82.

13. L. von Orlich, *Travels in India*, London, 1845, vol. 2, p. 181.

14. Cf. below, p. 178.

15. W. H. Carey, op. cit., vol. 1, p. 55. L. von Orlich, op. cit., vol. 2, p. 179, and H. R. Panchridge, *A Short History of the Bengal Club*, Calcutta, 1927.

16. Photographs in the possession of Bourne and Shepherd, Calcutta.

17. *Bengal, Past and Present*, vol. 17, July–December, 1918, p. 15.

18. The Asiatic Society, No. 57 Park Street. See *Centenary Review of the Asiatic Society of Bengal, from 1784 to 1883*, Calcutta, 1885, vol. 1, pp. 21 f. and W. K. Firminger, *Thacker's Guide to Calcutta*, Calcutta, 1906, pp. 82 f.

xi Country Residences near Calcutta, Madras and Delhi

1. H. D. Love, *Descriptive List of Pictures in Government House and the Banqueting Hall, Madras*, Madras, 1903, p. 35; cf. above, pp. 70 and 107.

2. See above, p. 69.

3. *Bengal, Past and Present*, vol. 29, January–June, 1925, pp. 207 ff., contains extracts from the records of the Government of India. 'The Garden front of Ghiretty House upon the banks of the River Hughley in Bengal', water-colour by S. Davis, dated 1782, WD. 968 in the India Office Library, Commonwealth Office.

4. L. O'Hier de Grandpré, *Voyage dans l'Inde et au Bengale . . . 1789 et 1790*, Paris, 1801, vol. 2, pp. 85 ff.

5. Cf. above, p. 29.

6. G. N. Curzon, Marquis Curzon of Kedleston, *British Government in India*, London, 1925, vol. 1, pp. 139 ff. Here Zoffany's portrait of the Hasting's couple is reproduced.

7. The quotation from the *Calcutta Gazette* is reproduced by Curzon, op. cit., vol. 1, p. 142.

8. The custom of living on the ground-floor is gradually introduced into town houses following experience in country houses. See below, p. 178.

9. G. N. Curzon, op. cit., vol. 2, pp. 1–47. Here there are several pictures and maps.

10. Ibid., facing p. 22, the Gothic aviary and menagery are reproduced. Re the church in Serampore, see above, p. 75.

11. See above, p. 29.

12. Examples of the 'heavy style' are the Catholic church in Dum Dum and the Mint in Calcutta. See above, pp. 117 and 128.

13. In Barrackpore, the servants lived in the basement of the house. L. von Orlich, *Travels in India*, London, 1845, vol. 2, p. 192.

14. 'Commillah, late the Residence of John Buller, Esqʳ.', drawing by J. Hunter, aquatint by H. Merke, published by E. Orme 1805; one copy No. R. 2314, in the Victoria Memorial Hall, Calcutta. 'Felicity Hall, late the residence of the Hon. David Anstruther Near Moorshedabad, Bengal', after a painting by T. Daniell, included in F. W. Blagdon, *A Brief History of Ancient and Modern India*, London, 1805. The latter engraving is also dealt with below, p. 187, in connection with the origin of the structure of the bungalow. In that connection it is not the European residence that is of interest, but the 'curvilinear huts' belonging to it.

15. H. Dodwell, *Dupleix and Clive, the beginning of Empire*, London, 1920, p. 170.

16. H. D. Love, *Vestiges of Old Madras*, London 1913, vol. 3, p. 55. G. Annesley, Viscount Valentia, *Voyages and Travels to India, Ceylon, the Red Sea . . . in the years 1802, 1803, 1804, 1805 and 1806*, London 1809–11, vol. 1, p. 389, describes the 'garden houses' of Madras, likewise M. Graham, *Journal of a Residence in India*, Edinburgh 1812, p. 124. Cf. the chapter on 'The Forms of Architecture as determined by the Climate', p. 177, below.

17. The water-colours, WD. 479, 1264, 1266, 1618, in the India Office Library, Commonwealth Office. Cf. above, p. 26 and fig. 1a.

18. 'The illustrated Map of Madras', printed 1866 by Higginbotham, Maps Collection No. 54570 (5), British Museum.

19. H. C. Fanshawe, *Delhi, Past and Present*, London, 1902, pp. 18 and 81 f. *List of Muhammedan and Hindu Monuments, Delhi province*, vol. 2, Calcutta, 1919, p. 281.

20. Photo 52, in India Office Library, Commonwealth Office.

21. Cf. below, p. 181.

22. Quotation from G. N. Curzon, op. cit., vol. 2, p. 1.

23. 'The Origin of the Dwelling-House', pp. 186–189 below.

xii Christian Churches

1. B. Little, *The life and work of James Gibbs*, London, 1955, pp. 179 ff. M. Whiffen, *Stuart and Georgian Churches*, London, 1948, pp. 40–41.

2. B. Little considers in the above op. cit. that St. George's in Cape Town was the last church built after the model of St. Martin-in-the-Fields, 1830–34. As our knowledge of colonial architecture increases, further examples come to mind. R. Lewcock has recently described the church I mention here, the Dutch Reformed Church in Cradock, in *Early Nineteenth Century Architecture in South Africa*, Cape Town, 1963, pp. 402 ff. I have not found any example in India later than the above.

3. J. Summerson, *Georgian London*, first published 1945, Pelican Books 1962, p. 62.

4. Cf. 'The Growing Towns: Calcutta', p. 63, above.

5. H. B. Hyde, *Parochial Annals of Bengal*, Calcutta, 1901, p. 155. With reference to the possibility of the Danish citizenship of M. B. de Melvell and J. Goldingham, see p. 108 above.

6. The description is made after the engraving 'Elevation of the Church called Beth-Tephillah, i.e., House of Prayer, built A.D. 1770, at Calcutta, Bengal. By the Revᵈ. John Zachariah Kiernander'. Dept. of Prints and Drawings, Topography, India, British Museum.

7. W. S. S. Karr, *Selections from the Calcutta Gazettes*, Calcutta, 1864–1959, vol. 1, p. 2.

8. 'Copy of a letter from the committee for building a church . . .' The National Archives of

India, New Delhi, Orig. Consultations of 16th December 1784. For localising the MS, see the Presslist of ancient documents preserved in the Imperial Record Room of the Govt. of India, 1780–84.

9. K. Blechynden, *Calcutta, Past and Present*, London, 1905, pp. 137 f. See also *List of Ancient Monuments in Bengal*, Calcutta, 1896.

10. H. B. Hyde, op. cit., pp. 174 ff. W. Hickey, *Memoirs*, London, 1925, vol. 4, pp. 47 f.

11. Engraving in The King's Topographical Collection CXV 46-c, British Museum. This is unsigned. Cf. T. Daniell, *Views of Calcutta*, Calcutta, 1786–88, plate 12, and W. Baillie, *Twelve views of Calcutta*, London, 1794, plate 6.

12. *Bengal, Past and Present*, vol. 16, January–June 1914, p. 33, loc. cit.

13. Letter in the National Archives of India, New Delhi. See Presslist etc. W. K. Firminger, *Thacker's guide to Calcutta*, Calcutta, 1906, pp. 130 f.

14. L. O'Hier de Grandpré, *Voyage dans l'Inde et au Bengale . . . 1789 et 1790*, Paris, 1801, vol. 2, p. 5.

15. See above, p. 75.

16. M. Martyn, 'Georgian architecture in Calcutta', *Country Life*, 3 December, 1948.

17. J. B. Fraser, *Views of Calcutta and its environs*, London, 1824. Cf. above, p. 100.

18. *Bengal, Past and Present*, vol. 9, July–December, 1914, p. 215.

19. H. D. Love, *Vestiges of Old Madras*, London, 1913, vol. 3, p. 436.

20. E. W. Sandes, *The Military Engineer in India*, Chatham, 1933–35, vol. 2, p. 89. C. S. Srīnivāsāchāri, *History of the City of Madras*, Madras, 1939, p. 224.

21. E. W. Sandes, op. cit., loc. sit., C. S. Srīnivāsāchāri, op. cit., p. 225. De Havilland was also active in Fort St. George, Madras, and in Seringapatam, where he built the 'Havilland Arch', now destroyed. C. R. Srīnivāsāchāri, op. cit., p. 224; H. D. Love, *Descriptive List of Pictures in Government House and the Banqueting Hall, Madras*, Madras, 1903, p. 34, and T. F. De Havilland, *Public Edifices of Madras*.

22. St. Mary's in Poona is reproduced in R. Cameron, *Shadows of India*, London, 1958, p. 170. St. Andrew's in Bombay is mentioned in C. L. Burns, *Victoria and Albert Museum*, Bombay, 1918.

23. *Bengal, Past and Present*, vol. 5, January–June, 1910, p. 175, note.

24. *Bengal, Past and Present*, vol. 11, July–December, 1915, p. 239.

25. J. B. Fraser, *Military memoirs of Col. James Skinner*, London, 1851, pp. 234 f. W. H. Carey, *The Good Old Days of Hon'ble John Company*, Simla 1882–87, vol. 2, p. 273 f., H. C. Fanshawe, *Delhi, Past and Present*, London, 1902, p. 17.

26. The churches in Goa have been dealt with in Carlos de Azevedo, *Arte Christã na India Portuguesa*, Lisbon, 1959.

27. K. Blechynden, op. cit., p. 139.

xiii General Martin's Palace-Tomb in Lucknow

1. S. C. Hill, *The life of Claud Martin*, Calcutta, 1901; Sidney Hay, *Historic Lucknow*, Lucknow, 1939, pp. 154–55; Roderick Cameron, *Shadows of India*, London, 1958, pp. 156–63; an early engraving of Martin's palace, published in the *European Magazine* 1790, is preserved in the Dept. of Prints and Drawings, Topography India, British Museum.

2. Thomas Twining, *Travels in India a hundred years ago . . .*, London, 1893, p. 310.

3. George Annesley, Viscount Valentia, *Voyages and travels to India, Ceylon . . . in the years 1802, 1803, 1804, 1805 and 1806*, London, 1809, vol. I, p. 162.

4. Cf. S. C. Hill, op. cit., Chapter II.

5. L. von Orlich, *Travels in India*, London, 1845, vol. II, pp. 98 f.

6. Cf. above, p. 119 and below, p. 164.

xiv Heroes' Tombs and Monuments

1. K. Blechynden, *Calcutta, Past and Present*, London, 1905, pp. 117 f.

2. The Banqueting Hall was 'built to commemorate the capture of Seringapatam'. C. W. Forrest, *Cities of India*, Westminster, 1903, p. 318.

3. 'Banks has finished a very fine model of Marquis Cornwallis for the purpose of making a statue in marble, which is to be sent to Madras. The figure is well conceived, and the attitude is heroic, without affectation.' The above quotation is taken from a notice in the *Calcutta Gazette* of 5 January, 1797. See W. S. S. Karr, *Selections from The Calcutta Gazettes*, Calcutta, 1864–1959, vol. 2, p. 462. Cf. H. D. Love, *Vestiges of Old Madras*, London, 1913, vol. 3, pp. 405 and 563.

4. See G. N. Curzon, Marquis Curzon of Kedleston, *British Government in India*, London, 1925, vol. 2, p. 171, and above, p. 116.

5. Description of the 'Statue in Honour of Marquis Cornwallis' painted and engraved by G. Dawe. Proof in The King's Topographical Collection, CXV 46–6, British Museum.

6. Four drawings for 'A Cenotaph proposed to be erected to the Memory of the most Hon'ble Charles Marquis Cornwallis, late Governor General of India', signed T. Fraser, all pen and water-colour 280 × 432 mm., WD. 521–524, India Office Library, Commonwealth Office, London. Re Fraser see further p. 156 below. The structure recalls somewhat the monument erected at St. John's church, Calcutta, in memory of 'Begum' Johnson, who died in 1812. See *Bengal, Past and Present*, vol. 4, July–December, 1909, plate facing p. 499.

7. 'Mausoleum erecting at Ghazepore, to the Memory of the Marquess Cornwallis', in J. Moffat, *Views from Calcutta, Berhampore, Monghyr and Benares*, London, 1805.

8. R. Heber, *Narrative of a Journey from Calcutta to the Upper Provinces of India, from Calcutta to Bombay, 1824–25*, London, 1828, vol. 1, pp. 261 f. Cf. below, p. 167.

9. L. F. Rushbrook Williams, ed., *A Handbook to travellers in India, Pakistan, Burma and Ceylon*, 19th ed., London, 1962, pp. 50 and 371.

10. L. von Orlich, *Travels in India*, London, 1845, vol. 2, p. 185. *Bengal, Past and Present*, vol. 61, July–December, 1941, p. 28.

11. C. S. Srīnivāsāchāri, *History of the city of Madras*, Madras, 1939, p. 234.

12. *Bengal, Past and Present*, vol. 4, July–December, 1909, plate facing p. 500.

13. Designs for the Cenotaph at Barrackpore Park, or 'Memorial erected in commemoration of the 24 officers who had fallen in the conquest of Java and Isle de France (Mauritius) in 1810 and 1811'. Two sets of drawings, showing alternative but related schemes, are to be found in the R.I.B.A. Drawings Collection, F 3/1:1–10: 1) 'Site plan showing position in Barrackpore Park and Lieut. Col. Reid's house'; 'A Plan showing the site of the Cenotaphe to be erected at Barrackpore by the Rt. Honoble. Lord Minto.' Signed G. Rodney Blane, pen and water-colour, 622 × 415 mm.; 2) 'Ground-Plan', pen and wash, 546 × 375 mm.; 3) 'Front Elevation with hexastyle Corinthian portico', pencil and sepia wash, 372 × 540 mm.; 4) 'Side elevation drawn

to a larger scale', signed G. R. B., pen and wash, 448 × 667 mm.; 5) 'Longitudinal Section', pen and wash, 375 × 543 mm.; 6) 'Plan drawn to a larger scale and showing moulding of internal walls', pen and wash, 673 × 457 mm., 7) 'Front Elevation drawn to a larger scale', signed G. R. B., pen and wash, 447 × 667 mm.; 8) 'Side Elevation drawn to a larger scale showing shutters closed over windows'; signed G. R. B., pen and wash, 451 × 673 mm.; 9) 'Longitudinal section', pen and wash, 457 × 673 mm.; 10) 'Transverse section of entrance end, interior and exterior', pen and wash, 457 × 673 mm. For dating of the actual structure see the chapter on 'Country Residences near Calcutta, Madras and Delhi'.

14. Inscriptions on the black marble slabs in the temple.

15. 'Church of St. John, in memory of those killed in Sind and Afghanistan', 1) Plan, S. elev., W. elev., plans and sections of tower, signed and dated 'H. Conybeare, October 1847', pen and water-colour, 593 × 934 mm.; 2) Transverse section of nave and aisles; elevation of compartment of nave and of chancel, pen and water-colour, 622 × 635 mm.; 3) Perspective from S.W., print; also prints of original drawings coloured with wash. X12/65 1–4, the Drawings Collection of the R.I.B.A., London. The history of the origin of St. John's is rather long; before Conybeare the architects J. M. Derick and Anthony Salvin had been given the task of making drawings.

16. G. N. Curzon, op. cit., vol. 1, p. 182.

17. See J. Johnson, *The Influence of Tropical Climates on European Constitutions*, London, 1827, and P. Spear, *The Nabobs*, first ed. 1932, London 1963; the chapter on 'Medicine', pp. 100 ff.

18. These are reproduced and described in H. G. Rawlinson, *British Beginnings in Western India 1579–1657*, Oxford, 1920. They were also noticed by earlier travellers. O. Toreen, *A Voyage to Suratte*, printed together with P. Osbeck, *A Voyage to China and the East Indies*, London, 1771, vol. 2, p. 177.

19. Such are to be found in the old cemetery in Patna.

20. The churchyard at Zion's church in Tranquebar has gravestones in Baroque style, while neo-Classical monuments are predominant in the churchyard by New Street. Cf. above, p. 62.

21. The first pyramid now stands by the High Court in Madras. Re the one in Soranghar erected over Alexander Eliot on the order of Warren Hastings, see *Bengal, Past and Present*, vol. 2, July–October, 1908, p. 415.

22. The cemetery has been described by many authors. Sir W. Hunter called it an 'aceldama of ancient animosities' in *The Thackerays in India*, London, 1897, p. 13. See also R. Pearson, 'A Calcutta Cemetery' in the *Architectural Review*, July 1957. I cannot, however, agree with Pearson's general description of the way the architects worked. Cf. 'The Training of the Architect', below, p. 156.

23. K. Blechynden, op. cit., p. 76.

24. M. Graham, *Journal of a Residence in India*, Edinburgh, 1812, p. 141.

25. *Bengal, Past and Present*, vol. 3, January–April, 1909, figs. facing pp. 276 and 280.

26. See S. Å. Nilsson, 'Pyramid på Gustav Adolfs torg', *Konsthistorisk tidskrift*, XXXIII, 1964, pp. 1–20, with an English summary.

27. *Bengal, Past and Present*, vol. 3, January–April 1909, pp. 142 f.

28. W. Chambers, *A Treatise on Civil Architecture*, London, 1759, and *The Works in Architecture of Robert and James Adam*, London, 1778–1822.

29. Cf. above, p. 128. It might naturally be supposed that Garstin himself had designed his memorial temple, but the structure is radically different from other works by his hand. The heavy Doric order which has been used would seem to belong to a generation other than Garstin's; he himself remained a Palladian. See also above, p. 94.

30. The Meta used as a death symbol in neo-Classical art has been dealt with by O. Reutersvärd. The manuscript is in the possession of the author in Lund, Sweden.

Three · The Indian Vitruvius

The Indian Vitruvius

THE introductory chapters of this book gave an idea of how travellers in the Romantic Age approached European architecture in India. Their points of view varied; some emphasized the material used in the buildings, others remarked on their associative values, others again criticized the architecture on the grounds that it did not suit the climate. Through describing the structures, we have gained a deeper knowledge of how the various patterns were built up and how they functioned. I shall now try to summarize the most important of these ideas and conclusions in five chapters. In each case the titles have been taken from Vitruvius's *Ten Books on Architecture*.

The connection with Vitruvius is deliberate. I considered that employing Vitruvius's approach to his material — his method — would emphasize the qualities that gave European architecture in India its distinctive character: its necessary dependence on fundamental considerations and factors, its discovery of solutions that come within the field of the engineer rather than of the architect.

The Europeans who built in India were obliged to take into consideration a number of factors that could have been ignored in a less extreme climate. The 'style' could not be applied quite simply in the new environment; there was far too great a difference between the theoretical projections of light and shade learnt in the drawing office and the tropical scene where buildings were erected. These had also to stand the great heat of sun, monsoons and rain. I shall describe the structural changes that were made under the headings: The Training of the Architect, The Fundamental Principles of Architecture, Building Materials and Methods, The Forms of Architecture as determined by the Climate, and The Origin of the Dwelling-House. Thus we can follow the change of European prototypes towards something that can be called a Euro-tropical or, in this case, a Euro-Indian architecture.

1 · The Training of the Architect

THE Danes who, at the end of the 18th century, prepared to colonize the Nicobar Islands in the Gulf of Bengal, considered that the following persons should head the project: a governor and a second, a clergyman and two clerks or writers, a captain and a lieutenant who should both be able to draw and should be acquainted with engineering and artillery, a competent engineer, etc.[1]

Thus the architectural work, the structural development of the new territory, was in the hands of officers and engineers. This organization can be described as typical of the whole period under review. The French architects in Pondicherry, whose activity we have followed, were all engineers and the same applies to those who solved the large construction tasks on British territory: Agg, Wyatt, Forbes, Russell, De Havilland, Cowper and Blane. And the Danes we have heard of in this connection were Kyhn, Passow, Mühldorff and Wickede. Their training was that of engineers and builders of fortifications. Their knowledge of civil architecture must have been rather limited in the beginning.[2]

However, the British, who had indisputably the most important body of engineers, were afforded an extra possibility of obtaining an insight into the elementary principles of architecture. In 1794, Michael Topping set up a surveying school in Madras which, even though it had no direct connection with architecture, became a springboard for talented draughtsmen with the 'right' attitude.[3] John Goldingham, as well as Thomas Fraser, was active there.[4] The College of Fort William in Calcutta was started in 1800.[5] This college was to train civil servants, and no instructions in housing construction were given. However, a number of handbooks were procured for the library which comprise, for example, James Gibbs's *A Book of Architecture* (printed in 1728 and obtained by the Library in 1801) and William Halfpenny's *Rural Architecture in the Chinese Taste* (printed in 1755 and procured in 1804).[6]

In 1809, a college was started at Addiscombe in England and in 1812 the institution for Royal Engineers was founded at Chatham.[7] The latter was headed by Major C. W. Pasley who outlined the training course in a handbook. By way of introduction he emphasized that those authors who so far had dealt with practical architecture, such as Peter Nicholson and Tredgold, had omitted many details which they perhaps considered to be generally known. 'My object has been to endeavour to fill up those deficiencies, an attempt, which, if successful, may be useful to the junior Officers of the Corps, who are often sent to the British colonies soon after they enter His Majesty's Service; and

156

are there required to perform duties, analogous to those or Architects of Civil Engineers, without having had any previous opportunity of acquiring a Practical Knowledge of the details of those duties.'[8]

This suggests, in the first place, that the instruction and training afforded referred to colonial conditions, and secondly, that the officers who had dealt so far with structural problems had been rather unprepared for their tasks.

Pasley's handbook is of a relatively late date (1826) and cannot have been used by many of the engineers we have dealt with. These engineers had thus to resort to self-instruction and from our investigation of the urban and individual patterns we already know which works they studied. In Tranquebar as well as in Pondicherry and Calcutta, Bélidor's *La Science des Ingénieurs* was used.[9] Gibbs's *A Book of Architecture* was used for the construction of St. John's in Calcutta in 1786 and several decades later in Madras and other places.[10] It seems that this treatise had reached most of the public which Gibbs referred to in his introduction to his book: 'such Gentlemen as might be concerned in Building, especially in the remote parts of the Country where little or no assistance for Designs can be procured.'

We have also found that the architectural productions of James Paine, the Adam brothers, William Halfpenny, William Chambers and Stuart and Revett were in use. In the National Library of Calcutta we find a whole collection of old treatises and hand-books preserved. They were certainly frequently consulted before they came to this Library. In addition to Gibbs, Bélidor and Halfpenny, whom I have already mentioned, we also find Leoni's editions of Alberti and Palladio, (1726 and 1742), *The Principle of Ancient Masonry* (1733), Colin Campbell's *Vitruvius Britannicus* (1767–1771), *Il Vignola Illustrato* (1770), Desgodetz's *The Ancient Buildings of Rome* (vol. 1, 1771), *The Builder's Magazine* (1788), Percier & Fontaine's *Choix des plus célèbres maisons de plaisance de Rome et de ses environs* (1809); *The Civil Engineer's and Architect's Journal* (from October 1837). The last works which should be included in our list are R. & J. A. Brandon's *An Analysis of Gothic Architecture* and Ruskin's *Seven Lamps of Architecture* (both published in 1849).[11]

Naturally, these handbooks were used not merely by engineers who wished to acquire more training. They were certainly read by many more people, if not by the general public. At that time architecture was a field still open to non-professionals, far more than just the engineers made use of the handbooks and put the knowledge they obtained to practical use.[12]

The governors of the colonies, such as Anker, Wellesley or Bie greatly influenced the building activity in their territories.[13] They can perhaps best be compared to the numerous amateurs in Europe who studied, discussed and sometimes even sketched and built according to classical principles. To this group also belongs the most headstrong of all European builders of palaces in India, Claude Martin,[14] as well as men like J. P. Parker, the designer of the Ochterlony column in Calcutta.[15]

But new ideas also came from other quarters; in this connection I would refer to the bricklayers and carpenters who were recruited by the Company for its constructions in Calcutta and who, in the course of time, created for themselves a position in the foreign environment. Thomas Lyon is the most famous of them all.[16] In many cases the European constructors seem to have taught the Indians, who assisted them and even worked on their own. The college in Serampore was constructed with such assistance[17] and William Hickey employed a 'Bengalee'.[18] In this connection the architectural drawings should be mentioned that have been dealt with by Mildred Archer and which represent Indian monuments placed in conspicuous Western perspectives; they emphasize another aspect of this co-operation.[19]

In spite of the free recruiting, the European structures in India bore the mark of the work and background of military engineers. The citadels, the fortified boundaries of the towns, the Maidans or the open grounds, the broad roads for parades, and the scattered pattern of the cantonments are all designed with a military purpose. When regarding the individual structures, the mark of the engineers is especially evident in those with Baroque features and the vast Doric structures which were erected in the beginning of the 19th century. As for the first group, we find that the engineers' conception of form was old-fashioned, and far too deeply rooted in the models as codified by Bélidor or Gibbs. The latter group of structures, on the other hand, is entirely in line with the spirit of that time. Even in Europe, architecture was then dominated by large-scale formal buildings which are perhaps most pronounced in Leningrad.

We have also considered some of the 'pure' products of engineering, such as the gola in Bankipur and the opium godown in Patna,[20] and hinted that there are more, including, for example, the bridges designed by John Garstin and John Rennie.[21] All these structures must be regarded as a 'civil' development of military architecture.

III THE INDIAN VITRUVIUS

The Training of the Architect: Notes

1. N. E. Møllers, *Beskrivelse over de Nichobariske eller Friedrichs Øerne i Ostindien,* Copenhagen, 1797, pp. 528 f.

2. We get an idea of their background from a list of the equipment and the books of reference used by the Danish engineers in Tranquebar. These included some twenty books on fortification, artillery, astronomy, optics, mathematics, mechanics and geometry as well as alidade rules, astrolabes, levelling instruments, water-levels, Det Kongl. Ostindiske guvernements arkiv, No. 1762, Ingeniørens regnskaber, 1785/86, National Archives, Copenhagen.

3. E. W. Sandes, *The Military Engineer in India,* Chatham, 1933–35, vol. 2, p. 353.

4. Ibid.; T. Fraser drew several maps of Candicottah, Goothy etc., in 1802, Western Drawings, large IV, India Office Library, Commonwealth Office, London. See also R. H. Phillimore, *Historical Records of the Survey of India,* Dehra Dun, 1945 and onwards, vol. 1.

5. F. C. Danvers, *An Account of the origin of the East India Company's Civil Service and their College in Hertfordshire*, London, 1894, p. 19.

6. These books are now included in The National Library, Calcutta; they are dated and inscribed 'College of Fort William'.

7. E. W. Sandes, op. cit., vol. 2, p. 348. W. Porter, *History of the Corps of Royal Engineers*, London, New York and Chatham, 1889–1915, vol. 2, p. 172.

8. C. W. Pasley, *Outline of a Course of Practical Architecture, compiled for the use of the Junior officers of Royal Engineers*, Chatham, 1826, the preface.

9. See above, pp. 56 and 97 and note 11 below.

10. See above, pp. 128 and 129.

11. In 1808 an advertisement was inserted in the *Calcutta Gazette* for books missing from the College of Fort William, among them being 'Gibbs's Designs'. W. S. S. Karr, *Selections from the Calcutta Gazettes*, Calcutta, 1864–1959, vol. 4, p. 429. The works to which the constructional engineers had access also included treatises and books of patterns as follows: *A Catalogue of Printed Books in European Languages in the library of the Asiatic Society of Bengal*, Calcutta, 1908, includes J. Gibbs, *Rules for Drawing the several parts of Architecture*, 2nd ed., London, 1738, W. Chambers, *A Treatise on Civil Architecture*, London, 1759, and J. Stuart and N. Revett, *The Antiquities of Athens*, London, 1762–87; *Catalogue of the Library of the Bombay Branch of the Royal Asiatic Society*, Bombay, 1845, includes as No. 2349, Campbell's *Vitruvius Britannicus*, No. 5407, Palladio's, *Architecture*, No. 5436, Williams *Views in Greece*, No. 5450, Bélidor, *Dictionnaire Portatif de l'Ingénieur*, No. 5538, Pasley, *Course of Instruction for the Royal Engineers; Catalogue of the Royal Engineers' Corps Library at the Horse Guards, Whitehall, London*, Chatham, 1929, includes under the heading of '$\frac{B}{7}$ 60: — Architecture' as No. 26 J. Gibbs, *A Book of Architecture*, 1737, No. 51, Isaac Ware, *A Complete Body of Architecture*, 1756, No. 85, Andrea Palladio, *Four Books of Architecture*, translated by I. Ware, 1738, No. 141, *L'Architectura Militare, o Sia Maniera di Fortificarsi le Piazze*, by C. di Lucca, M.S. Venice, 1704, No. 180, Peter Nicholson, *Principles of Architecture*, 1795, No. 215, William Chambers, *Treatise on the Decorative Part of Civil Architecture*, 1825, No. 227, Colin Campbell, *Vitruvius Britannicus*, 1731, and No. 50, *The Civil Architecture of Vitruvius, Comprising those books which relate to the Public and Private Edifices of the Ancients*, 1812. The Book Collection in Chatham was formed in 1845, but a rudimentary library had already existed since 1813.

12. The conditions were for a long time the same as in Europe. See J. Summerson, *Georgian London*, first published 1945, Pelican Books 1962, pp. 70 ff. For a comparison with other colonies, see R. Lewcock, *Early Nineteenth Century Architecture in South Africa*, Cape Town, 1963, pp. 351 ff. Here Lewcock makes the following surmise: 'many an architect made his reputation in the East and doubtless was consulted on current work as he passed through Cape.' This appears very plausible, but I have not found any proof of it in my research. An engineer officer such as Robert Smith (1787–1873), who was active as an architect in Delhi and, among other things, repaired the Jama Masjid there, left for the Cape on 8th February 1830, but we know nothing about his work, if any, in South Africa. See R. H. Phillimore, op. cit., vol. 2, p. 442. T. H. H. Hancock, on the other hand, has indicated architectural contacts *east* of Calcutta with Batavia and Singapore; 'Coleman of Singapore', *Architectural Review*, March, 1955.

13. See above, pp. 55, 68 and 72.

14. See above, p. 130.

15. See above, p. 134.

16. See above, p. 100.

17. See above, p. 75.

18. W. Hickey, *Memoirs*, London, 1925, vol. 4, p. 117.

19. M. Archer, 'Company architects and their influence in India', *R.I.B.A. Journal*, August 1963. M. and W. G. Archer, *Indian painting for the British*, Oxford, 1955, pp. 16 f. Here we can read, amongst other things, that the engineers used Indian craftsmen to make maps, drawings and even architectural models.

20. See above, pp. 98 and 99.

21. See above, p. 98 and below, p. 169.

2 · Fundamental Principles of Architecture

WE can assume from the start that Euro-Indian architecture was based on principles laid down in the prototypes, and in the treatises and handbooks which I have mentioned above. These codes do not, in fact, form any clear basis for continuous work, as they offer such different alternatives as Serlio's Mannerism, Gibbs's late-Baroque and Stuart's and Revett's direct acceptance of the Greek models. Nevertheless, it can perhaps be said that together they form a syncretism, a special language of Classicism that can be learned and used with a certain freedom and can include both foreign words and constructions without losing its special character.[1]

Wherein does this special character lie and how far can one go in making changes without disturbing it? Critics with a classical education have always been severe in their judgments and have regarded even small deviations as an unforgiveable sin. India's European structures have scarcely found favour in anyone's eyes. Are there any possibilities of passing a different judgment on them? Yes, indeed, if we take into account their background and their special situation, and no longer regard them as something that is not sufficiently European or something that should be Indian!

We shall start by examining the syntactic, or rather the semantic aspect of the architecture, and consider the question of the *purity* of the style. These aspects are both considered by Vitruvius, but naturally we shall not lay down any general rules, as he did, but transfer the discussion to a concrete level where a firm grasp of the context we are dealing with can be obtained.

In his first book on architecture, third paragraph, Vitruvius gives his famous interpretation of the characters of the column orders. The masculine Doric is said to be suitable for warlike divinities such as Minerva, Mars and Hercules; the delicacy of the Corinthian order is connected with Venus and Flora, and the Ionic, which lies between these two, should be used for buildings dedicated to Juno, Diana or Father Bacchus.

This doctrine of character was to hold significance for much European architecture, from the Renaissance onwards. The system was adapted to suit the new functions that developed and was applied with a certain flexibility, but also with great persistence. It was first violated by the artists of neo-Classicism, who by using the Greek Doric in all connections turned the theory upside down, and by their concentration on simple forms and functions gave the incentive to an autonomous mode of expression.[2] A Vitruvian conception of form was found in the prototypes and was taken over with these by the

European architects in India. We have no proof that they did this very consciously, but in practice they built in the Tuscan and Doric styles in the great majority of cases when it was a question of military constructions. This was displayed to full advantage in the gateways that adorned the towns and the walls of the forts. In one case, that of Chandernagore, the shafts of the columns were actually replaced by *gun-barrels*, an element that indicated very directly the fortifying purposes of the structures.[3] The houses of private traders and other more 'peaceful' buildings were often constructed in Ionic or Corinthian style. Their basement storey, which was long used as a godown, was, however, characterized by rough rustic work, etc.

In general this pattern was common until the end of the 18th century and was used in the British as well as in the Danish and French areas. But then the uniformity ceases. We find churches that are Doric or Ionic (although in both cases they are dedicated to the warrior, St. George), soldiers' tombs, government houses and private buildings likewise in different styles. We are confronted with a large number of forms that seem to have been chosen at random, borrowed from one context and applied in another. The significance of the form according to Vitruvius is no longer of importance; more attention is paid to the *effect* of the style than to its inherent characteristics. Or so it appears.

It is almost impossible to state when this change took place. In subsequent years also, the Doric style was predominant and was applied in such completely adequate contexts as in the Banqueting Hall in Madras and the Mint in Calcutta,[4] but one would very much like to date them about 1780, which is approximately the time when the British began their political domination.

If we connect the architecture with the political events, we should be able to read a *new* significance into the structures, but that would mean destroying their individuality or original 'integrity'.

The new characteristic was a feeling of *growing domination*, of a superiority on two levels, the military and political on the one hand and the cultural on the other.[5] From these points of view it is no longer of any importance that the style should express intricate functional ideas; it is sufficient if it is magnificent, has large dimensions and a sharp profile. It does not need to allude to specific gods or characteristics, but it must be associated with their general background, to Greek and Roman antiquity which was regarded as the richest inheritance of the West.

We have drawn attention to a politically conscious use of architecture by governors such as the Frenchman Dupleix and the Dane Bie;[6] in the latter case we have evidence that the buildings were intended to make an impression both on the neighbouring European nations and the Indian population. We find such a function of architecture in a still more pronounced form among the British, who were to dominate the whole of the immense scene.

In 1780 Robert Orme wrote the history of Clive's period as governor, and asserted that the British successes were the results of military superiority and that the conquerors

FUNDAMENTAL PRINCIPLES OF ARCHITECTURE

were also by nature given 'superior talents of mind'.[7] The British continued to act according to such a line of thought. Under Cornwallis, regulations were introduced, for the appointment of civil servants among other things, which contributed to the creation of a white ruling class.[8] And Cornwallis himself was represented in a sculpture in antique dress, as a Roman pro-consul, bringing prosperity to his province by means of law and the power of arms.[9]

Allegories of this kind were common. For instance, John Bacon Jr., who designed Cornwallis's monument, also represented George III in Roman dress and, what is more, in no less a place than on the pediment of East India House in London.[10] But in India this masquerading had a special significance. Cornwallis represented at one and the same time an ancient European power which had subdued part of Asia, and a modern nation which felt itself strong enough to dare to do likewise.

British expansion acquired decisive momentum under Wellesley, who from the start was encouraged in his policy by Henry Dundas, President of the Board of Control.[11] In addition to his successful campaigns, Wellesley tried to carry out an architectural advance. This, to be sure, was not wholly successful but, as we know, it made an impression both on Orientals and Westerners and was regarded as wholly adequate for a person 'who had subverted the throne of Tippo, humbled the power of the Mahrattas, and numbered among his protégés the Great Mogul of Delhi'.[12] It was W. H. Carey who interpreted his situation in this way; we know that Lord Valentia and Lord Ellenborough were of the same opinion.[13] From Wellesley's time as governor-general we also have a report from Hyderabad declaring that the splendour around the British Ambassador could function as an alternative to the practical exercise of power.[14]

In 1810 the Daniells summed up the change that had taken place and which had transformed Calcutta from an insignificant trading centre into the metropolis of a growing empire. They wrote thus:

'The splendour of the British Arms produced a sudden change in its aspects; the bamboo roof suddenly vanished; the marble column took the place of brick walls; princely mansions were erected by private individuals. . . .'[15]

It was natural for these assiduous observers of architecture to describe the change in such terms, to see in the buildings, *in the columns*, symbols of commercial, military and political progress.

In the above we have learned a great deal about the forms alluding to the Antique which the British spread over the Indian sub-continent. We have seen their 'temples', their heroes' tombs, their military camps; we have followed their progress *via* their monuments. Perhaps these conquerors, who were constantly crossing new frontiers, identified themselves with the Romans, who 'erected trophies and superb buildings of every kind in all those countries which had felt the power of their arms'.[16] Perhaps they considered themselves to be like the Greek armies. When they finally reached the Indus in 1838, says Cyril Northcote Parkinson, 'during the Afghan expedition, the boast was made that, for the first time since Alexander the Great, the banners of a civilised nation waved along that river.'[17]

On this occasion, the expedition to Afghanistan was not exactly a success and J. W. Kaye, who wrote its history, has been compared to Thucydides.[18] Even if this last quotation indirectly tells of a military defeat, it nevertheless has a note of triumph when it mentions 'the banners of a *civilised* nation'. Here we come across another element in the imperial policy of the British: the belief in their superiority in the sphere of culture.

This attitude of superiority has certainly never found clearer expression than in Macaulay's speech in the House of Commons, in 1833, when he used phrases such as 'the pacific triumph of reason over barbarism' and constructed an 'imperishable empire of our arts and our morals, our literature and our laws'.[19]

Unfortunately, Macaulay's opinions were widely accepted in spite of counter moves by the 'Romantic generation' and men like Thomas Munro and John Malcolm. Many, like Macaulay, were convinced that Greek and Latin surpassed both Arabic and Sanskrit, and that the Indians could find an excellent basis for their education in these classical languages.

The fashion for things Western had many strange consequences in the architectural field. Indian princes began to adopt a Western style for their residences. In 1804 the Nawab of Murshidabad ordered designs for a palace from Wellesley's architects,[20] and many followed suit. 'The wealthy natives now all affect to have their houses decorated with Corinthian pillars and filled with English furniture,' writes Bishop Heber of the Calcutta of the 1820's.[21] All this was superficial and had the character of a reverse exoticism. The Orientals experimented with the strange forms in the same way as Europeans; from 1815–18 John Nash constructed the Royal, and Indian, Pavilion in Brighton.

But the game took a more serious turn in India. When a building such as the Calcutta Madrasha, an Islamic college, is erected, and given a Doric style, the power of the conqueror is felt over educational life.[22] This power recalls the words of Macaulay, who considered in his Minute on Education that *one* Madrasha, namely the one in Delhi, should be sufficient for India.[23]

For the rest the European influence on architecture is most noticeable in mixed styles. These can be found in many places, in Jaipur, Calcutta, etc.,[24] but the best known are to be found in Lucknow, and the one we have studied most in detail is La Martinière.[25] We also find among the hybrid structures in Lucknow, some with an Indian skeleton structure, but which express on the surface European and classical forms. Such are the different components of the British Residency.[26] I have already put forward the idea that this was due to a conscious purpose — to keep the style pure. I cannot prove that this is actually the case, but in other connections we come across expressions of fear of the Oriental form world and a desire for 'purity'.[27] There was a desire to be European even in the façades of the buildings. Classicism acquired a racial character.

Percival Spear, who has described the social life of the Europeans in India, has shown

FUNDAMENTAL PRINCIPLES OF ARCHITECTURE

that the colonists first adopted Indian customs and associated with Indians, but that later, from about 1780, they avoided such intercourse.[28] When they felt their power growing, the colonists also wished to display it through emphasizing their background. Contrary to previous conquerors of the country, they strove consciously *not to be absorbed* in the oriental mass. In architecture thay had an instrument by means of which they could manifest their status and their ideals — so long as they kept the style pure.

To return to our starting-point, we can now state that political and social conditions in India gave a new significance to European architecture. The classical forms began to contain forces that were not to be found in the prototypes; they stood as the symbols of conquering militarism and a culture and race which considered themselves superior.

In other respects too, the architecture was to be changed in the foreign environment. There were factors in the materials and in the climate that were against the original principles, but which caused important innovations and enriched the classical language of architecture with a unique dialect.

2. *Fundamental Principles of Architecture:* Notes

1. This characterization links up to a certain extent with J. Summerson, *The classical language of architecture*, London, 1964. Re the evaluation of similar 'liberties' in American neo-Classicism, see T. Hamlin, 'The Greek Revival in America and some of its Critics', *The Art Bulletin*, XXIV, September, 1942, and H. D. Eberlein and C. V. D. Hubbard, *American Georgian Architecture*, London, 1952.

2. This strictly speaking 'Vitruvian' conception of form has been particularly studied by E. Forssman, *Dorisch, Jonisch und Korinthisch*, Uppsala, 1961.

3. The example is, of course, not unique; a similar gate is known, amongst others, from Copenhagen's 17th-century fortifications. See L. de Thurah, *Hafnia Hodierna*, Copenhagen, 1748, Tab. V.

4. See above, pp. 108 and 117.

5. I believe that such a change will always occur when styles of architecture are taken out of their original environment to function under different conditions. Alan Gowans has recently regarded the neo-Classical architecture in North America as an expression of the feeling of freedom and power on the part of the colonists after independence, *Images of American living*, Philadelphia and New York, 1964.

6. See above, pp. 94 and 72.

7. R. Orme, *A History of the Military Transactions of the British Nation in Indostan*, 3rd ed., London 1780. Cf. G. D. Bearce, *British attitudes towards India, 1784-1858*, Oxford, 1961, p. 47.

8. See 'The consolidation of Direct Rule', in M. Edwardes, *A history of India, from the earliest time to the present day*, London, 1961, pp. 221-23.

9. See above, p. 133.

10. M. Archer, 'The East India Company and British Art', in *Apollo*, Nov. 1965, p. 407.

165

11. H. C. Philips, *The East India Company 1784–1834*, first published 1940; Manchester 1961, p. 103.

12. W. H. Carey, *The Good Old Days of Hon'ble John Company*, Simla, 1882–87, vol. 1, p. 62.

13. See above, p. 105.

14. See above, p. 115. We have also come across statements which indicate that attempts had been made to *avoid* extravagance so as not to upset trading interests. This controversy arose in Calcutta and Madras. See above pp. 104 and 109.

15. T. and W. Daniell, *A Picturesque Voyage to India*, London, 1810, p. ii.

16. J. Soane, *Lectures on Architecture*, publication of Sir John Soane's Museum, No. 14, London 1929, p. 27.

17. See C. Northcote Parkinson, *East and West*, London, 1963, p. 191. It may be said in passing that the interpretation of the attitude of the Georgian aristocracy to Gothic which is given by the author here, is far from being correct.

18. G. D. Bearce, op. cit., p. 269.

19. See the chapter entitled 'Social Reform and the Beginnings of English Education', in M. Edwardes, op. cit., pp. 254 ff. Macaulay's speech in the House of Commons is quoted here.

20. See above, p. 110.

21. R. Heber, *Narrative of a Journey from Calcutta to the Upper Provinces of India; from Calcutta to Bombay 1824–25*, London, 1828, vol. 2, p. 306.

22. See above, p. 118.

23. Macaulay's Minute on Education of 1835 is reproduced in the extract in M. Edwardes, op. cit., pp. 260 ff.

24. An example in Jaipur is the Sawai Man Singh Town Hall. Cf. below, p. 171. For an example in Calcutta, see plate 2 in T. and W. Daniell, *Oriental Scenery. Twenty-four views in Hindoostan*, London, 1797. The engraving shows a house in Chitpore Road and has the following text: 'the style of architecture in its ornamental parts is Mohammedan, except in the turret which is an unsuccessful attempt at the Grecian . . . These incongruities very frequently occur in modern Indian buildings whose owners have intercourse with Europeans.' M. Archer has dealt with a mixed style drawing from Tanjore in 'Company Architects and their Influence in India', *R.I.B.A. Journal*, August 1963, p. 321.

25. Above, p. 131. Another famous example is the Begum Kothi built in 1844, reproduced in M. Edwardes, op. cit., fig. 42 and described by J. Fergusson, *History of the Modern Styles of Architecture*, London, 1862, pp. 420 f.

26. See above, p. 113.

27. Such a statement was made regarding an arsenal in Fort St. George, Madras, 1772. The architect, Lieut. Col. Patrick Ross, 'came under severe criticism for the design, which was peculiar in many ways, and he was blamed for ornamenting the exterior with a hybrid type of decoration much favoured by the old Nawabs of Oudh in Lucknow; though the orders of the Board were that those Buildings should be as plain as they could consistently be made'; E. W. Sandes, *The Military Engineer in India*, Chatham, 1933–35, vol. 2, p. 88.

28. P. Spear, *The Nabobs*, first ed. 1932, London 1963, pp. 34 ff. Cf. Philip Woodruff, *The Men Who Ruled India*, first ed. 1953, London, 1963, vol. 1, p. 383, 'Notes on the Authorities'.

3 · Building Materials and Methods

THE travellers of the Romantic era readily allowed themselves to be deceived by the architectural scenery. We can recall their dazzling visions of the waterfront of Madras and the line of palaces along the Esplanade and the Chowringhi in Calcutta.[1] But just as often they saw the buildings as concrete substances. Cracks in the plaster of the façades exposed the bricks and mortar. They could study, as in an anatomy lecture, the basic composition of the structures.

Surprisingly, many of the travellers were interested in the building materials from a purely practical point of view. Even the female travellers described these things almost with passion, at least as long as they were talking about the *chunam*, the white plaster of Madras. The most detailed account was given by Thomas Williamson. His *East India Vade-Mecum* (1810), based on the conditions around 1800, contains much information on the various materials and their application.[2]

With the help of the notes made by Williamson and others, I shall make a survey which, in spite of its limited subject, contains many essential conditions for European architecture in an Oriental environment. The modifications and alternatives which arise are of special interest, as is also the close co-operation between Indians and Europeans on this elementary level.

Stone. When St. John's was built in Calcutta in the 1780's and the tower erected in pink ashlar from Chunar, this was so unique that, at least for some time, it was called 'Pathar Girja', the stone church.[3] The greater part of European architecture in India was to be erected in brick, mortar and plaster, and structures or elements in a heavier material were scarce. The hero Cornwallis was honoured with two architectural monuments in *everlasting* material: a circular temple of the Ionic order in Madras and the gigantic cenotaph in Ghazipur which I have described in the chapter on the individual patterns. Its style was commented on by Bishop Heber, who also remarked on the material as 'being some of the finest free-stones I ever saw'.[4]

In 1803, the main flight of steps of the Residency in Hyderabad was constructed of light granite.[5] Completely black granitic gneiss was used for the Tuscan columns which for a long time stood in front of Fort St. George in Madras, forming a passage from the water up to the entrance. That they really were extremely rare is emphasized by the fact that they were captured by the French and moved to Pondicherry and then retaken by the British in 1761. In the same way cannons and standards were captured in campaigns, and the black columns thus functioned as a sort of display of triumph.[6]

Marble. The genuine stone was difficult to come by and the same applied to marble which had to be fetched a long way. The grey floor slabs of Wellesley's Government House came from as far away as China.[7] However, as a rule marble was shipped as ballast in unhewn blocks or slabs and in the form of sculptures from Italy and England. The magnificent floor of St. Andrew's in Madras and the numerous inscription tablets on tombstones all over India were obtained in this way.[8] And even to-day it is possible to buy amongst a great many other things *Italian* marble in the streets of Calcutta; this is marble which was saved when houses were pulled down.

Brick. The Indian workers built for Europeans in the same way as they had built for the invading Mughal princes. A characteristic feature of their work is the bricklaying technique which was carried out with great care and which required relatively small, thin and almost square bricks. The first Fort William in Calcutta was constructed of such diminutive elements,[9] as well as many structures in Lucknow. It is the latter place that we can best study the technique employed, as the buildings were destroyed and now have the character of anatomical specimens.[10]

However, the conditions in Lucknow are rather special, as the town was for a long time under Indian rule. English bricklayers were recruited at an early stage to a European centre like Calcutta. They were to serve as instructors and at the same time altered the dimension of the structural elements.[11] As early as in 1754, Colonel Scott advertised for bricks measuring $11 \times 5\frac{1}{2} \times 2\frac{1}{2}$ inches when burnt.[12] And in 1790 we can read a notice in the *Calcutta Gazette* also about 11 inch bricks, which was in future to be the standard size.[13] It appears that the strength of the bricks was also experimented with and longer burning demanded than the Indians usually permitted. 'The best bricks I ever saw in India were made by an engineer officer who had some extensive public works to carry on', says Thomas Williamson.[14]

From the turn of the century (1800) these products of European engineers were also used for simpler buildings, such as bungalows where previously *sun-dried* Indian bricks, so-called *cutcha*, had been regarded as satisfactory.[15]

A more original novelty can be observed in the Danish towns, where from the 1780's colonnades were erected in special 'column stone' of quarter-circle shape. Four of these stones form one 'layer' of the shaft.[16]

Tiles. Tiles are used for roofs especially on the rainy Malabar coast and in Bihar.[17] Their manufacture and application have been described by Toreen, a Swede, who was also a pupil of Linnaeus. During a visit to Mangalore in 1751, he found, to start with, that the roofing-tiles looked the same as those of Surat and Cadiz (!):

'The brickmaker forms a hollow cylinder about twelve inches long, and four in diameter; this is cut into two equal parts lengthways, and burnt in little kilns. They tile here by single rows, and when one row of tiles is laid so that the concave part comes uppermost, the next is inverted, and so cover the ridges.'[18]

Terracotta. When the paint flakes off balustrades in Barrackpore, Calcutta or Pondicherry it can be seen that the balusters are made of terracotta: thrown like jars and filled with mortar in order to obtain the necessary bearing capacity. Terracotta is also used for acroteria in Panjim which once was Portuguese. Thus the material is put to the same use as in the architecture of antiquity.[19]

European tiles were probably used to some extent in the Dutch territories. In *Bengal, Past and Present* we can read about a consignment of tiles which went astray and which was rediscovered adorning a Hindu temple in Murshidabad as late as 1920 (not far from the old Dutch factory of Cozimbazaar).[20]

Lime. The greater part of the lime used for construction work in the Calcutta area was brought from the Morungs and transported downstream in big boats. It was slaked before it came on board the boats, otherwise the rain would have achieved the same result, as the voyage sometimes took up to one month.[21]

The lime from the Morungs was in many respects inferior to a type of lime which was produced on the Coromandel Coast and to a lesser extent also on the Malabar Coast. This lime was produced by burning shells.[22] It was used both in mortar and in the white plaster *chunam*. When transported to Bengal, this lime was rather sensitive to the salt-petre content of the air.[23]

Sand was taken from beaches and river banks; both the Ganges and the Jumna can form gigantic sandbanks. The sand thus obtained was washed and purified.

Timber. In the same way in which wood — deal from the Baltic countries and mahogany from the West Indies[24] — used in 18th-century England was imported, much of the timber necessary for the construction work in the European colonies in India — mainly teak — was imported. This material was shipped across the Gulf of Bengal from the coast of Pegu near Rangoon. The material was transported in large beams, spars and planks of all sizes.[25] The market area and import towns were mainly Calcutta and Madras. In the south of India, timber was imported from Ceylon. The engineers' accounts in Tranquebar include 'beams from Trincomalee'.[26] However, Indian material was also used, such as mahogany, palm, mango and saulwood.[27]

Bamboo, ratan and cuscus grass. Bamboo was not only used for scaffoldings, but also in bungalows and when cut for various types of sun protection. Light screens were made of ratan and cuscus.[28]

Iron. The freight lists of Danish East Indiamen include quantities of bar iron,[29] and in the *Calcutta Gazette* we can see many sales notices concerning consignments including iron, both in the form of semi-finished and finished products.[30] Finally all those cast-iron elements which were so popular in Europe during the 19th century were to be imported into India, but in the beginning, iron was scarce. An iron bridge constructed by John Rennie, who also designed Waterloo Bridge, was sent out from England in 1815, but was not mounted before 1844, in Lucknow.[31] The college in Serampore, which was commenced in 1819, was supplied with a cast-iron fence, fanlights and a large staircase, all made in Birmingham.[32] And in 1831 iron supports had been inserted in a brick colonnade in Calcutta.[33]

Glass, oyster shells. When Lord Teignmouth came to Calcutta in 1769, he remarked that hardly any house had glass windows. Instead, solid wooden shutters or plaited ratan were used.[34] Other substitutes were oyster shells, *placuna placenta*, which were mounted in wooden frames and let a dim light through. This type of window is known also from Ceylon and China. Numerous windows of this kind are preserved in Goa which is old-fashioned in other respects too. [35]

However, when it was possible to get glass, it was used. In 1786 we can read about the purchase of glass windows for houses in the Danish town of Serampore;[36] they were bought in Calcutta. Around 1800, the replacement had been completed in the British territories.[37]

Methods of building. I have divided up the buildings into their structural components. Before we proceed, I shall assemble them again in the same way as the architects did. In order to get to know the *methods* we must, of course, know how the various materials were combined.

The mortar which jointed the bricks into walls and colonnades was mixed of brick dust, water, coarse sand and cut hemp.[38] A house constructed in this way was a *pucka* building as opposed to the *cutcha* houses which were erected of sun-dried brick. The terms *pucka* and *cutcha* are later to be used in many connections, but always with the original meaning, *pucka* used for something that lasts, something to rely on.[39]

The brick construction also contained wooden elements in the shape of door and window frames and the architraves of the columns as well as the roof girders were of wood.[40] Teak was usually preferred, since termites generally did not attack this material, but palm and saulwood were also used.[41]

Bricks, mortar and wood formed the skeleton of the building, an organic whole which gave strength and height, but which was never allowed to be visible from the outside. The aesthetic spirit of that time demanded a display of structural principles which were not identical with those used, but were based on the study of Antique architecture. For this purpose the buildings were given a finish which disguised the substructure. The customary brick bonding, the voussoirs of the arched window heads and the inserted wooden frames were covered with a homogenous layer of lime plaster. The building was to convey the impression of having been made entirely of stone, and we know that the spectator was disappointed when this illusion was not complete.[42]

Thus the European architect in India worked in the same way as his colleague in the mother-country. He was like John Nash, who thought of his structures in 'terms of Bath-stone' even if he was not in a position to use such material.[43] Incidentally, it is significant that C. W. Pasley referred to one of John Nash's terraces in Regent's Park when he taught the Junior Officers of the Royal Engineers how to disguise a heterogeneous structure with stucco.[44] However, the engineers in India did not always follow the advice of the European creators of prototypes. It could be said that they confronted Antique with neo-Classical construction when they emphasized the *architrave* on the outside of the building. As I have mentioned before, the architrave was made of wood, usually teak, and these beams were painted in a special colour, generally Spanish green.

170

But in order to explain this phenomenon we must place it in a wider context and must write something about the *overall* colour effect of the buildings. By doing this we definitely enter upon a stage where the substantial qualities of the material are of secondary importance as compared with its radiance.

The first colour engravings of Calcutta, those of the Daniells and of Baillie, display a colour-scheme which still belongs to the traditions of the Baroque.[45] White quoins and mouldings stand out against pink and ochre-coloured wall panels. The key-stones in the arcade of the ground floor are emphasized with white paint and the window shutters are paler. This façade treatment can still be studied in its most extreme form in Panjim, where the houses are not merely pink, but of a dark ox-blood red; not merely blue, but of a brilliant ultra-marine. In the once French Pondicherry, the colour scale is somewhat paler. Grey alternates with white on the portals, which are of the Tuscan order; the overall colour impression is pink and yellowish that deepens sometimes to a golden-ochre colour.

This diversity of colour was replaced at the end of the 18th century in the British colonies by a more stereotype colouring. 'The good taste of a few individuals, chiefly gentlemen in the corps of engineers, overcomes this vile imitation of Dutch and Portuguese finery,' writes Williamson, and thus professes himself a follower of the aesthetics of neo-Classicism which were to dominate from that time onwards.[46]

It is difficult to determine when the transition took place. As early as in the 1770's colouring-matter was shipped to the Danish colonies which, so to speak, indicates the new look. The East Indiaman *Prins Frederik* sailed on January 1st, 1771, to Tranquebar, the load including the following:

Bunting in white and red	760 ells	95 rixdollars[47]
White chalk	1550 pounds	16 rixdollars
Smoke-black	30 pounds	10 rixdollars
Yellow-ochre	225 pounds	16 rixdollars
Spanish-green	406 pounds	287 rixdollars

The white and red were to be used for making Danish flags, a colour combination not liable to changes of fashion. But the others, the chalk, smoke-black, yellow-ochre and Spanish green were meant for the architectural elements of neo-Classicism. There are no examples of this colouring preserved in Tranquebar, but they exist in other places, one of which is the Judge's Court in Alipur, Calcutta. Here the colonnades of the portico and the veranda are painted white, and the architraves and all the other *wooden* elements green, the walls yellow and the iron bars black.

As an alternative and successor to this colour-scheme there was the *chunam* or the entirely white façade plaster mixed with lime of burnt shells, the white of eggs, milk and other ingredients. After special treatment it received a very hard and shiny surface.[48]

The entirely white building was a product of the marble cult of neo-Classicism.[49] The Sawai Man Singh Town Hall in Jaipur recalls another very popular 'material', Wedgwood; like the majority of buildings in Jaipur, this town hall has received a pink plaster. Against this background the white markings and ornaments stand out, and through their delicate colour scheme show some resemblance to the nearby Palace of the Winds.

The exterior of the neo-Classical buildings boldly interacted with the surrounding milieu, with the vegetation and the water, with the strong daylight of the tropics and the warm colour of the sunset which was reflected in the façades. The interiors were not so rewarding to work with, as here the contrast of light killed much of the effect. In spite of this, approximately the same colour-scheme as in the exterior was employed. The interiors also alternated between two alternatives: the marble white and the Wedgwood type. In Fort St. George, Madras, William Hodges found rooms 'presenting to the eye only white walls'.[50] We have found similar examples in the Danish Serampore.[51] This was, however, the simplest colour-scheme. It could be improved by brownish-red wood elements or with gold, as was the case in the official rooms in the Government Houses in Calcutta and Madras.[52]

When Lord Mayo came to Calcutta he found the colonnades in Wellesley's marble hall painted *black*.[53] They had obviously been changed (from white) in order to conform with the strict fashion which had been in vogue in London during the first years of the 19th century. It could also be said that the interiors were in a way coloured like the ships of the line of that time.[54]

The well-preserved interiors in the Residency in Hyderabad correspond with the general description made by Williamson:

'Some paint the beaded, or moulded, edges of the door panels, also the rounded corners of the joists, with some delicate colour; such as a very light sky-blue, a very light verdi-gris-green, or a lilac; and by way of conformity, ornament the mouldings of the wall panels with similar tints. In the upper provinces, it is a very prevalent fashion to colour the panels with some native ochres of beautiful hues, leaving the mouldings, cornices &c. white.'[55]

This play with delicate colour effects still has a resemblance to the decorative style of the Adam school. The architects of the Greek Revival demanded interiors of quite a different type, built strictly and simply. Here the contrast between light and shade could really be aesthetically utilized and, as we know, such compositions were made, e.g. the Town Hall in Bombay. The light is thrown down in white cones through circular or oval openings in the roof, and the colour scheme is dark. The emphasis is on the white marble figures.[56]

3. *Building Materials and Methods:* Notes
   1. See above, p. 26.
   2. T. Williamson, *The East India Vade-Mecum; or Complete Guide to Gentlemen intended for the Civil, Military, or Naval Service of the Hon. East India Company*, London, 1810. For a

comparison with other colonial conditions, see R. Lewcock, *Early Nineteenth Century Architecture in South Africa*, Cape Town, 1963, pp. 378 ff.

3. Cf. above, p. 128.

4. R. Heber, *Narrative of a Journey from Calcutta to the Upper Provinces of India; from Calcutta to Bombay 1824–25*, London, 1828, vol. 1, p. 261. Cf. above, p. 133.

5. *Some Notes on the Hyderabad Residency; collected from original records in the Residency Office*, 1918, p. 3. Cf. above, p. 114.

6. See H. B. Hyde, *Parochial Annals of Bengal*, Calcutta, 1901, pp. 174 ff. and above, p. 108.

7. G. N. Curzon, Marquis Curzon of Kedleston, *British Government in India*, London, 1925, vol. 1, p. 94.

8. Re St. Andrew's, Madras. See above, p. 129. It should be noted that it had been planned from the beginning to use marble in St. John's in Calcutta, from the Kings' tombs in Gour; this shows how difficult it was to obtain marble and how brutally those who wanted it were prepared to act in order to get it. W. K. Firminger, *Thacker's Guide to Calcutta*, Calcutta, 1906, p. 130. It is also rather remarkable that in India they had not thought of using 'Coade-stone' as a substitute. Reliefs in this special material still adorn the façades of many London houses and one would think that such elements would have been easy to export. Cf. J. Summerson, *Georgian London*, first ed. 1945, Pelican Books 1962, pp. 130–32.

9. C. R. Wilson, *Old Fort William in Bengal*, Indian Record Series, London 1906, vol. 2, p. 225, plate XXV. Cf. above, p. 46.

10. See above, p. 113.

11. E. W. Sandes, *The Military Engineer in India*, Chatham, 1933–35, vol. 1, p. 192. K. Blechynden, *Calcutta, Past and Present*, London, 1905, pp. 86 f. Cf. the chapter on 'The Training of the Architect', and p. 64 above.

12. C. R. Wilson, op. cit., vol. 2, p. 16.

13. W. S. S. Karr, *Selections from the Calcutta Gazettes*, Calcutta, 1864, vol. 2, p. 15.

14. T. Williamson, op. cit., vol. 2, p. 15. For a comparison with English conditions, see J. Summerson, op. cit., p. 80.

15. T. Williamson, op. cit., vol. 1, pp. 514 f. Cf. the chapter on 'The Origin of the Dwelling-House', p. 188 below.

16. Det Kongl. Ostindiske guvernements arkiv, A. Ingeniørens regnskaber 1785 ff., National Archives, Copenhagen.

17. Re the sloping tiled roofs used on the West coast of India see the chapter on 'The Forms of Architecture as determined by the Climate'.

18. O. Toreen, *A Voyage to Suratte*, printed together with P. Osbeck, *A Voyage to China and the East Indies*, London, 1771, vol. 2, p. 209.

19. See, for example, A. Mau, *Pompeji in Leben und Kunst*, 2nd ed., Leipzig, 1908.

20. *Bengal, Past and Present*, vol. 20, January–June 1920, pp. 111 f. The writer emphasizes that the Biblical motif of the tiles is not particularly suitable for ornamenting a Hindu temple.

21. T. Williamson, op. cit., vol. 2, p. 12.

22. Ibid., vol. 2, p. 13.

23. Mrs. Kinderley gave this information which is quoted by J. Macfarlane, *Hartly House, Calcutta*, Calcutta, 1908, p. 296 in the notes.

24. J. Summerson, op. cit., p. 81.

25. T. Williamson, op. cit., vol. 2, p. 55.

26. Det Kongl. Ostindiske guvernements arkiv, A. Ingeniørens regnskaber 1785 ff., National Archives, Copenhagen.

27. T. Williamson, op. cit., pp. 64 ff.

28. Cf. above, the heading 'Glass, oyster shells' and the chapter 'The Forms of Architecture as determined by the Climate'. On the use of cuscus, see P. Spear, *The Nabobs*, first ed. 1932; London, 1963, p. 50.

29. A. A. Rasch and P. P. Sveistrup, *Asiatisk Kompagni i den florissante periode 1772–1792*, Copenhagen, 1948, Appendix V.

30. W. S. S. Karr, op. cit., vol. 1, p. 117.

31. This information is to be found also in L. F. Rushbrook Williams, editor, *A Handbook for Travellers in India, Pakistan, Burma and Ceylon*, 19th ed., London 1962, p. 299.

32. Cf. above, p. 75.

33. *Bengal, Past and Present*, vol. 61, July–December, 1941, p. 28. This concerns the School Chapel of St. Thomas built by J. P. Parker.

34. J. Long, *Peeps into social life of Calcutta a Century ago*, Calcutta, 1868, also quoted by K. Blechynden, op. cit., p. 114.

35. Tampalakamam Bay near Trincomalee on Ceylon is a place where these oysters are found. O. Toreen tells of their use in Goa and in China, op. cit., p. 229. Cf. J. Douglas, *Bombay and Western India*, London, 1893, vol. 1, p. 10. *Nova Goa*, or Panjim, first developed into a town in the first decades of the 19th century under rulers such as Dom Manuel de Portugal e Castro, Conde das Antas and Visconde des Torres Novas. It is therefore surprising that its buildings show such old-fashioned features. See F. C. Danvers, *The Portuguese in India*, London, 1894, vol. 2, pp. 456 ff.

36. p. 72 above.

37. T. Williamson, op. cit., vol. 2, p. 45.

38. The constituents of the mixture is given, for example, by A. Hamilton, *A New Account of the East Indies*, Edinburgh, 1727, vol. 2, p. 9, which also includes 'Molasses'. See H. D. Rawlinson, *The British Achievements in India*, London, 1948, p. 12.

39. 'Pukka (i.e. brick and mortar)', says G. N. Curzon, op. cit., vol. 1, p. 2. See further *Hobson-Jobson* under 'Pucka' and 'Cutcha'.

40. This combination can be studied to advantage on the destroyed Baillie Guard in Lucknow and also on houses which are still inhabited. In Government House, Calcutta, 'the beams, doors and window frames are . . . of *saul* wood, while the floors of the upper storey [are] of teak;' G. N. Curzon, op. cit., vol. 1, p. 44, note 1.

41. The use of wood on the façade of the building was condemned on grounds of safety in the London Building Acts of 1707 and 1709. See J. Summerson, op. cit., p. 68. The criticism of the European architecture in India should be seen against this background. See W. H. Carey, *The Good Old Days of Hon'ble John Company*, Simla, 1882–87, vol. 2, p. 154 f., and J. Fergusson, *History of the Modern Styles of Architecture*, London, 1862, p. 420. Fergusson states that 'wooden architraves are the worst possible mode of construction in a climate where wood decays so rapidly, even if spared by the white ants.' Against this it can be said that the teak beams in many houses in India are very well preserved. An attempt was made, however, to reduce the element of wood in neo-Classical houses. T. Lyon and De Havilland made such experiments

in Berhampur and Madras. See T. Williamson, op. cit., vol. 2, pp. 55 and passim, and T. F. De Havilland, *Public Edifices of Madras*.

42. See above, p. 28. The layer of plaster had, of course, also a protective function. See E. B. Havell, *Indian Architecture*, London, undated, pp. 197 f.

43. J. Summerson, op. cit., p. 130.

44. C. W. Pasley, *Outline of a Course of Architecture, compiled for the use of the Junior Officers of Royal Engineers*, Chatham, 1826, pp. 229 ff. and figs. 321 and 322.

45. T. and W. Daniell, *Oriental Scenery. Twenty-four views in Hindoostan*, London, 1797. W. Baillie, *Twelve views of Calcutta*, London, 1794.

46. T. Williamson, op. cit., vol. 2, p. 16.

47. A. A. Rasch and P. P. Sveistrup, op. cit., loc. cit. It should be noted that the Spanish green is valued very highly. It was an expensive colour used because of its good preserving properties on wood. R. Lewcock has told of its occurrence in colonies other than those in India, op. cit., p. 418.

48. E. W. Sandes, op. cit., vol. 1, p. 82. T. Williamson, op. cit., vol. 2, p. 13. In some letters translated from Bengali a story is told of a *chunam*-maker, Paul Stratey, who was agent for Alexander Paniotty; Original Consultations, December 1788, The National Archives of India, New Delhi. For localization of the letters, see Presslist of ancient documents preserved in the Imperial Record Room of the Government of India.

49. Cf. p. 26, above.

50. W. Hodges, *Travels in India during the years 1780, 1781, 1782 and 1783*, London, 1793, p. 9.

51. Above, p. 73. Older houses in Pondicherry and Tranquebar also have this interior decoration.

52. See above, p. 107.

53. G. N. Curzon, op. cit., vol. 1, p. 97.

54. Steen Eiler Rasmussen who in his capacity as an architect had practical experience of the effect of colour in buildings, has devoted special attention to this 'medium' in his writings. *London, the unique city*, first published 1934; Pelican Books 1963, p. 191. The interplay of black and white is in this case not compared with the colour of the ships of the line, but with the fashion created by Beau Brummel!

55. T. Williamson, op. cit., vol. 2, p. 30.

56. The Town Hall, Bombay, was finished in 1833. Cf. above, p. 117. In Calcutta also sky-lights were used at the beginning of the 1830's. See *Bengal, Past and Present*, vol. 61 July-December, 1941, p. 28.

4 · The Forms of Architecture as determined by the Climate

THE climatic aspects of architecture are self-evident, and much discussed at present. Our attention has been drawn to them repeatedly by architects with a world-wide field of activity such as Le Corbusier, Maxwell Fry and Louis Kahn, and during recent years they have been the subject of experiment and research. Only two examples of the literature on the subject can be mentioned here: Jane Drew and Maxwell Fry's *Tropical Architecture in the dry and humid zones* and Victor Olgyay's *Design with Climate*.[1] The authors of the first mentioned book base their work on experience in India and West Africa, while Olgyay uses mainly American material, but also gives examples from countries such as Iraq and Australia.

Even if our attitude to the problems is new, the problems as such are ancient. Victor Olgyay quotes Vitruvius; so did the neo-Classicist, John Soane, who made the following observation in one of his *Lectures on Architecture*:

'A good living room in Egypt might, as it has been well observed, make an excellent wine cellar in England.'[2]

The problems became particularly obvious, of course, when a type of building was transferred from one climate to another, as occurred in the period we are dealing with.

The Danes, British and Dutch who tried to apply their European experience in their tropical colonies necessarily encountered great practical difficulties. They were also obliged to redesign buildings and change functions almost in the way suggested by Soane, though not necessarily implying that the wine cellar always became a living-room. In our study of urban patterns and individual buildings, we have already seen a number of solutions to these problems, but it seems essential to consider all of them against a more clearly defined background.

Thus the background is climatological and is mainly determined by the monsoons which give the sub-continent of India a rainy season and a dry season. The former occurs in summer, when the south-west monsoon is blowing, and the latter in winter with the dry, north-east monsoon. The temperature and the intensity of the rain vary greatly according to the topographical conditions. In such an enormous land area comprising seas, rivers, plateaux and mountains, a number of *microclimatic* phenomena occur which directly affect the possibility of people adapting themselves to the climate and living and building there. The difference in situation between places such as

176

Ootacamund and Madras offer very different alternatives and, as we know, these were utilized.

The variations are numerous, but here we must limit ourselves to studying the architecture in two main types of climate, the hot–humid region, represented by places as different as Calcutta, Madras, Tranquebar, Bombay and Panjim, and the hot–arid region, represented by two inland towns, Delhi and Lucknow.[3] These are of course the towns we have been investigating in previous chapters and know something about, and on the basis of the results of the research of Olgyay and others they can be appraised in greater detail.

For a town in the hot–humid zone Olgyay prescribes a high situation, a loose and scattered structure which allows of air movements round the houses which stand separate, vegetation that provides shade and lakes or rivers that give air flow.[4]

If we look at the European buildings in India, we find that they are very seldom situated on heights. Hill stations such as Mahabaleshwar and Ooty are exceptions.[5] We find, however, a strikingly scattered pattern in Calcutta from the middle of the 18th century, where the Maidan, Tank Square with its open reservoir, and the river basin give scope for the wind. 'The most salubrious parts of the city are the Chowringhee, the Esplanade and Tank Square,' writes Leopold von Orlich and further points out that:

'the hot or dry season begins in the middle of June, when the wind blows very regularly from the south or south-west, the thermometer then rises in the shade to 95°F. and in the open air to 100° or 110°F.'[6]

The spaciously planned residential districts near Calcutta counteracted the heat to a certain extent. Here it was also possible for the inhabitants to make use of vegetation which provided shade and of water (e.g. Garden Reach and Barrackpore).[7] At the same time a similar pattern developed in Madras, where the town of Fort St. George was deserted by Europeans, who built themselves garden houses on the outskirts of the town.

'One can ride and drive as one will, the roads are excellent, one flies on one's way, the air we breathe is balsamic, invigorating. We drive past one fine villa after another. All are situated in beautifully laid out and well kept parks and gardens,' writes Steen Bille in 1845.[8]

In Tranquebar the houses were arranged according to the old 17th-century plan which was softened, however, by means of avenues which also led out into the country.[9] In Bombay the European population moved out into garden houses which were spread over areas such as Malabar Hill.[10] And the most spacious of all urban patterns, the cantonment, was probably created in the hot–humid climate of Bengal.[11]

Distances in these scattered towns were considerable, and those who went from one building to another were subjected both to heat and rain. Europeans avoided these by travelling in carriages or (more usually) being carried in palanquins which gave them shelter.[12] The porticos of the houses then function as passages. Through these transport was effected from one shady spot to another.[13]

The effort to obtain space, shade and ventilation also dictated the design and distribution of the individual structures. The houses in the Chowringhi district have large rooms and high ceilings. Bishop Heber describes a hall in the house at 5 Russell Street as a double cube, almost 80 ft. long, i.e. almost 12 metres high![14] Here the rooms lay in rather compact formation inside the walls. A structure such as Government House in Calcutta, built by Wyatt, shows another possible lay-out in a hot climate. This lay-out is really one suited to country residences and is shown to best advantage in the residential suburbs of Madras, where the architects worked with very spread out buildings: a system of units connected by long corridors which allow the air to stream round the corners and cool every part of the building.[15] Finally the units can be detached, as in the governor's residence on Malabar Point, Bombay, which consists of a collection of freely grouped bungalows.[16]

It was long the custom to live on the first floor of the house, while the ground floor was used as a godown, servants' living quarters and offices, even as stables, writes Thomas Williamson from Calcutta.[17] The ground floor was also constructed in the shape of a heavy podium with arcades and rustic work. But in about 1780 the family's living rooms were moved to the ground floor, probably following the experience in country residences, where practically all families lived on the ground floor and found it very satisfactory.[18] The same change took place elsewhere; during the last decades of the 18th century we see in Madras newspapers advertisements for the sale of both *upper-* and *lower-*roomed houses.[19]

Parts of neo-Classical buildings which could not be utilized fully in Northern Europe were made to function in India; I refer to the porticos, loggias and flat roofs. The porticos were certainly a protection against rain (possibly also snow) in a cold climate, but they were still more necessary in India, where the rains are so torrential and where the sunlight strikes with overwhelming power. The porticos were usually placed on the shady northern front of the house, while the south façade was occupied by a loggia. This might be one storey high, as at 9 Russell Street, Calcutta,[20] or be repeated on several floors and thus form a real *screen* in front of the wall, as in Government House, Triplicane.[21] It was used in the evening as a sitting-room and at night as a bedroom. The flat roof enclosed by a balustrade was used in the same way; there the lightest breeze could be caught. Thus the residents slept in the open air, or rather in the open air under mosquito nets. Sometimes a special small room was built for the purpose, a small house on top of the actual house, like a belvedere.[22]

The functions to which I have just referred would indicate numerous uses of the building, where, unlike Europe, a distinction is not always made between the inside and the outside, but in India the functions of the structure are *adaptable* to either of these aspects. This quality — flexibility — is extremely desirable in buildings in the hot-humid region and requires special lightness in the structural members. 'The customary distinction between walls and openings disappears,' says Olgyay, 'Ventilation is needed 85% of the year.'[23]

Flexible walls are produced in India by changing the classical loggia into a veranda.

178

The intercolumniation is widened, the proportions of the columns are changed; Indian architecture has clearly functioned as a source of inspiration, and the result is a structure which both screened the sun's rays and allowed the wind to penetrate. James Johnson wrote about these qualities: the verandas 'afford a pleasing shade from the sun, and keep the inner apartments cool and refreshed by the draught of air under them,'[24] and Maria Graham said: 'The viranda keeps off the too great glare of the sun, and affords a dry walk during the rainy season. It is about twenty feet wide, and one side of it is one hundred feet long; the roof is supported by low arches, which are open to the garden.'[25]

Both these descriptions are from the beginning of the 19th century and from Bombay, but at that time the veranda was found everywhere in the hot–humid zone. We know from Tranquebar, Serampore and Calcutta that it was used and that it was often added to older houses as a shade from the sun.[26] One of the best known enthusiasts for verandas was certainly William Hickey, who moved into a house in Calcutta in April 1794, and soon provided the south façade with what he regarded an absolutely necessary complement. He also showed in sketches how the change was made.[27]

Smaller additions, such as balconies, can be noted in Panjim especially. Their origin is, of course, Iberian. An 'iron cage' of the type frequently found on London houses, which provide a daring and Eastern touch to the dark Georgian brick façades, was added to the upper storey of the Residency in Hyderabad in the 1810's.

Between the supports of the veranda thin elements were placed for breaking the sunlight, screens of wooden ribs or cloven bamboo, *tatties* or curtains of split bamboo, or plaited cuscus grass; if kept moist, they emitted an aromatic fragrance.[28] These tatties were in general use, and it is still possible to see how the verandas in Madras and the deep south are filled with such green sails.

Wooden screens were also used, the ribs being laid in a simple chequered pattern or, occasionally, more intricately designed.[29] Some walls of this kind are to be found in the governor's bungalows in Bombay, where they actually recall the pierced marble screens of the Mughal period.

As can be gathered from the quotations above, the verandas contributed to the ventilation of the houses. The height of the rooms could be utilized by making ventilation openings near the ceiling — the 'mezzanines' or 'attics' which are to be found in many houses function in this way — and an attempt was made to increase the circulation of air by additional means. One was the *punka*, a large cloth fan hung from the ceiling and drawn slowly to and fro by a servant; another was the mechanical *thermantidote*.[30]

At first the window openings were kept small and protected by plaited work of rattan. Inside these were heavy shutters that could be closed during the monsoon. Lord Teighmouth describes this arrangement in Calcutta in the 1760's,[31] and it was still in use in smaller places far into the 19th century.[32] Conditions in the larger towns were soon changed. There glass was introduced which gave good protection against dust-carrying winds and driving rain, but which became extremely hot if directly exposed to the sun. It was therefore necessary to have double elements, and shutters were normally used to protect the glass. The Danes in Tranquebar made a compromise between these solutions, probably according to Dutch models, by dividing the window, having glass in the top part and rattan in the lower which was more exposed to the sun.[33] The Portuguese in Panjim also achieved this double effect by joining together oyster shells and glass by means of wooden laths.[34]

The window elements were usable so long as they could be utilized in different combinations; they had to have two or three functions. Great demands were made on them when the window openings increased towards the end of the 18th century, and they also changed in the direction of greater flexibility. 'Almost every house has folding Venetians to each window, or outward door; these are sustained by very strong hinges, which allow each fold, or shutter, to open outwards, and to lie back flat upon the exterior wall,' writes Thomas Williamson in 1810.[35] Now the solid shutters had been changed into ribbed elements, Venetian blinds, which always let in wind and which could be completely opened when the sun was not in that direction. The Venetian blinds, often placed on enormous Venetian windows, were characteristic elements of the Euro-Indian architecture. When such openings were placed opposite each other they gave a maximum air flow through the room.[36]

Like the entrances to the houses, the window openings also required external protection against rain and sun. Here the pediments of Classicism were altogether insufficient, as they were placed high above the window openings like Japanese eyebrows.

Elements were, however, constructed which formed a more effective sun-break. Such sunbreakers or *jhilmils* were often fixed to the house later, if they were found to be necessary.[37] An exception to this was the Town Hall in Bombay, which was equipped with these from the start. They are placed over the windows, and also over the doors in the portico, and in this way actually act as *corrigenda* of the neo-Classical building.[38]

Bombay is perhaps the town in India where one notices the *jhilmils* most, and in some cases they cast their shadows over the front of a house several storeys high. Then it can be realized that they act as a protection, not only against sun, but also against rain. For the same reason the roofs have been made slanting with a large overhang.

Bombay lies on a strip of coast in the west of India which is specially exposed during the rainy season, and the slanting tile roofs which can soon dispose of the rainwater may be regarded as typical of this area.[39] They can also be studied in towns such as Panjim and Mangalore.[40]

Terraced roofs, which dominate the east side and Bengal, are constructed, on the other hand, not only to get rid of rainwater, but also to collect it. The water runs through small pipes in the partition walls projecting above the roof and then through rainwater pipes to be collected in large jars.[41]

The violent monsoon rains in India pose a special problem, as they make the fronts of the houses scale off. The damp causes great damage. The following, signed by initials, was written in the *Calcutta Gazette* on 29 November, 1798:

'For . . . twenty years have I been witness to our pillars beginning to crumble away at the base, ere the superstructure they were intended to support was well finished; our houses after the same manner to all appearance giving way just above the foundation! It is the outer surface only I grant, but what a lamentable deformity, both within and without, to see the plaister strained and discoloured, and scaling off some three or four feet above the foundations. How perverse and vexatious to have the bricks laid bare, at once, destroying the pleasing delusion of beholding a building of stones! How unthrifty to construct apartments that are neither fit to breathe in nor be converted even to a store-room with any degree or security. . . . We all know how bibulous the terraced roofs are of this country, and although ever so sound and free from cracks, after a constant rain of eight or nine days, they drop and leak all over.'[42]

The anonymous critic also made concrete suggestions for improvements;[43] usually people managed with annual repairs. The outside finish was replaced after every rainy season.[44] And the light coloured stucco or *chunam* covering the building was very suitable as a sun radiator during the hot season. 'The more like a mirror the more efficient the house would be,' writes Maxwell Fry on the basis of his modern experience.[45] Investigations which have been made in Baghdad, show that a white coating of lime plaster reflects a very high percentage of the heat of the sun; to get a higher coefficient aluminium or silver must be used.[46]

We do not have so many subjects for study from the hot–arid region; there are no large urban patterns, and actually only a couple of examples of individual houses. In their construction, however, these give concrete information on the specific climate of this zone, which is dry with a very high summer temperature and wide differences between day and night temperatures during the winter months. These extreme conditions also make extreme architectural solutions necessary. To protect themselves, people had to fight the climate.[47]

Metcalfe House in Delhi has already been mentioned. It was described in detail by Lady Clive Bayley, daughter of Thomas Metcalfe. She said that all the rooms were large and airy, and the study, the 'Napoleon Gallery', and the library were in a row on the north side of the house. To the south were a number of bedrooms and Lady Metcalfe's sitting-room. A veranda ran round the whole building. It was supported on stone pillars and was between four and six feet wide, thus forming quite a large outside room.[48]

So far the description conforms well with the structures we know from the hot–humid region. But we have not yet come to the point. Metcalfe House was situated beside the River Jumna, and the position was utilized in a radical way. The veranda on the south side of the house, which faced the river, was formed as a terrace, and beneath this, in the actual river bed, a room was dug out which would afford the greatest possible coolness. The same arrangement was made in Lucknow, doubtless after Indian models. Mr. Bank's House and the British Residency had suites of *tykhanas* below the main storeys,[49] and General Martin's palace had underground catacomb-like chambers which admitted no daylight, but were lit with oil lamps.[50]

The underground or basement room was kept cool by soil embankments, thick walls and the whole mass of the building. It was turned away from the sun, but also from the wind and from most possibilities of air flow. To remedy this defect, Martin arranged a ventilation system for his palace of a type still used in Hyderabad in West Pakistan.[51]

'Great pillars run at intervals from top to bottom of the building. Down the centre of each is driven an air shaft with holes communicating with the various rooms through which it passes, thus enabling the hot air to rise and the cool air to take its place.'[52]

It seems, however, that this system worked badly. Thomas Twining has mentioned the heat and the thick oily smoke in the rooms of La Martinière.[53]

From other places in the country we also hear about underground rooms in which the hottest part of the day was spent; such a report comes from Jalalabad.[54] In other quarters people did not perhaps go underground, but constructed veritable forts against the sun, solid buildings with closed shutters. There was a house of this kind at Safirabad, just off the Dacca road. The roof was several feet thick, the rooms were small and stuffy. This building was not particularly suitable in the hot, wet climate of this area. The building style was probably due to an idiosyncrasy: the orientalist, William Jones, who lived in the house, once wrote that he only kept his health through his resolve never to see the sun, 'or suffering him to see me'.[55]

With regard to lythosphere arrangements, it might be said that the architects in the hot–arid zone followed Victor Olgyay's general advice, but the overall construction did not get the appearance which is now considered to be the best. In such a case the different parts of the structure would have been arranged in a *closed* formation around a courtyard or patio. Prototypes for such lay-outs are to be found in Indian architecture, but Europeans used these models only on exceptional occasions.[56] Government House in Tranquebar and the Palais de Justice in Pondicherry are two such examples — in the hot–humid region! — which were cooled by means of a system of inner courtyards and corridors.[57]

These examples of construction to suit the climate may be considered sufficient to demonstrate the situation and manner of working of the European engineers in the days of the Companies in India. As can be seen, they dealt with their tasks in a very practical way. While architectural models nowadays are tested according to the same principles as models of ships and aeroplanes (in wind tunnels, and taking into account diagrams of air humidity and the heat of the sun), in the century with which we are dealing the engineers had to experiment and practise on the houses themselves.[58] The architects worked, so to speak, on full scale models, risking failures, which were also on a full scale. Building in those days had the character of trial and error.

The work was based on prototypes which had been taken from Europe and which the architects made to work by means of additions and functional changes. The neo-Classical building was suitable for the climate, but not even this type of structure with its loggia, portico and flat roof could be successful without alterations. The changes were made in conformity with Indian models, but it was mostly individual elements that were adopted. There was hesitation in making large structural changes, except on one point that led to the construction of the bungalow.

4. *The Forms of Architecture as determined by the Climate:* Notes

1. Jane Drew and Maxwell Fry's book was published in London, 1964. It was preceded by another publication, *Tropical architecture in the humid zone,* London, 1956. Victor Olgyay's book was written in collaboration with Aladar Olgyay, Princeton, New Jersey 1963. It contains an instructive bibliography of this special subject.

2. V. Olgyay quotes Vitruvius, op. cit., p. 4 and passim. J. Soane, *Lectures on Architecture,* publication of Sir John Soane's Museum, No. 14. London 1929, p. 115.

3. In characterizing the various types of climate I have followed V. Olgyay, op. cit., and through the latter Köppen-Geiger, *Handbuch der Klimatologie,* Berlin, 1930–39.

4. V. Olgyay, op. cit., p. 173.

5. Cf. above, p. 70.

6. L. von Orlich, *Travels in India,* London, 1845, vol. 2, p. 178. Cf. above, p. 68.

7. See the chapter on 'The Growing Towns: Calcutta', above, pp. 69 f.

8. S. Andersen Bille, *Beretning om Corvetten Galathea's Reise omkring Jorden 1845, 46 og 47,* Copenhagen, 1849–51, vol. 1, p. 166. Cf. the chapter on 'Country Residences near Calcutta, Madras and Delhi', p. 125 above.

9. See above, p. 58. The plantations in Tranquebar were certainly made according to the model of those in Madras, which were described by travellers such as C. P. T. Laplace, *Voyage autour du Monde . . . pemdant les années 1830, 1831 et 1832,* Paris, 1833–39, vol. 1, pp. 244 f. W. H. Carey writes about avenues of *neem* trees in *The Good Old Days of Hon'ble John Company,* Simla, 1882–87, p. 63.

10. M. Graham, *Journal of a Residence in India,* Edinburgh, 1812, pp. 19 f. In the 1830's it also became a fashion to live in tents or in bamboo houses on the Esplanade during the fine season. See *Old and New Bombay, A Historical and Descriptive Account of Bombay and its Environs,* Bombay, 1911, p. 38.

11. See above, p. 76.

12. P. Spear writes about the palanquin in *The Nabobs,* first ed. 1932; London 1963, p. 100.

13. The large flight of steps on the north side of Government House in Calcutta also served as a portico. See above, p. 102. Cf. the custom in towns in the West Indies, where the arcades on the ground floor of the houses formed sheltered passages along streets and squares. See above, p. 61.

14. *Bengal, Past and Present,* vol. 63 January–December, 1943, p. 22. C. P. T. Laplace, op. cit., vol. 1, p. 245 talks of 'vastes apartements, disposés contre la chaleur', and W. Hodges of buildings 'on a large scale, for the necessity of having a free circulation of air'; *Travels in India during the years 1780, 1781, 1782 and 1783,* London, 1793, p. 15.

15. M. Graham, op. cit., p. 137, points out that Government House, Calcutta gets the breeze from all quarters on account of its pavilion system. The spacious arrangement of the country residences around Madras have been described above on p. 125.

16. Cf. below, p. 188.

17. T. Williamson, *The East India Vade-Mecum*, London, 1810, vol. 2, p. 9. 'In all the good houses the apartments are up stairs', writes J. Kindersley from Madras. *Letters from the East Indies*, London, 1777, p. 77.

18. Examples of this have been given in the description of Hastings' House p. 122 above, and Government House, Triplicane. Two exceptions are the Governor General's country residence in Barrackpore and 'Comillah', where the ground floor was inhabited by the servants. See above, the chapter on 'Country Residences near Calcutta, Madras and Delhi'.

19. W. S. S. Karr, *Selections from the Calcutta Gazettes*, Calcutta 1864–1959, vol. 1, p. 109; H. D. Love, *Vestiges of Old Madras*, London, 1913, vol. 3, p. 448.

20. See above, p. 120.

21. See above, p. 107.

22. I have indicated such examples in the Danish town of Tranquebar, see p. 58 above. These additions often have the character of thatched huts. Cf. K. Blechynden, *Calcutta, Past and Present*, London, 1905, p. 73.

23. V. Olgyay, op. cit., p. 174.

24. J. Johnson, *The Oriental Voyager*, London, 1807, p. 337.

25. M. Graham, op. cit., p. 21.

26. See p. 58 above. Cf. the conditions in other tropical environments. M. D. Ozinga writes: 'These galleries, which in the beginning, as can still be seen in some of the oldest houses, were mere accidental additions, became an essential, functional part of the large merchants' houses, where they also contained the staircase to the upper storeys.' *De Monumenten van Curaçao in Woord en Beeld*, The Hague, 1955, p. 140. See also R. Lewcock, *Early Nineteenth Century Architecture in South Africa*, Cape Town, 1964, pp. 111 ff.

27. W. Hickey, *Memoirs*, London 1925, vol. 4, figs. facing page 117. Verandas made of wooden elements can be found especially in Bombay. Here we can trace influences from the wooden architecture of Gujarat. Cf. below, p. 190, note 16.

28. In the accounts of the engineers in Serampore from the 1780's and onwards 'tatties' or material for such are often mentioned. See above, p. 72. Cf. T. Williamson, op. cit., vol. 2, p. 10; L. von Orlich, op. cit., vol. 2, p. 214 and P. Spear, op. cit., p. 50.

29. In J. K. Stanford, *Ladies in the Sun*, London, 1962, a photo taken before 1860 is reproduced showing a military bungalow with such additions, facing p. 119. Cf. R. Lewcock, op. cit., figs. 189 and 190.

30. P. Spear has a special chapter, 'The Punkah', op. cit., pp. 26 ff. He says there that it cannot have been used before 1780, that it was first used in Calcutta and then introduced into Madras and Bombay; see also the same work, p. 50, and T. Willamson, *The European in India; from a Collection of Drawings by Charles D'Oyly* etc., London, 1813.

31. See above, pp. 169 f.

32. K. E. Møhl, *Breve fra Indien*, Copenhagen, 1940, p. 42. Cf. above, p. 72.

33. 'die obere helfte von denen Fenstern von Glass, die untere helfte von Rottingen — und dieses um des wissens, damit man zur heissen Zeit wegen des starken Landwindes, und wegen des vielen mit sich führenden Sandes, zur Regenzeit aber wegen des starken Regens die Rottings Fenster mit denen Laden zumachen und dennoch um Licht zubekommen die obere Glass Fenster seyn möchten', B. Ziegenbalg and J. E. Gründler, *Grundlegung, Bau und Einweihung der neuen Missionskirche in Tranquebar, gennant Neu-Jerusalem*, Tranquebar, 1719, A. 3. Cf.

G. Annesley, Viscount Valentia, *Voyages and Travels to India, Ceylon, the Red Sea . . . in the years 1802, 1803, 1804, 1805 and 1806*, London, 1809–11, vol. 1, p. 267.

34. Many such windows are still in use. Cf. above, p. 170.

35. T. Williamson, op. cit., vol. 2, p. 71.

36. Thus the large halls in Government House Calcutta were arranged and the palace planned in Murshidabad; V. Olgyay, op. cit., p. 111, shows in a picture how the use of 'venetian blinds result in well-directed, diffused air pattern'.

37. They may be shaped as small sloping roofs covered with tiles. During the Victorian era they were frequently elaborately decorated.

38. See above, p. 117.

39. The annual amount of rain reported by the observatory on Colaba has been over 78 ins. during the last few years.

40. Cf. above, p. 168.

41. T. Williamson, op. cit., vol. 2, p. 25. Cf. T. and W. Daniell, *Oriental Scenery, Twenty-four views in Hindoostan*, London, 1797, text to plate 3. The rainwater is also collected in the 'tanks'.

42. W. S. S. Karr, op. cit., vol. 3, pp. 215 ff.

43. Ibid., loc. cit.; by way of improvement it is proposed that the humidity in the soil should be kept out with 'Gool' which is 'nothing more than a mixture of oil and lime that been slaked'.

44. See, for example, above, p. 62.

45. J. Drew and M. Fry, *Tropical Architecture in the humid zone*, London, 1956, pp. 57 f.

46. V. Olgyay, op. cit., p. 114. Cf. the opinion that Hastings' House was 'milky white and dazzling'. See above, p. 122.

47. Re the general characteristics of this type of climate and the guiding principles for the architecture, see V. Olgyay, op. cit., pp. 166 ff.

48. *List of Muhammedan and Hindu Monuments*, Calcutta, 1919, vol. 2, p. 291. Cf. above, p. 126.

49. See above, p. 112, and S. Hay, *Historic Lucknow*, Lucknow, 1939, p. 120. As far back as the 17th century, F. Bernier described underground rooms in Delhi; *Travels in the Mogul Empire, 1656–1668*, Oxford, 1891, p. 247.

50. See above, p. 131.

51. V. Olgyay, op. cit., fig. 182.

52. S. Hay, op. cit., p. 155.

53. T. Twining, *Travels in India a hundred years ago*, London, 1893, p. 310.

54. Quoted under the heading 'Tyconna' in *Hobson-Jobson*.

55. William Jones's house has been measured twice with rather different results and is described in *Bengal, Past and Present*, vol. 15, October–December, 1917, pp. 57 ff.

56. Plans for Indian houses arranged with a courtyard in the middle surrounded by galleries have been described by R. Heber, *Narrative of a Journey from Calcutta to the Upper Provinces of India; from Calcutta to Bombay 1824–25*, London, 1828, vol. 1, pp. 37 f., and S. Andersen Bille, op. cit., vol. 1, p. 241. J. Johnson gives a detailed account of a South Indian house of one storey, op. cit., pp. 302 f. J. Forbes finds similarities between Indian houses and Roman villas (!), *Oriental Memoirs*, London, 1813, vol. 2, pp. 326 f.

57. See above, pp. 56 and 96.

58. The only climatological book to which I found any reference is James Capper, *Observations on the Winds and Monsoons*, London, 1801, mentioned in J. Johnson, op. cit., p. 78.

5 · The Origin of the Dwelling-House

JOB CHARNOCK, as well as the first French and Dutch colonists in India, is said to have used Indian-style dwellings. No contemporary pictures exist of these houses, but they must have been simple structures with walls of clay or bamboo and thatched roofs.

In the middle of the 18th century, where the present investigation starts, the style of living is quite different; as far as possible, the colonists now build and reside after European models. Only occasionally does the architecture employed show a connection with the local pattern, and on the whole it adheres to an imported system of forms with specific features and with a long tradition. When employing this type of architecture, it would seem that tradition was of particular importance. The Europeans in exile wanted to keep the memory of their mother-country alive and their preference for certain prototypes would seem to have an undertone of sheer nostalgia.

Towards the end of the century, when a growing interest in rustic architecture arose in Europe, we can discern in India also an approach to native types of buildings.[1] This development may have a sentimental basis, but in most cases it results from purely practical reasoning.

The construction which is thus created as a kind of fusion between the European and the Indian pattern is the bungalow. The name is derived from the Hindustani *banglā* and means something originating in Bengal.[2] The word bungalow has been used in so many places and in so many connections that its meaning has become both diffuse and varied. In this connection I shall make an attempt to trace it back to its original context and place it in relation to the buildings.

Of the ancient Bengal types of houses, two are specially interesting.[3] The first is the so-called 'curvilinear hut' which is a rectangular building with a special roof structure: wooden ribs are bent and jointed together to form a grid which is covered with straw. This roof protrudes over the walls and forms curves resembling a crescent moon on its sides. At the front, the protruding part of the roof may be supported by wooden poles, thus forming a gallery.

The curvilinear hut greatly influenced Mughal architecture during the 17th century. The best example is perhaps Shahjahan's *Naulakha* or *Bangla* in Lahore.[4] This is a fine little building in which the architect adopted the characteristic form of the prototype, but used material which is far from primitive. The building is constructed of marble with inlaid work in *pietra dura*. When taking a close look at the walls it is, however, possible to trace some of the original structural composition in the decoration.[5] The

186

curvilinear hut was also used in combination with European architecture, for out-offices of country residences, probably as living quarters for the Indian servants.[6] It was not, however, to influence European architecture to the same degree as it did the Oriental; its shape was far too complex. The origin of the bungalow must be ascribed to another Bengal feature, 'the double-roofed house'.

This structure is also rectangular and the thatched roof is divided into two sections, a feature from which the building derived its name. The entrance may be designed as an open vestibule, and in this case the roof above this space is supported by a couple of wooden posts. The roof may protrude over the walls in the same way as in the curvilinear hut and together with its posts forms a gallery on one or more sides of the house.

The double-roofed house was also erected in intimate connection with European 18th-century architecture. A large painting in the Victoria Memorial Hall in Calcutta shows two such buildings which, to judge by appearances, were erected as out-offices and dwellings for servants beside a neo-Classical structure.[7] One of them lies in the same compound as the main building. It is not quite certain from where the painter found his motif, but it may be presumed that it was taken from Alipur or Garden Reach, or in any case from one of the residential areas that grew up around Calcutta. Advertisements in the *Calcutta Gazette* inform us that as far back as the 1780's British houses had such annexes.[8]

This type of building was also to function in another connection where it was used, so to speak, instead of tents. I refer to the suburban pattern described in the chapter on cantonments.[9] Although we do not know what the first small houses in Barrackpore or Dum Dum looked like, we know the camp in Ballyganj from a water-colour showing Lord Wellesley 'reviewing his Body-guard'. Here the barracks simply consist of a collection of double-roofed houses arranged in two rows. They have exactly the same design as their counterparts in the residential areas, i.e. a veranda on three sides and a small out-house on one of the short sides, probably a privy.[10]

The bungalow can best be regarded as a European version of the Bengal double-roofed house. The lightest structural properties of the prototype were made use of, and in the beginning its semi-temporary character also. Such houses were built in many places. Henry Roberdeau, a young man who was posted in Mymensingh in Bengal in 1801, described this country station as follows:

'There are no brick houses in the district except the jail and those of the half-dozen officials. Thatch and dried mud does for the rest. Even the Englishmen live in what are really stationary tents which have run aground on low brick platforms. They are 'Bungalows', a word I know not how to render unless by a Cottage. These are always thatched with a straw on the roof and the walls are sometimes of Bricks and often of mats. Some have glass windows besides the Venetians but this is not very common ... To hide the sloping Roofs we put up a kind of artificial ceiling made of white cloth ... There are curtains over the doorway to keep out the wind ... I have two Bungalows near to each other, in one I sleep and dress and in the other sit and eat.'[11]

To start with, Roberdeau supplies us with important information on the materials and structural elements used. The result was an extremely flexible structure with light screen walls. In a description of a more elegant bungalow interior than the above, we can read that two rooms were divided by 'a large screen of red silk',[12] and we recall that many Indian miniatures show just such freely hanging or rolled-up cloth walls.

The British adopted the simplest elements and functions of the Indian houses. The exterior character of the buildings does not indicate any profound structural changes on the part of those who lived there. The difference in the way of living remained. Roberdeau continues to say that 'the natives will not eat or drink with us nor partake of anything from our Tables.'[13]

In the majority of cases, the bungalow only represented a convenient solution to a practical problem. It was cheap and quick to build and was suitable for the climate. Consequently it was used for many purposes, as barracks, out-offices, annexes for guests and even as a dwelling-house, when the various functions were distributed over *several* bungalows. We have read above that the Residency in Hyderabad and the country residence of the governor-general in Barrackpore were arranged in this way,[14] but in the former case these scattered and 'temporary' structures were replaced in 1803 by a building with purely European features. And even in Barrackpore a large main building was added which changed the status of the bungalows to what they generally were, a complement.[15] However, on Malabar Point in Bombay, a group of bungalows was to preserve its function and to have it enhanced when they were turned into the permanent residence of the governor towards the middle of the 19th century.[16]

The change-over from something temporary to something more permanent is on the whole significant of the later history of the bungalow. The building *itself* undergoes such a metamorphosis as regards the material. The sun-baked Indian brick, which according to Thomas Williamson is the most frequently used material around 1800, is replaced by fired brick of the European type. Instead of wooden supports, columns or pillars support the tiled roof. Thus the primitive Indian building is integrated into the system of forms of neo-Classicism.[17] We need not, however, presume that this strengthened building is better and more resistant than the original Indian construction. It did not represent a perfection of the type imagined by William Hodges when he wrote his treatise on architectural prototypes. The use of heavier materials changed the balance and stresses between the various parts of the building and the adaptation of the construction was not always successful. Unexpected weather phenomena could occur and destroy the delicate building. In June 1803 an account appeared in the *Calcutta Gazette* of a bungalow that collapsed on account of a strong gust of wind:

'The supporters were not posts, as is commonly the case in bungalows, but pillars made of substantial masonry, though not, as the event proved, sufficiently strong to sustain an extraordinary large roof under the pressure of such severe gusts of winds . . .'[18]

In this case the roof must have had the shape of a large pyramid and not been divided into sections. Both alternatives occurred. However, the most elegant and most functional solution was undoubtedly the double roof, where the wall section between the sloping elements could be supplied with small windows and thus function as a clerestory. Otherwise the interior would be extremely dark, as the verandas cut off the light from the side. Many military and *dāk* bungalows were also built according to this model.

During the following century, the bungalow was to be built in various shapes and in different parts of the world.[19] But from the beginning it was to stand out as the specific contribution of the Bengal engineers to the cottage architecture of Romanticism. It is original in the same way as, let us say, J. M. Gandy's rural projects,[20] as it was created as an interpretation and a synthesis based on the functional possibilities of the prototypes, both Indian and European.

5. *The Origin of the Dwelling-House:* Notes

1. C. R. Wilson, *Old Fort William in Bengal*, Indian Record Series, London, 1906, vol. 1, p. 16; on p. 42 of the same book the following is stated: 'The Right. Hon. Company having been at a vast charge by building with mudd, and thatch which is removed.' See also *Hobson-Jobson* under the heading 'Bungalow'.

2. *Hobson-Jobson*, loc. cit.

3. See B. Ghose, *Primitive Indian Architecture*, Calcutta, 1953, and A. Ray, *Villages, towns and secular buildings in ancient India*, Calcutta, 1964.

4. See, for example, J. Burton-Page, 'Lahore-Fort', in *Splendours of the East*, edited by Mortimer Wheeler, London, 1965, p. 91, with a good photograph.

5. Cf. B. Ghose, op. cit., p. 47: 'India is a classical land for the translation of wood into stone.'

6. Thus it is reproduced in an engraving published by E. Orme 1805. See the chapter 'Country Residences near Calcutta, Madras and Delhi', above, p. 125.

7. 'House at Calcutta', oil painting, No. 999A., in the Victoria Memorial Hall, Calcutta.

8. See above, p. 123.

9. p. 77.

10. The painting is reproduced in G. N. Curzon, Marquis Curzon of Kedleston, *British Government in India*, London, 1925, vol. 1, facing p. 244.

11. Roberdau's description can be found in *Bengal, Past and Present*, vol. 29, January–June, 1925, but it is dealt with in great detail by Ph. Woodruff, *The men who ruled India*, first published 1953; London 1963, vol. 1, pp. 163 ff.

12. D. Kincaid, *British social life in India*, London, 1938, p. 143.

13. Ph. Woodruff, op. cit., p. 166.

14. p. 124.

15. G. N. Curzon, op. cit., vol. 2, pp. 18 ff. Here Bishop Heber is quoted concerning Barrackpore 1828; he gives the following general description, 'Bungalow', a corruption of Bengalee, is the general name in this country for *any structure in the cottage style, and only of one floor* (my italics). Some of these are spacious and comfortable dwellings, generally with high thatched roofs, surrounded with a verandah, and containing three or four good apartments, with bath- ·

rooms and dressing-rooms, enclosed from the eastern, western, or northern verandahs. The south is always left open.'; *Narrative of a Journey from Calcutta to the Upper Provinces of India; from Calcutta to Bombay 1824–25*, London, 1828, vol. 1, p. 29.

16. The bungalows on Malabar Point are of varying design and year of origin. A bungalow for guests has the shape of a 'double-roofed house' with many wooden elements, a phenomenon which is usual in this part of India. The residency was made permanent under Lord Reay and Lord Harris. See Cecil L. Burns, *Victoria and Albert Museum, Bombay*, Bombay, 1918, p. 86.

17. Of this more stationary type of bungalow, which was much erected up country, Ph. Woodruff gives a detailed description also with regard to furniture, etc., op. cit., p. 315. Several such bungalows are preserved in Patna on Fraser Road and adjacent streets. In 1825, Charles D'Oyly included in his sketch book a 'View of the Bungalow attached to the House of Maharajah Mutrefeyt Singh'. This house has a tiled roof in the form of a pyramid and columns on the veranda or the open vestibule. WD. 2060, No. 79, India Office Library, Commonwealth Office.

18. W. S. S. Karr, *Selections from the Calcutta Gazettes*, Calcutta, 1864–1959, vol. 3, p. 382.

19. Re 'bungalows' in the Dutch colonies in Indonesia and in the Caribbean, see V. I. van de Wall, *Oude Hollandshe Buitenplaatsen van Batavia*, Deventer, 1943, and M. D. Ozinga, *De Monumenten van Curaçao in Woord en Beeld*, The Hague, 1959. The Spanish colonist in the southwestern parts of the U.S.A. developed a building style which recalls the Caribbean, and as regards the material also the Indian cutcha buildings. See D. R. Hannaford and R. Edwards, *Spanish Colonial or Adobe Architecture of California 1800–1850*, New York, 1931. The American bungalow and its origin is described by C. Lancaster in the *Art Bulletin*, September 1958, pp. 231–53. J. L. Kipling reproduces later types of Indian bungalows, adaptations of the Bengal 'double-roofed house' in 'The Origin of the Bungalow', *Country Life in America*, XIX, 8, February 1911. During the period of Romanticism 'bungalows' were also built in Northern European countries, prototypical houses with wooden supports and thatched roofs which, even when called 'Norwegian huts', recall the primitive architecture of the Tropics. *'Liselund'* on the island of Møen in Denmark has been described in a monogram, Copenhagen, 1918. See further Chr. Elling, *Klassicisme i Fyn*, Copenhagen, 1939, pp. 28 ff., plate 35, and the same author *Den Romantiske Have*, Copenhagen, 1942.

20. J. Summerson, 'The Vision of J. M. Gandy', in *Heavenly Mansions and other Essays on Architecture*, first ed. 1948; New York 1963, p. 122.

Appendix

Jaipur — a Fusion of Eastern and Western Town Planning

IN the chapter on the enclaves we were confronted with a number of examples of European town planning in India.[1] They all have in common the fact that the town is surrounded by a wall protecting the inhabitants and their trade. Almost without exceptions these are fortified towns, either completely built like fortresses or with a citadel in the centre. Even the originally peaceful factories were changed in this way when the political situation so required.

I have said that these towns are in accordance with European patterns and in several cases pointed out parallels and models. It should, however, be emphasized that this form of town planning, as regards the main features, is not an original or new element in the world of Indian culture. Several of India's old towns, such as Ahmedabad or Bijapur developed in the same way. As regards Bijapur, the 'citadel' in the centre is indeed a fort in the fortress. And even the simpler settlements show similar features. 'Every village that I passed had something like a wall or a fort to defend it,' writes Lord Valentia during his journey through South India.[2]

The originality of the European towns is the uniform lay-out of the houses within the walls, the uniform blocks and streets which intersect at right angles and make quick communication possible. In this respect the Indian towns are quite different; they present a more organic development with a winding road network, and recall medieval Europe again in their lay-out of complete quarters for special castes and occupational groups.[3]

There is, however, a town which does not fit into this general description — Jaipur in Rajasthan.

Jaipur was founded in 1728 by the Maharajah Jai Singh II, the famous astronomer.[4] He planned his town according to the same functional geometry that characterized the enormous observatories which he erected in various places in his realm. The design and execution of the work are also said to have been carried out by a Bengalee, Vidyadhar, who was a most prominent coadjutor of the Maharajah in his astronomical and historical research.[5]

Jai Singh had close contacts with Europeans who supplied him with the astronomical works he was interested in. In the City Palace of Jaipur, copies of *Stellarium* and *Historiæ Coelestie*, both published in London in 1719, are still kept to-day. However,

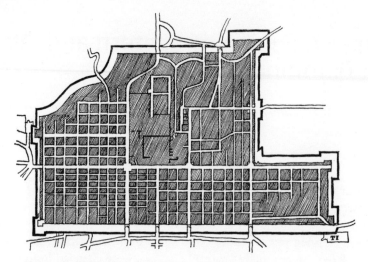

13. Jaipur in Rajasthan, founded by Jai Singh II in 1728. (1 : 40000)

these are merely some fragments of the Maharajah's large library, which most probably also included some European town plans.[6] The plan of Jaipur corresponds in many respects to European patterns. Broad streets paved with stone run through the town from one gate-way to the other and where they cross, open rectangular squares are formed.[7] Within these frames lie the quarters in the shape of squares and rectangles. The palace of the Maharajah, the City Palace, as well as the observatory lie in the centre of the town.

This is, however, not the whole truth about the plan of Jai Singh, as he also got ideas from other quarters, namely from *Śilpa-Śāstra*, the old Hindu architectural treatise. The design of Jaipur contains a rather unique fusion of the Western and Eastern art of town planning.

The *Śilpa-Śāstra* texts say that the town should lie beside a hill, a river or by the sea.[8] Jaipur is situated near a chain of hills. The general rule is that the town should have a square or rectangular design and that four gateways should be connected with main streets. Furthermore, a division into occupational groups and castes is laid down. The ruler should live in the centre, as is the case in Jaipur. The rules are idealistic and abstract, and in this way correspond to the European projects of the Renaissance. It may be said that for this reason they were hardly ever completely applied. Jaipur is a fine exception to the rule.

Appendix. Jaipur — a Fusion of Eastern and Western Town Planning: Notes

1. See above, pp. 40–47.

2. G. Annesley, Viscount Valentia, *Voyages and Travels to India, Ceylon, The Red Sea . . . in the years 1802, 1803, 1804, 1805 and 1806*, London, 1809–11, vol. 1, p. 480.

3. Re fusion of this type in another connection, see the analysis of Pondicherry's first town plan in the chapter on 'The Enclaves', above, p. 44. Cf. B. B. Dutt, *Town planning in ancient India*, Calcutta, 1925.

4. J. Tod, *Annals and Antiquities of Rajasthan*, London, 1832, vol. 2, p. 367.

5. A. Garrett, *The Jaipur Observatory and its builder*, Allahabad, 1902, p. 11.

6. Ibid., p. 12.

7. See again Pondicherry's first town plan, above, p. 44. Cf. Bishop Heber's description of Jaipur, *Narrative of a Journey from Calcutta to the Upper Provinces of India; from Calcutta to Bombay, 1824–25*, London, 1828, vol. 2, p. 12.

8. See D. N. Shukla, *Vástu-śāstra*, Lucknow, 1960, vol. 1, and Amita Ray, *Villages, towns and secular buildings in ancient India*, Calcutta, 1964, pp. 52 f.

Notes on Archives and Collections

ARCHITECTURAL DRAWINGS, PAINTINGS, WATER-COLOURS, SKETCHES, PRINTS and PHOTOGRAPHS OF ARCHITECTURE, MAPS and RECORDS have been studied in the following archives and collections:

H.M. the King's Private Library, The Royal Library, The School of Architecture's Collection of Measured Drawings, Royal Academy for the Fine Arts, National Archives, all in *Copenhagen*. The Commercial and Maritime Museum in Kronborg Castle, *Elsinore*. Ib Andersen's Collection of Architectural Drawings, *Fredensborg*. The Ethnographical Museum, *Oslo*. The British Museum, The Drawings Collection of the R.I.B.A., India Office Library, Commonwealth Office, Mildred and W. G. Archer Collection, all in *London*. Bibliothèque de la Section Outre-Mer des Archives Nationales, *Paris*. Tropen-museum, *Amsterdam*. The National Archives of India, *New Delhi*. The National Library, Victoria Memorial Hall, Photographers Bourne & Shepherd, all in *Calcutta*. Record Office, *Madras*. The Public Library, *Pondicherry*. The Victoria and Albert Museum, *Bombay*.

For full details refer to the Notes.

List of Printed Works Consulted

PUBLISHED BEFORE 1850

Abu Talib Ibn Muhammad Khan, *Voyages de Mirza Abu Taleb Khan*, Paris, 1811.

Adam, R., and J., *The Works in Architecture of Robert and James Adam*, London, 1778–1822.

Alberti, L. B., *Della Architettura*, London, 1726.

Annesley, G., Viscount Valentia, *see* Valentia.

A Visit to Madras, London, 1821.

Baillie, W., *Twelve Views of Calcutta*, London, 1794.

Barozzi, G., called Vignola, *Il Vignola Illustrato*, Roma, 1770.

Bélidor, B. F. de, *La Science des Ingénieurs*, Paris, 1719, and later editions.

Bille, S. Andersen, *Beretning om Corvetten Galathea's Reise omkring Jorden 1845, 46 og 47*, Copenhagen, 1849–51.

Blagdon, F. W., *A Brief History of Ancient and Modern India*, London, 1805.

Blondel, J-F., *De la distribution des Maisons de plaisance et de la décoration des édifices en général*, Paris, 1737–38.

Brandon, R., and J. A., *An Analysis of Gothic Architecture*, London, 1849.

Broecke, P. van, *Korte Historiael ende Journaelsche Aenteyckeninghe*, Haarlem, 1634.

Calcutta, Views 1756, London, 1778.

Campbell, C., *Vitruvius Britannicus*, London, 1767–71.

Capper, J., *Observations on the Winds and Monsoons*, London, 1801.

Catalogue of the Library of the Bombay Branch of the Royal Asiatic Society, Bombay, 1845.

Chambers, W., *A Treatise on Civil Architecture*, London, 1759.

College for the Instruction of Asiatic Christian and Other Youth in Eastern Literature and European Science, Serampore, 1818.

Cramp, W. B., *Narrative of a Voyage to India*, London, 1823.

Daniell, T., *Views of Calcutta*, Calcutta, 1786–88.

Daniell, T. and W., *Oriental Scenery, Twenty-four Views in Hindoostan*, London, 1797.
   A Picturesque Voyage to India, London, 1810.

De Havilland, T. F., *Public Edifices of Madras*.

Desgodetz, A., *The Ancient Buildings of Rome*, London, 1771.

D'Oyly, C., and Williamson, J., *The European in India*, London, 1813.

LIST OF PRINTED WORKS CONSULTED

Ebert, J. J., *Beschreibung und Geschichte der Hauptstadt in den Holländischen Ostindien, Batavia*, Leipzig, 1785.

Fenger, I. F., *Den Tranquebarske Missions Historie*, Copenhagen, 1843.

Forbes, J., *Oriental Memoirs*, London, 1813.

Fraser, J. B., *Views of Calcutta and its environs*, London, 1824–26.

Gandy, J. M., *Designs for Cottages, Cottage Farms, and other Rural Buildings*, London, 1805.

Gibbs, J., *A Book of Architecture*, London, 1728.

Graham, M., *Journal of a Residence in India*, Edinburgh, 1812.

Grindlay, R. M., *Scenery, Costumes and Architecture*, London, 1826–30.

Halfpenny, W., *Rural Architecture in the Chinese Taste*, London, 1755.

Hallische Missionsberichte, Halle, 1710 and onwards.

Hamilton, A., *A New Account of the East Indies*, Edinburgh, 1727.

Heber, R., *Narrative of a Journey from Calcutta to the Upper Provinces of India; from Calcutta to Bombay 1824–25*, London, 1828.

    An Account of a Journey to Madras and the Southern Provinces, 1826, published as an addition to the afore-mentioned work.

    The Life of Reginald Heber by his Widow, together with a Journal of his Tour in Norway, Sweden, Russia, Hungary and Germany, London, 1830.

Hennings, A., *Gegenwärtiger Zustand der Besitzungen der Evropäer in Ostindien*, Copenhagen, Hamburg & Kiel, 1784–86.

Hodges, W., *A Dissertation on the Prototypes of Architecture*, London, 1787.

    Travels in India during the years 1780, 1781, 1782 & 1783, London, 1793.

Johnson, J., *The Oriental Voyager*, London, 1807.

    The Influence of Tropical Climates on European Constitutions, London, 1827.

Jombert, C.-A., *Architecture moderne ou l'Art de bien bâtir pour toutes des personnes*, Paris, 1764.

Kindersley, J., *Letters from the Island of Teneriffe, Brazil, the Cape of Good Hope and the East Indies*, London, 1777.

Langlès, L., *Monuments anciens . . . de l'Hindoustan*, Paris, 1821.

Langley, B., *The City and Country Builder's and Workman's Treasury of Design*, London, 1745.

Laplace, C. P. T., *Voyage autour de Monde . . . pendant les années 1830, 1831 et 1832*, Paris, 1833–39.

    Campagne de Circumnavigation de la frigate l'Artémise pendant les années 1837, 1838, 1839 et 1840, Paris, 1842.

Le Gentil de la Galasière, G. J. H. J. B., *Voyage dans les mers de l'Inde*, Paris, 1779–82.

Moffat, J., *Views from Calcutta, Berhampore, Monghyr and Benares*, London, 1805.

Møllers, N. E., *Beskrivelse over de Nichobariske eller Friedrichs Øerne i Ostindien*, Copenhagen, 1797.

Nicholson, P., *Principles of Architecture*, London, 1795.

O'Hier de Grandpré, L. de, *Voyage dans l'Inde et au Bengale . . . 1789 et 1790*, Paris, 1801.

Orlich, L. von, *Travels in India*, London, 1845.

Orme, R., *A History of the Military Transactions of the British Nation in India*, 3rd ed., London, 1780.

Paine, J., *Plans, Elevations and Sections of Noblemen's and Gentlemen's Houses*, London, 1783.

Palladio, A., *The Architecture of Andrea Palladio*, London, 1742, and other editions.

Pasley, C. W., *Outline of a Course of Practical Architecture, compiled for the use of the Junior Officers of Royal Engineers*, Chatham, 1826.

Percier, C., and Fontaine, P. F. L., *Choix des plus célèbres maisons de plaisance de Rome et de ses environs*, Paris, 1809.

Quarenghi, G., *Edifices construits à Saint-Pétersbourg*, St. Petersburg, 1810.

Roberts, E., *Scenes and Characteristics of Hindostan*, London, 1835.

Ruskin, J., *Seven Lamps of Architecture*, London, 1849.

 The Stones of Venice, London, 1853.

Stavorinus, J. C., *Reise nach dem Vorgebürge der guten Hoffnung, Java und Bengalen*, Berlin, 1796.

Stuart, J., and Revett, N., *The Antiquities of Athens*, London, 1762–87.

Tayler, W., *Sketches illustrating the Manners and Customs of the Indians and Anglo-Indians*, London, 1842.

The Builder's Magazine, or a Universal Dictionary for Architects, Carpenters, Masons, Bricklayers, London, 1788.

The Civil Architecture of Vitruvius, London, 1812.

The Civil Engineer's and Architect's Journal, London, 1837, and onwards.

The Principles of Ancient Masonry, London, 1733.

Thurah, L. De, *Den Danske Vitruvius*, Copenhagen, 1746.

 Hafnia Hodierna, Copenhagen, 1748.

Tod, J., *Annals and Antiquities of Rajasthan*, London, 1832.

Toreen, O., *A Voyage to Suratte*; published together with Osbeck, P., *A Voyage to China and the East Indies*, London, 1771.

Valentia, Viscount, *Voyages and Travels to India, Ceylon . . . in the years 1802, 1803, 1804, 1805 and 1806*, London, 1809.

Ware, I., *A Complete Body of Architecture*, London, 1756.

Williamson, T., *The East India Vade-Mecum*, London, 1810.

Wood, R., *The Ruins of Palmyra, otherwise Tedmor, in the Desert*, London, 1753.

 The Ruins of Balbec, otherwise Heliopolis, in Coelosyria, London, 1757.

Ziegenbalg, B., and Gründler, J. E., *Grundlegung, Bau, und Einweihung der neuen Missionskirche in Tranquebar, genannt Neu-Jerusalem*, Tranquebar, 1719.

LIST OF PRINTED WORKS CONSULTED

PUBLISHED AFTER 1850

A Catalogue of Printed Books in European Languages in the Library of the Asiatic Society of Bengal, Calcutta, 1908.

A Descriptive List of the Pictures in the Viceroy's Residences at New Delhi, Simla and Calcutta, Calcutta, 1936.

Archer, M., 'Forgotten Painter of the Picturesque, Henry Salt in India 1802–1804', *Country Life*, 19 November, 1959.

    'Company Architects and their influence in India', *R.I.B.A. Journal*, August, 1963.

    'The East India Company and British Art', *Apollo*, November, 1965.

    'Aspects of Classicism in India; Georgian Buildings of Calcutta', *Country Life*, 3 November, 1966.

Archer, M., and W. G., *Indian Painting for the British 1770–1880*, Oxford, 1955.

Azevedo, C. de, *Arte Cristã na India Portuguesa*, Lisboa, 1959.

Bearce, G. D., *British attitudes towards India 1784–1858*, Oxford, 1961.

Bengal, Past and Present, periodical published by the Historical Society of Calcutta, Calcutta, 1907 etc.

Bernier, F., *Travels in the Mogul Empire, 1656–1668*, Oxford, 1891.

Blechynden, K., *Calcutta, Past and Present*, London, 1906.

Bluhme, C. A., 'Af en Ostindifarers Breve', edited by H. Müller, *Tilskueren*, September, 1934.

Bocarro, A., *Livro das plantas de tôdas as fortalezas, citades e provoações do Estado da India Oriental, 1635*, published in *Arquivo Português Oriental, Tomo IV*, Bastorá-Goa, 1935.

Boxer, C. R., *The Portuguese in the East*, Oxford, 1953.

Bredsdorff, P., Engqvist, H. H., Jein, B. and Licht, K. de Fine, 'Kunstakademiets studier over byer og bygningskunst paa de dansk-vestindiske øer', *Arkitekten*, no. 24, 1960.

Buck, E., *Simla, Past and Present*, Calcutta, 1904.

Bulsara, J. F., *Problems of rapid urbanization in India*, Bombay, 1964.

Burns, C. L., *Victoria and Albert Museum, Bombay*, Bombay, 1918.

C. A. Ehrensvärds Skrifter, published by the Swedish Society for Belles-Lettres, Stockholm, 1922, 23 and 25.

Calendar of a Volume containing notifications, 1774 to 1824, issued by the Danish Administration at Tranquebar, Madras, 1908.

Cameron, R., *Shadows of India*, London, 1958.

Carey, W. H., *The Good Old Days of Hon'ble John Company*, Simla, 1882–87.

Catalogue of Danish Records, Madras, 1952.

Catalogue of Pictures destined for the Victoria Memorial Hall and now exhibited in the Indian Museum, Calcutta, 1908.

Catalogue of the Royal Engineers Corps Library at the Horse Guards, Whitehall, London, Chatham, 1929.

Centenary Review of the Asiatic Society of Bengal, from 1784 to 1883, Calcutta, 1885.

Churchill, W. S., *My early life,* London, 1930.

Colvin, H., *Biographical Dictionary of English Architects, 1660–1840,* London, 1954.

Curzon, G. N., Marquis Curzon of Kedleston, *British Government in India,* London, 1925.

Danvers, F. C., *The Portuguese in India,* London, 1894.

    An Account of the Origin of the East India Company's Civil Service and their College in Hertfordshire, London, 1894.

Dodwell, H. H., *Dupleix and Clive, the beginning of Empire,* London, 1920.

    Nabobs of Madras, London, 1926.

Dollfus, J., *Les Aspects de L'architecture Populaire dans le Monde,* Paris, 1954.

Douglas, J., *Bombay and Western India,* London, 1903.

Dutt, B. B., *Town planning in ancient India,* Calcutta, 1925.

Eberlein, H. D., and Hubbard, C. V. D., *American Georgian Architecture,* London, 1952.

Edwardes, M., *Asia in the European Age 1498–1955,* London, 1961.

    A History of India, From the Earliest Time to the Present Day, London, 1961.

    Battles of the Indian Mutiny, London, 1963.

Edwards, R., *Spanish Colonial or Adobe Architecture of California 1800–1850,* New York, 1931.

Elling, C., *Arkitekten Philip de Lange,* Copenhagen, 1931.

    Klassicisme i Fyn, Copenhagen, 1939.

    Danske Herregaarde, Copenhagen, 1942.

    Den Romantiske Have, Copenhagen, 1942.

    Rom, Arkitekturens Liv fra Bernini til Thorvaldsen, Copenhagen, 1956.

Fanshawe, H. C., *Delhi. Past and Present,* London, 1902.

Fay, E., *Original Letters from India;* first published 1819; with an introduction by E. M. Forster, London, 1925.

Fergusson, J., *History of the moderne styles of architecture,* London, 1862.

Firminger, W. K., *Thacker's Guide to Calcutta,* Calcutta, 1906.

Forrest, G. W., *Cities of India,* Westminster, 1903.

Forssman, E., *Dorisch, Jonisch und Korinthisch,* Uppsala, 1961.

Foster, W., *The Founding of Fort St. George, Madras,* London, 1902.

    The English Factories in India 1618–23, Oxford, 1906.

    British Artists in India, 1760–1820, London, 1931.

Fraser, J. B., *Military Memoirs of Col. James Skinner,* London, 1851.

Fry, M., and Drew, J., *Tropical Architecture in the Humid Zone,* London, 1956.

    Tropical Architecture in the Dry and Humid Zones, London, 1964.

Furber, H., *Bombay Presidency in mid-eighteenth century,* London, 1965.

Garrett, A., *The Jaipur Observatory and its Builder,* Allahabad, 1902.

Germann, W., *Ziegenbalg und Plütschau. Die Grüdungsjahre der Trankebarschen Mission*, Erlangen, 1868.

Ghose, B., *Primitive Indian Architecture*, Calcutta, 1953.

Glachant, R., *Historie de l'Inde Français*, Paris, 1966.

Gowans, A., *Images of American Living*, Philadelphia & New York, 1964.

Hamilton, G. H., *The Art and Architecture of Russia*, the Pelican History of Art, 1954.

Hamlin, T., 'The Greek Revival in America and some of its Critics', *The Art Bulletin*, XXIV, September, 1942.

Hancock, T. H. H., 'Coleman of Singapore', *Architectural Review*, March, 1955.

Hanotaux, G., and Martineau, A., *Histoire des Colonies Françaises*, vol. 5, l'Inde et l'Indochine, Paris, 1932.

Hauser, P. M., editor, *Urbanization in Asia and the Far East*, proceedings of the joint U.N./Unesco Seminar, Calcutta, 1957.

Hautecoeur, L., *Histoire de l'architecture classique en France*, Paris, 1943–57.

Havell, E. B., *Indian Architecture*, London, undated.

Hay, S., *Historic Lucknow*, Lucknow, 1939.

Hickey, W., *Memoirs of William Hickey*, London, 1925.

Hill, S. C., *The life of Claud Martin*, Calcutta, 1901.

Hodson, V. C. P., *List of the Officers of the Bengal Army, 1758–1834*, London, 1927–47.

Humlum, J., 'St. Croix, St. Thomas og St. Jan', *Kulturgeografi*, October, 1964.

Hunter, W. W., *Annals of Rural Bengal*, London, 1868.
    The Thackerays in India, London, 1897.

Hvass, T., *Dansk Vestindien*, Ældre Nordisk Architektur, vol. IV, Copenhagen, 1925.

Hyde, H. B., *Parochial Annals of Bengal*, Calcutta, 1901.

Ihle, A., *Under Sydkorset*, Copenhagen, 1894.

Journal and Proceedings of the Asiatic Society of Bengal, Calcutta, 1899 and onwards.

Karr, W. S. S., *Selections from the Calcutta Gazettes*, Calcutta, 1864–1959.

Kaufmann, E., *Von Ledoux bis Le Corbusier. Ursprung und Entwicklung der autonomen Architektur*, Vienna, 1933.

Kaye, J. W., *History of the War in Afghanistan*, London, 1851.

Kincaid, D., *British social life in India*, London, 1938.

Kipling, J. L., 'The origin of the bungalow', *Country Life in America*, XIX, February, 1911.

Köppen, W., and Geiger, R., *Handbuch der Klimatologie*, Berlin, 1930–39.

Lancaster, C., 'The origin and evolution of the bungalow', *The Art Bulletin*, September, 1958.

Langberg, H., *Danmarks Bygningskultur*, Copenhagen, 1955.
    Arkitekturens oprindelse og andre perspektiver, Copenhagen, 1963.

Larsen, K., *De dansk-ostindiske Kompagniers historie*, Copenhagen, 1907–08.

Lavedan, P., *Historie de l'Urbanisme, Renaissance et Temps Modernes*, Paris, 1941.

Lawrence, A. W., *Trade Castles and Forts of West Africa*, London, 1963.

Lewcock, R., *Early Nineteenth Century Architecture in South Africa*, Cape Town, 1963.

Liselund, Copenhagen, 1918.

List of Ancient Monuments in Bengal, Calcutta, 1896.

List of Muhammedan and Hindu Monuments. Delhi Province, vol. II, Calcutta, 1919.

Little, B., *The life and work of James Gibbs*, London, 1955.

Long, J., *Peeps into social life of Calcutta a century ago*, Calcutta, 1868.

Lorenzen, V., and others, *Christian IV:s Byanlæg*, Copenhagen, 1937.

   'L'Urbanisme Hollandaise au Danemark', *Actes du XVIIIme Congrès International d'Histoire de l'Art*, The Hague, 1955.

Love, H. D., *Descriptive List of Pictures in Government House and the Banqueting Hall, Madras*, Madras, 1903.

   Vestiges of Old Madras, London, 1913.

Macfarlane, J., *Hartly House, Calcutta*, Calcutta, 1908.

Mahārāna, B., *Śilpa-Śāstra*, Cuttack, 1908.

Majumdar, R. C., *History of the Freedom Movement in India*, Calcutta, 1962.

Marshman, J. C., *The Lifes and Times of Carey, Marshman and Ward*, London, 1859.

Martin, J. R., 'Official Report on the Medical Topography and Climate of Calcutta', *The Medico-Chirurgical Review*, no. 67, Westminster, 1840.

Martyn, M., 'Georgian Architecture in Calcutta', *Country Life*, 3 December, 1948.

Massey, M., *Recollections of Old Calcutta*, Calcutta, 1918.

Mau, A., *Pompeji in Leben und Kunst*, 2nd ed., Leipzig, 1908.

Mitterwallner, G. von, *Chaul, eine unerforschte Stadt an der Westküste Indiens*, Berlin, 1964.

Mejer Antonsen, I., 'Researches on the Domestic Culture of the Danish West Indies', *Dansk Folkemuseum & Frilandsmuseet, History and Activities*, 1966.

Møhl, K. E., *Breve fra Indien*, Copenhagen, 1940.

Nielsen, Y., 'Guvernør Peter Anker', *Norsk Historisk Tidskrift*, I, Kristiania, 1871.

Nilsson, S. Å., 'Pyramid på Gustav Adolfs torg', *Konsthistorisk tidskrift*, XXXIII, 1964.

Nørregaard, G., 'The English purchase of the Danish possessions in the East Indies and Africa 1845 and 1850', *Revue d'Histoire des Colonies*, no. 3, 1933.

Oaten, E. F., *European Travellers in India*, London, 1909.

Olafsson, J., *Oplevelser som Ostindiefarer . . .* , Copenhagen, 1907.

Old and New Bombay, A Historical and Descriptive Account of Bombay and its Environs, Bombay, 1911.

Olgyay, V., and A., *Design with Climate, bioclimatic approach to architectural regionalism*, Princeton, New Jersey, 1963.

Ozinga, M. D., *De Monumenten van Curaçao in Woord en Beld*, The Hague, 1959.

Panchridge, H. R., *A short History of the Bengal Club*, Calcutta, 1927.

Parasnis, D. B., *Mahabaleshwar*, Bombay, 1916.

Parkinson, C. N., *East and West*, London, 1963.

Pearson, R., 'A Calcutta Cemetery', *Architectural Review*, July, 1957.

LIST OF PRINTED WORKS CONSULTED

Philips, C. H., *The East India Company 1784–1834*; first ed. 1940; Manchester, 1961.

Phillimore, R. H., *Historical Records of the Survey of India*, Dehra Dun, 1945 and onwards.

Porter, W., *History of the Corps of Royal Engineers*, London, New York & Chatham, 1889–1915.

Ram Gopal, *How the British occupied Bengal*, London, 1963.

Rasch, A. A., and Sveistrup, P. P., *Asiatisk Kompagni i den florissante periode, 1772–1792*, Copenhagen, 1948.

Rasmussen, S. E., *London, the unique city*: first ed. 1934; Pelican Books, 1961.
  Experiencing Architecture, London, 1959.

Rawlinson, H. G., *British Beginnings in Western India 1579–1657*, Oxford, 1920.
  The British Achievements in India, London, 1948.

Ray, A., *Villages, towns and secular buildings in ancient India*, Calcutta, 1964.

Regional Seminar on Public Administration Problems of New and Rapidly growing Towns in Asia, New Delhi 1960, New York, 1962.

Reid, D. M., *The Story of Fort St. George*, Madras, 1945.

Rendtorff, C., *William Carey, Pionermissionæren under dansk Flag*, Copenhagen, 1943.

Reynolds, G., 'British Artists Abroad, T. and W. Daniell in India', *Geographical Magazine*, November, 1947.

Robert-Gaebelé, Y., *Creole et Grande Dame, Joanna Bégum, Marquise Dupleix*, Pondicherry, 1934.

Sandes, E. W., *The Military Engineer in India*, Chatham, 1933–35.

Sastri, K. A. N., *A History of South India*, Madras, 1955.

Selections from the Letters, Despatches and other State Papers, preserved in the Foreign Department of the Government of India, 1772–85, edited by G. W. Forrest, Calcutta, 1890.

Sen, S. N., *Eighteen Fifty-Seven*, New Delhi, 1957.

Sen, S. P., *Farmans and Parawanas for the Establishment of the French in Bengal*, Indian Historical Record Commission Proceedings, 1946.
  The French in India, Calcutta, 1948.

Shukla, D. N., *Vāstu-śāstra*, Lucknow, 1960.

Soane, J., *Lectures on Architecture*, Publication of Sir John Soane's Museum no. 14, London, 1929.

Some Notes on the Hyderabad Residency, collected from original records in the Residency Office, 1918.

Sovani, N. V., *Urbanization and Urban India*, London, 1966.

Spear, P., *The Nabobs*; first ed. 1932; London, 1963.

Srīnivāsāchārī, C. S., *History of the city of Madras*, Madras, 1939.

Stanford, J. K., *Ladies in the Sun*, London, 1962.

Straub, H., *A History of Civil Engineering*, London, 1960.

Summerson, J., *Georgian London*; first ed. 1945; Pelican Books, 1962.

Heavenly Mansions and other Essays on Architecture; first ed. 1948; New York, 1963.

Architecture in Britain, 1530–1830, The Pelican History of Art, London, 1953.

The Classical Language of Architecture, London, 1964.

Sutton, T., *The Daniells, Artists and Travellers*, London, 1954.

Svensson, O., *Three Towns, Conservation and Renewal of Charlotte Amalia, Christiansted and Frederiksted of the U.S. Virgin Islands*, Copenhagen, 1964.

The Cambridge History of India, vol. 5, British India 1497–1858, Cambridge, 1929.

Turner, R., editor, *India's urban future*, Berkeley, 1962.

Twining, T., *Travels in India a hundred years ago*, London, 1893.

Tyrwhitt, J., *Patrick Geddes in India*, with an introduction by H. V. Lanchester, London, 1947.

Vitruvius, *The Ten Books on Architecture*, transl. by Morris Hicky Morgan, New York, 1960.

Vladimirov, V. N., *Starye arkhittekurnye proekty*, St. Petersburg, 1913.

Vore Gamle Tropekolonier, Copenhagen, 1952.

Vos, F. H. de, 'Monumental Remains of the Dutch East India Company in Ceylon', *Journal of the Royal Asiatic Society, Ceylon Branch*, 1898–1910.

Wall, V. I. van de, *Oude Hollandshe Buitenplaatsen van Batavia*, Deventer, 1943.

Watson, W. C., *Portuguese Architecture*, London, 1908.

Weilbach, F., *Arkitekten Lauritz de Thurah*, Copenhagen, 1924.

Wheeler, J. T., *Early Records of British India*, London, 1878.

Wheeler, M., *Rome beyond the Imperial Frontiers*, London, 1954.

editor, *Splendours of the East*, London, 1965.

Whiffen, M., *Stuart and Georgian Churches*, London, 1948.

Wieder, F. C., *Monumenta Cartographica*, The Hague, 1925–33.

Williams, L. F. R., editor, *A Handbook for Travellers in India, Pakistan, Burma and Ceylon*, 19th ed., London, 1962.

Wilson, C. R., *Old Fort William in Bengal*, India Record Series, London, 1906.

Wonen in de Wijde Wereld, catalogue no. 49, Tropenmuseum, Amsterdam, 1963.

Woodruff, Ph., *The men who ruled India*; first ed. 1953; London, 1963.

Yule, H., and Burnell, A. C., *Hobson-Jobson*, 2nd ed., London, 1903.

For the rest I refer to the bibliographies contained in Mildred and W. G. Archer, *Indian Painting for the British 1770–1880*, and Percival Spear, *The Nabobs*, both mentioned above.

Index to persons, places and structures

INDEX

INDEX

INDEX

212

INDEX

Plates

1a. The sea-front of Madras. Water-colour by John Gantz.

1b. The greenhouse at Pushkin, U.S.S.R., designed by V. P. Stasov, 1819–21.

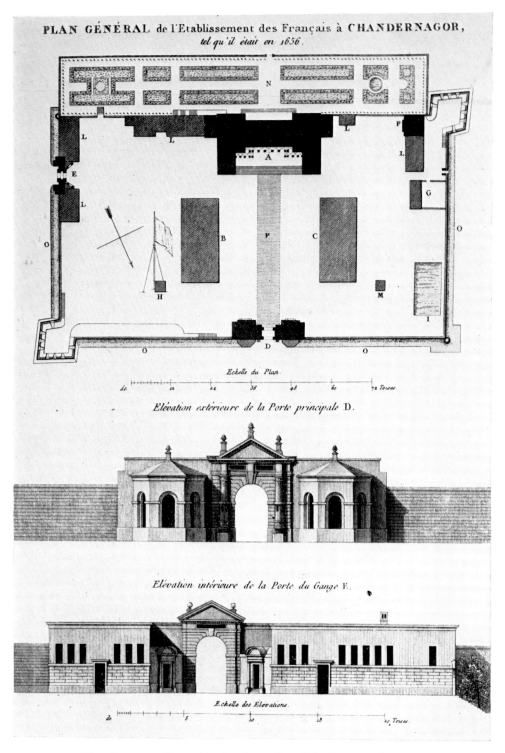

2. Chandernagore. Engraving showing a plan of the factory and two gates.

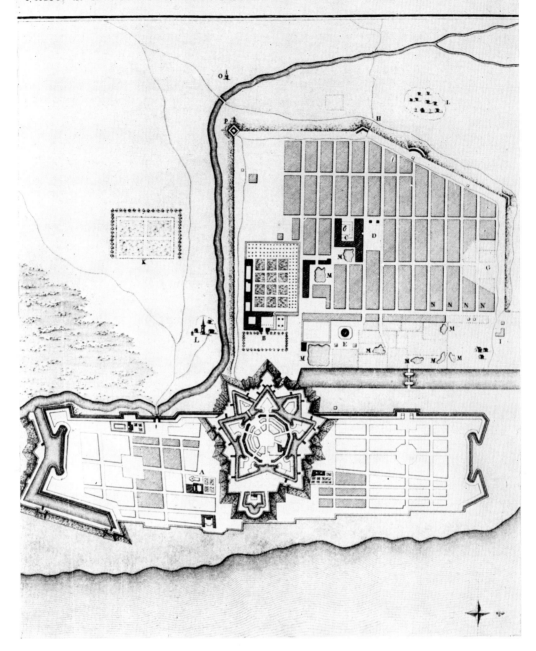

3. Pondicherry.

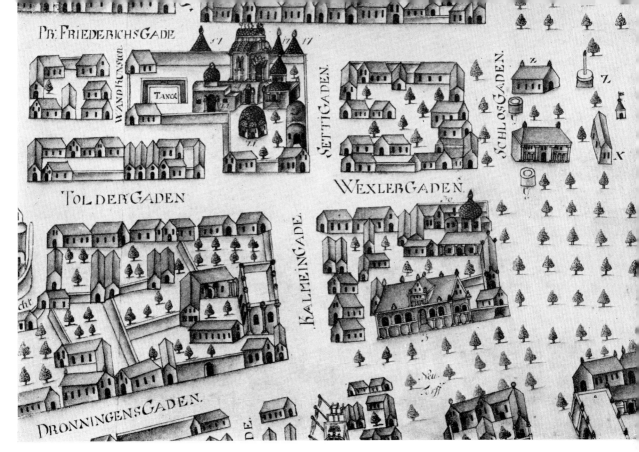

PR. FRIEDERICHSGADE

WANDKUSMON.

TANCA

SETTIGADEN.

SCHLOSGADEN.

TOLDERGADEN.

WEXLERGADEN.

KALMEINGADE.

Neu Coff.

DRONNINGENSGADEN.

5a. Tranquebar. Part of a map drawn in 1733 by
Gregers Daa Trellund.

4. (*Opposite*) Euro-Indian baroque. Detail of a school-
house in Admiralgade (Admiral's Street) Tranquebar.
The building was completed in 1741.

5b. Nygade (New Street) in Tranquebar. Houses
dating from 17th century with porticos added later.

Façaden af den Nije Land Sort, ud til Landet.

6a. The western gate of Tranquebar, erected in 1792. Drawing, showing the outer façade.

6b. (*Below*) Kongens gade (King Street) in Tranquebar. Photograph from about 1920.

7. (*Opposite*) Kongens gade (King Street) in Tranquebar. Photograph taken in 1965. Detail of a portico showing Tuscan capital, architrave and gargoyle. On the other side of the street is The Convent.

8. House in Prins Christians gade (Prince Christian Street) in Tranquebar. Detail showing an ionic pilaster and an engrailed arch above the
window.

9a. Calcutta, the Esplanade Row
and Council House.

9b. Calcutta, the area around Tank
Square (now Dalhousie Square).
Detail of a map published in 1794 by
A. Upjohn.

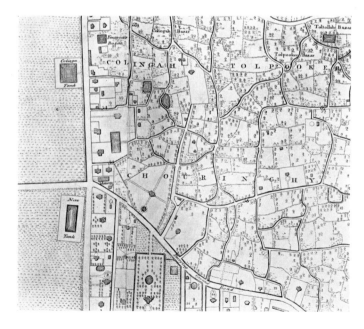

10a. Chowringhi, Calcutta.

10b. Chowringhi, Calcutta. (Detail
of a map published in 1794 by
A. Upjohn.)

11a and b. Houses in Chowringhi.
Photographs taken in 1965.

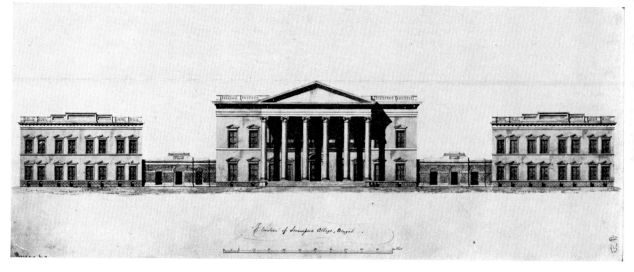

12a. Serampore College. (English
architectural drawing — here
somewhat cut down — in Samlingen
af Land-og Søkort.)

12b. Serampore College, the main building.   13. (*Opposite*) Serampore College, detail of the portico.

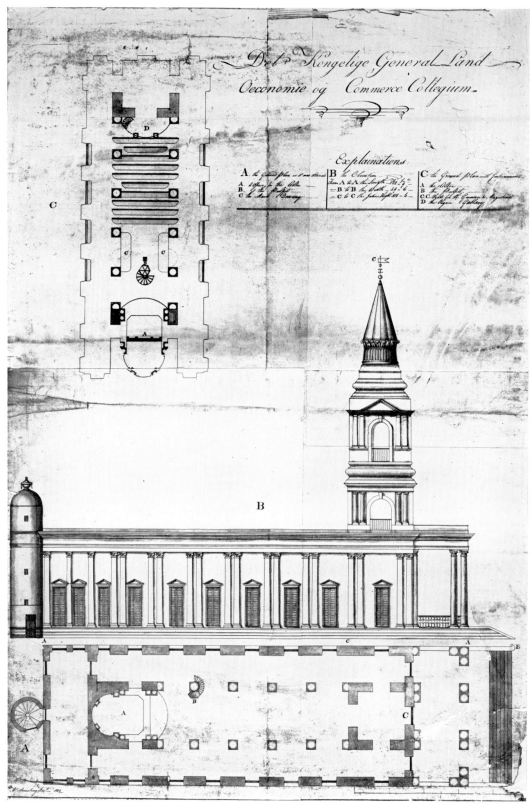

14. St. Olav's Church, Serampore.
(Architectural drawing by 'Lt.
Armstrong, 1806'.)

15. St. Olav's Church, Serampore,
1800–1821. Detail of the portico and
the steeple.

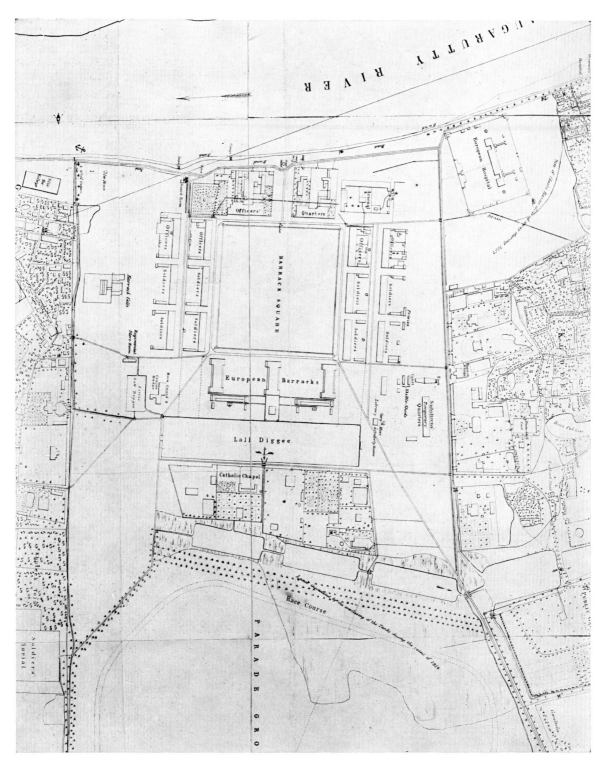

16. 'The Cantonment and Civil
Station of Berhampoor, surveyed in
1851–52.'

17. Arched gallery of a barracks in
Fort St. George, Madras. Situated at
the north-western corner of the Fort
Square, and erected before 1825.

18a. Barracks at Chinsura, built by the British after 1825.

18b. Officers' Mess at Dum Dum.

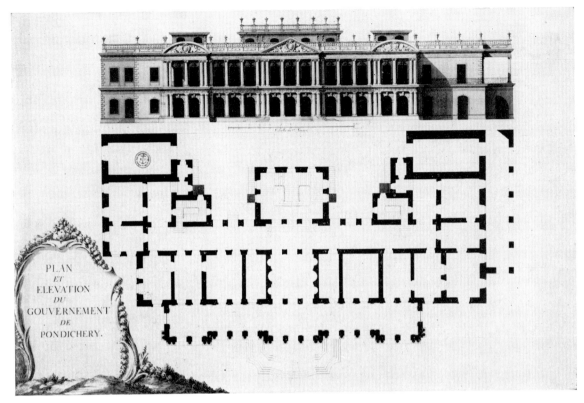

19a and b. Old Government House, Pondicherry, built by the engineer,
Dumont, and completed in 1752. a, front elevation and plan of ground
floor; b, section and back elevation.

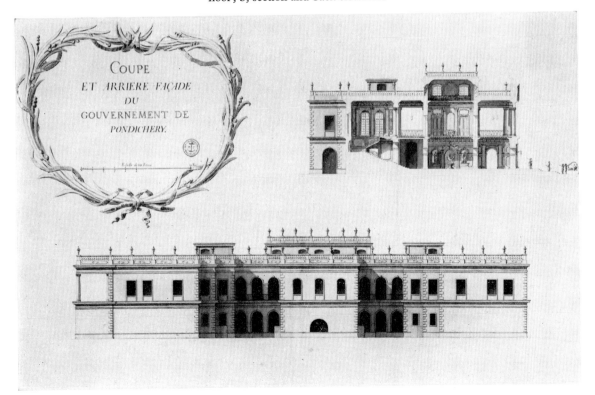

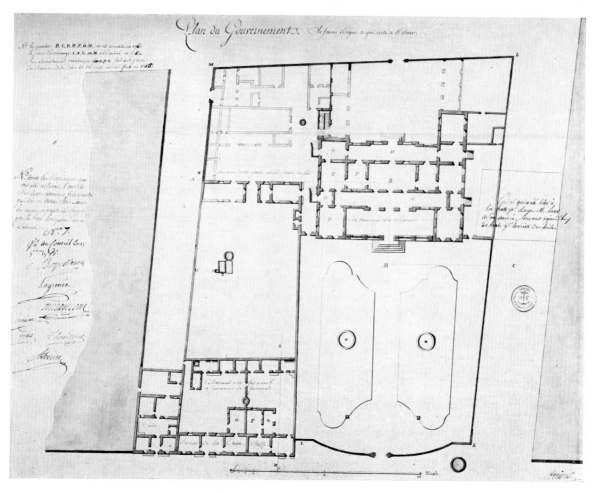

20a. New Government House, Pondicherry. Plan by Bourçet, 1766.

20b. New Government House, Pondicherry. Architectural drawing by Bourçet, 1766, showing the front elevation and sections.

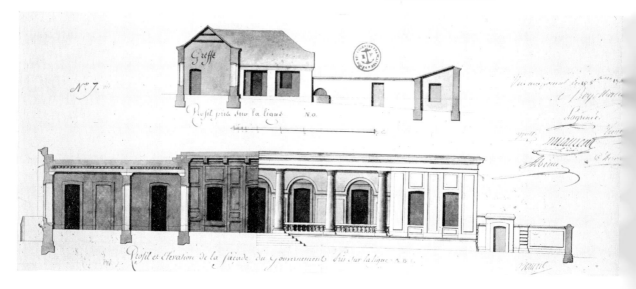

21a. Plan of a town house on irregular site. (Engraving — here somewhat cut down.)

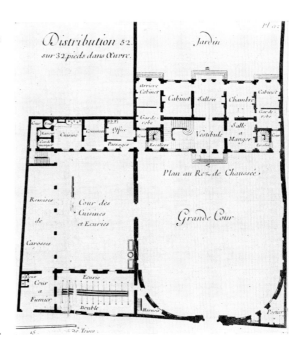

21b. Palais de Justice, Pondicherry.

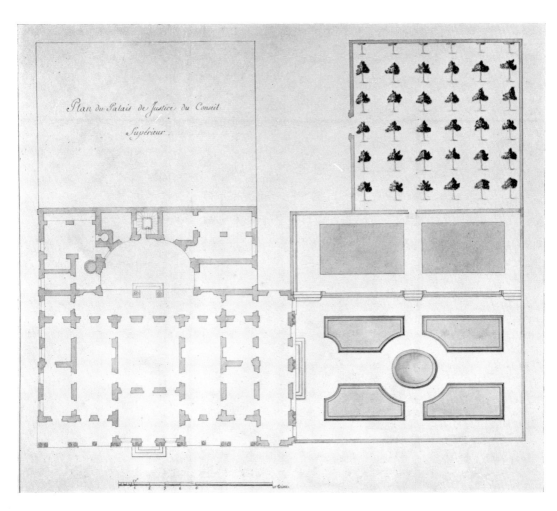

22a. Town gate.

Echelle de la 2.e porte.

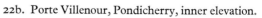

22b. Porte Villenour, Pondicherry, inner elevation.

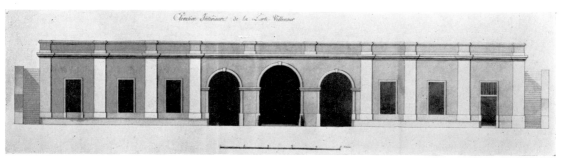

23a and b. The gates of Pondicherry.
a, Porte Madras; b, Porte Villenour,
outer elevation. (Architectural
drawings by La Lustière, 1788.)

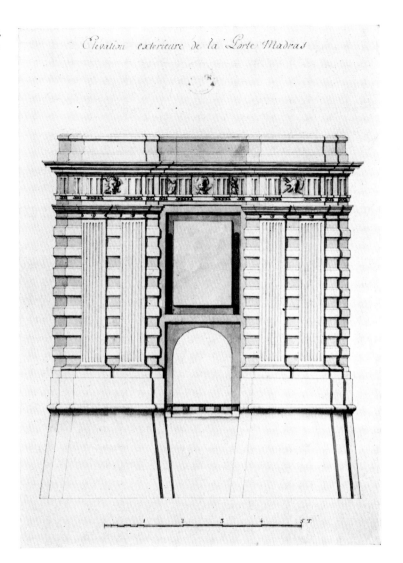

Elevation extérieure de la Porte Madras

24a. The 'Gola', Bankipur, erected by John Garstin and completed in 1786.

24b and c. The 'Gola', Bankipur, plan and section.

PLAN of the GRANARY at PATNA.

SCALE of FEET.

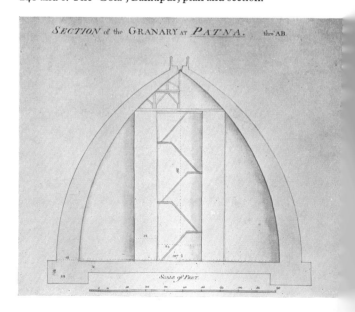

SECTION of the GRANARY at PATNA.   thro' AB.

SCALE of FEET.

25. Writer's Buildings, Calcutta, erected by Thomas Lyon in 1780.

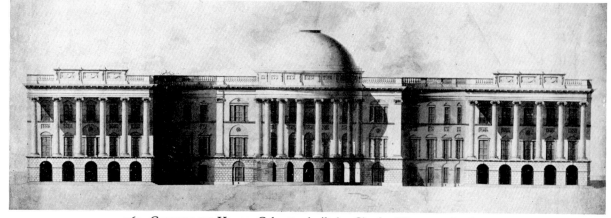

26a. Government House, Calcutta, built by Charles Wyatt 1798–1803, south-west elevation. (Architectural drawing — here somewhat cut down.)

26b. Government House, Calcutta, north-west elevation. (Architectural drawing by James Best.)

26c. Government House, Calcutta. Detail of the north-west front, photograph 1965.

27a. Kedleston Hall, Derbyshire, south elevation as projected by James
Paine in 1761.

27b. Government House, Calcutta. (Aquatint by J. Clarck and H. Merke,
published by Edward Orme in 1805.)

29a. (*Above*) Government House,
Calcutta. One of the gates facing
Council House Street.

28. (*Opposite*) Government House, Calcutta. Detail of
one of the gates facing Council House Street.

29b. Syon House, Middlesex. The
gate facing West Road, erected by
Robert Adam in the 1760's.

30a. Government House and Banqueting Hall, Triplicane, Madras. The buildings were altered and erected by John Goldingham in 1800 and subsequently. (Aquatint by H. Merke, published by Edward Orme in 1807.)

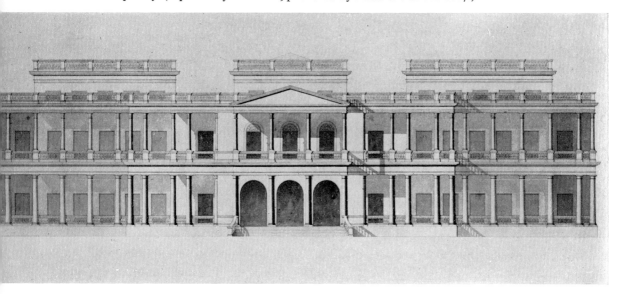

30b. Government House, Triplicane, Madras. (Architectural drawing —
here somewhat cut down.)

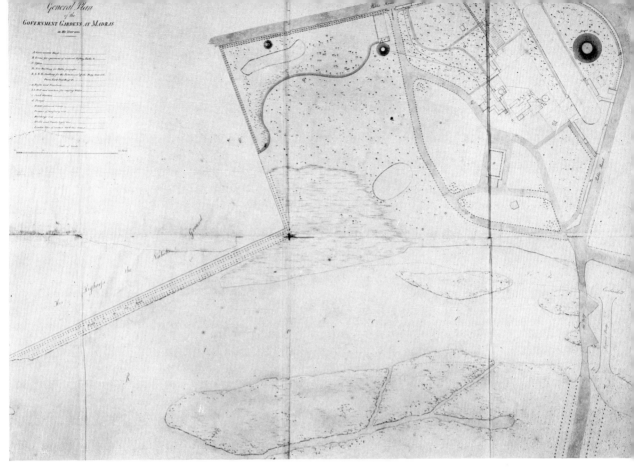

31a. The park of Government House, Triplicane, Madras. (Drawing —
here somewhat cut down.)

31b and c. Banqueting Hall, Triplicane, Madras.
Details from the interior; b, detail of the decorated
ceiling; c, detail of the bannisters leading to the gallery.
The photographs were taken, in 1965, by courtesy of
Public Works Department, Madras.

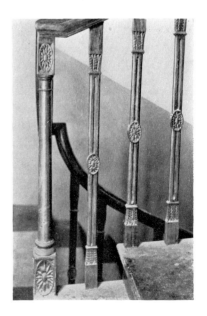

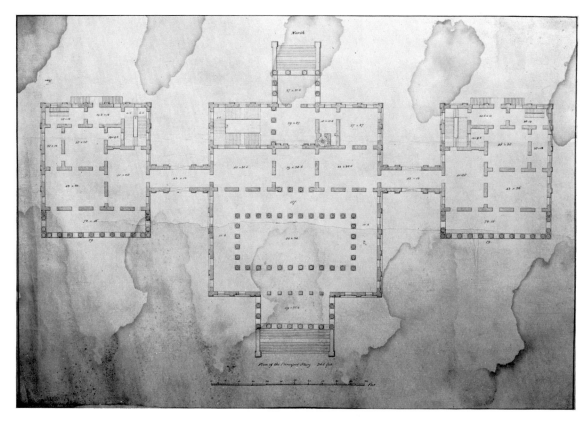

32a. Plan of a palace, projected for the Nawab of Murshidabad.
(Architectural drawing by Edward Tiretta.)

32b. Plan of a palace, projected for the Nawab of Murshidabad.

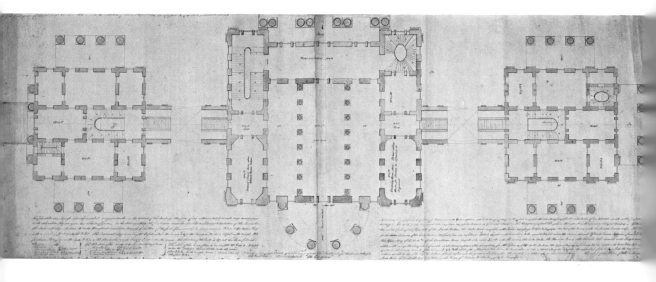

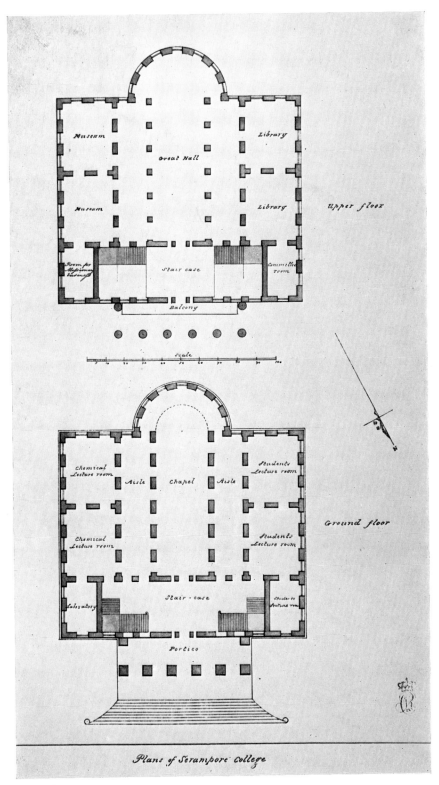

Museum

Great Hall

Library

Museum

Library

Upper floor

Room for
Missionary
Students

Stair case

Committee
room

Balcony

scale

Chemical
Lecture room

Aisle

Chapel

Aisle

Students
Lecture room

Chemical
Lecture room

Students
Lecture room

Ground floor

Laboratory

Stair-case

Students
Lecture room

Portico

Plans of Serampore College

33. Serampore College, plan of the first and second floors. (Architectural
drawing — here somewhat cut down.)

34. (*Opposite*) The Banqueting Hall of the British Residency in Lucknow. Erected in the beginning of the 19th century, demolished in 1857.

35. The Banqueting Hall of the British Residency in Lucknow. Part of the interior.

36. House in Clyde Road, Lucknow, showing mixed European and Indian decoration. The house was built about 1800.

37a. The British Residency in Hyderabad, erected in 1803 and subsequently after plans by S. Russell. Photograph of the north front of the main building.

37b. The British Residency in Hyderabad. Aquatint showing south front, yard and head gate.

38. The British Residency in
Hyderabad. Mirror and (reflected in
the mirror) parts of the interior of the
hall of the main building.

39a. Staircase of Home House (now the Courtauld
Institute), Portman Square, London. Erected by
Robert Adam, 1773–77.

39b. Staircase of the main building of the British
Residency in Hyderabad.

39c. Staircase of the main building of the British
Residency in Hyderabad. Detail showing the
bannisters.

40. Town Hall, Calcutta, erected by John Garstin 1807–13.

41. The Mint, Calcutta, erected by W. N. Forbes
1824–31. Detail of the colonnades facing Strand Road.

42. (*Opposite*) Town Hall, Bombay, erected by Thomas Cowper and others and completed in 1833. Detail of the portico of the south front.

43. Town Hall, Bombay. Detail showing south portico of the main front.

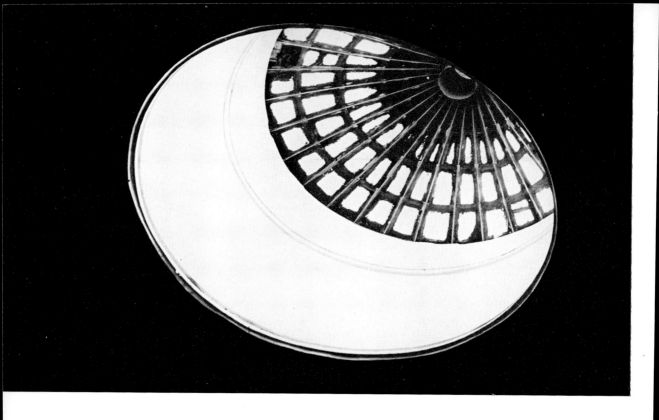

44a and b. Town Hall, Bombay. a, skylight in the vestibule; b, part of the vestibule including the statue of John Malcolm.

45. (*Opposite*) Town Hall, Bombay. Detail showing the flight of steps leading to the main portico.

To the Chairman, Deputy Chairman, and Directors of the Hon'ble the United East India Company
THIS VIEW of a HOUSE, MANUFACTORY, and BAZAR, in CALCUTTA
is most respectfully dedicated by their humble and obedient Servant, Francis Jukes.

46a. A merchant's house in Calcutta. (Aquatint by
F. Jukes, published in 1795.)

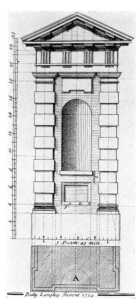

46b. Gate pier, designed by Batty Langley.

47. (*Opposite*) Gate pier and rusticated wall of a house
in Harrington Street, Chowringhi area, Calcutta.

48. (*Opposite*) No. 9, Russell Street, Calcutta. The house was built around 1820 and is now used by the Calcutta Turf Club. Detail showing the upper veranda of the south front.

49a and b. No. 9, Russell Street, Calcutta. a, south front; b, the 'porte cochère' of the north front.

50a. The Bengal Club, Calcutta.

50b. The New Club, Calcutta.

51. Hastings House, Alipur, Calcutta. Erected at the end of the 1770's. The portico and the wings were added later.

52a, b, c and d. (*Opposite*) Country residences. a, The 'Ghiretty House' in Bengal. (Watercolour — here somewhat cut down — by S. Davis, 1782); b, 'Felicity Hall' in Bengal; c, and d, country houses near Madras. (Water-colours — here somewhat cut down — by Justinian Gantz, 1832 and 1834.)

53a. Country Residence of the British Governor-General at Barrackpore, north front.

53b. 'Bungalow'. One of the smaller buildings surrounding the country residence of the British Governor-General at Barrackpore.

54. The Cathedral of Bom Jesus in Old Goa, erected in 1594. Detail of the west front.

55. (*Opposite*) St. John's Church, Calcutta, erected by James Agg, 1784–87.

56. St. Andrew's Church,
Calcutta,
erected in 1815.

57. St. Andrew's Church,
Madras, erected by
Thomas Fiott De Havilland,
1818–20.

58. (*Opposite*)
St. Andrew's Church,
Madras.
The portico.

59a and b. St. Andrew's
Church, Madras.
a, detail of the east
front; b, the east front.

61a. The Catholic Church in Patna, erected 1772–79, probably by Edward Tiretta.

61b. Skinner's Church in Delhi, erected in the 1830's.

60. (*Opposite*) St. George's Church, Madras, designed by James Caldwell, erected by T. F. De Havilland, and consecrated in 1816. Detail showing one of the aedicules of the south front.

62a and b. 'La Martinière', Lucknow, designed by Claude Martin and erected in the 1790's. a, column in front of the main building; b, main building facing the park.

63. (*Opposite*) 'La Martinière'. Detail showing one of the lions of the front facing the park.

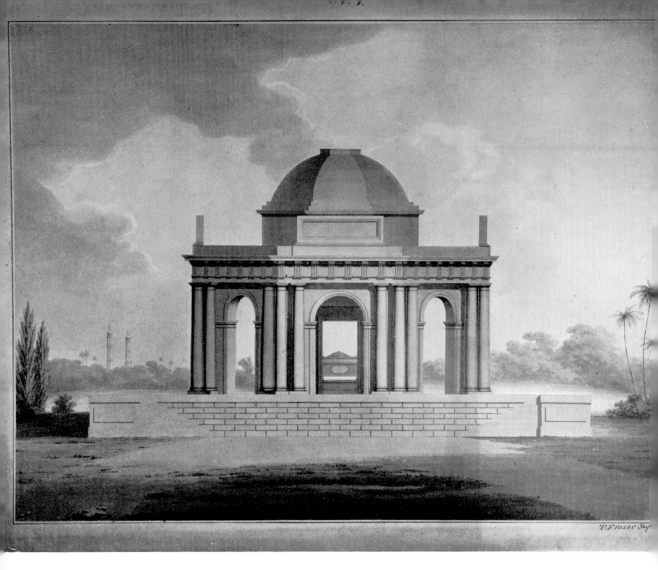

64a. Cenotaph, intended to be erected to the memory of Lord Cornwallis in Ghazipur. (Architectural drawing by T. Fraser.)

64b. Statue of Lord Cornwallis by John Bacon Jr., 1803. (Aquatint by G. Dawe.)

65. (*Opposite*) Doric Column, erected as a monument to the memory of General David Ochterlony in the Calcutta Maidan, 1828. The Monument was designed by J. P. Parker.

66. (*Opposite*) Doric circular temple, erected near St. John's Church, Calcutta, in memory of those killed in the second Rohilla war, 1794.

67a. Dalhousie Institute, erected in Dalhousie Square, Calcutta, in the 1850's.

67b. (*Left*) The 'Temple of Fame' in Barrackpore Park. (Architectural drawing — here somewhat cut down — by George Rodney Blane, showing transverse section of entrance end, interior and exterior.)

67c. The 'Temple of Fame' in Barrackpore Park, facing the Hooghly.

68a. The 'main street' of South Park Cemetery, Calcutta. The cemetery
was opened in 1767 and was subsequently used towards the middle of the
19th century.

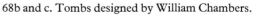
68b and c. Tombs designed by William Chambers.

69a and b. Tombs in South Park Cemetery, Calcutta. a, no name and no date; b, erected to the memory of John Garstin, the architect, who died in 1820.

70a, b, c and d. Tombs in South Park Cemetery, Calcutta. a, truncated pyramid, to the memory of Joannis Caulfield who died in 1804; b, Ionic circular temple to the memory of Maria Elisabeth Ricketts who died in 1824; c, Tuscan temple having no name — probably erected in the 1820's; d, pyramid to the memory of Elisabeth Barwell (Miss Sanderson), who died in 1778.

71. Tomb in South Park Cemetery, Calcutta, to the memory of Henry
Wilkins Hicks who died in 1812. Detail showing Ionic capital and other
ornaments.

72. Fragment of a marble slab showing Thanatos motif. South Park
Cemetery, Calcutta.

73. (*Opposite*) The Old Cemetery in Patna. Tombs from about 1800.

74a and b. a, 'Two European officers being entertained at a nautch in an Indian house'; b, 'A European presiding over a musical performance in his house'. Indian paintings, 'company style (perhaps Delhi)'.

75a. House of a distinguished
Indian, Serampore. (Water-colour
dated 1845.)

75b. Indian houses in Chitpur
Road, Calcutta, showing influences
from European architecture.

76. Indian palace showing influences from European
architecture. Project, architectural drawing from
Tanjore, probably executed in the 1830's.

77. (*Opposite*) Sawai Man Singh Town Hall, Jaipur,
erected about 1790. Detail of the front facing Siredeori
Bazaar.

78a. Acroterion, made of terra-cotta. From a house in
Panjim, built by the Portuguese about 1820.

78b. Veranda with a cast iron railing, probably from
the 1820's. From a Danish house in Serampore.

79. Window with shutters composed of wooden laths and oyster-shells. From a house in Panjim, built by the Portuguese in the beginning of the 19th century.

80. (*Opposite*) Limestone columns from a Portuguese building in Old Goa, erected about 1600 and later demolished.

81a. Cast iron columns from a Portuguese building from the middle of the 19th century. Later demolished.

81b. Balusters made of terra-cotta and filled with mortar, from a house at Barrackpore, near the Hooghly. The building was erected about 1820.

82. Fragments of columns and walling composed of Indian burnt bricks. From Baillie Guard, the British Residency in Lucknow.

83a. Figure showing the composing of neo-Classical elements of brick and mortar to be covered with plaster. (From *Outline of a Course of Practical Architecture, compiled for the use of Junior Officers of Royal Engineers*, 1826.)

83b. Fragment of a column composed of 'column-bricks' and mortar. From the ruin of a Danish house in Tranquebar.

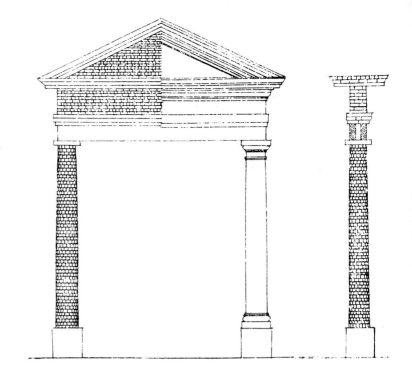

84. Wooden screens in the Governor's Bungalow,
Malabar Point, Bombay.

85. Screens cut out of sandstone slabs. Detail of the
tomb of Imam Zamin, erected in the 1530's near the
Qutb Minar, Delhi.

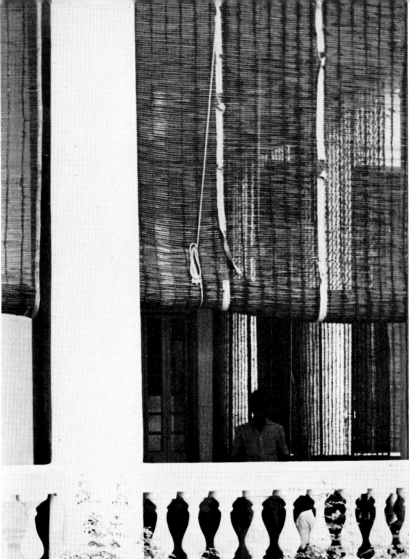

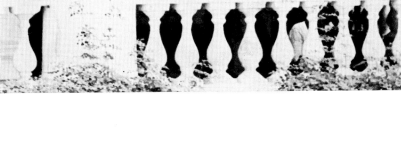

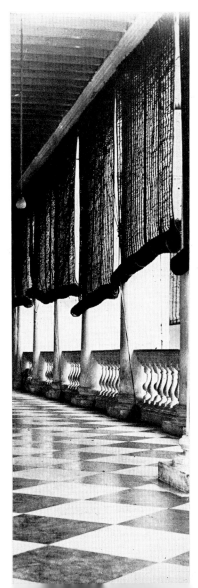

87a and b. 'Tatties' in the verandas of Government House, Triplicane, Madras.

86. (*Opposite*) Portico of a house in Kongens gade (King Street), Tranquebar. The Tuscan columns were erected about 1800, the supporters of the upper storey were later added (cf. figure 7).

88a. Doorways of the basement storey of a house in Fort St. George, Madras, protected by iron bars and to be closed up with wooden shutters.

88b. Doorway of the basement storey of a house in Fort St. George, Madras, protected by wooden fanlight, venetian blinds and shutters.

89. (*Opposite*) Doorway of the house No. 9 Russell Street, Calcutta, protected by a projection supported by brackets, and to be closed up with glassed wooden doors and venetian blinds.

90a, b and c. William Hickey's House, Calcutta; the same house with verandas added by Hickey; and Hickey's country residence at Chinsura.

90d. Part of Lall Bazar, Calcutta. The houses have additions of Indian as well as European type.

90e. Terrace roofs in Pondicherry on the Coromandel Coast.

91a. Wooden verandas of a house in Marine Street, Bombay.

91b. Tiled sloping roofs in Panjim, on the west coast of India.

92a. Guest bungalow attached to the Residence of the
Governor of Maharashtra, Malabar Point, Bombay.

92b. Bungalow in Fraser Road, Patna, built in the
beginning of the 19th century.

93a. 'Curvilinear huts', bungalow and European country residence in Bengal.

93b. 'Double-roofed house' in a European housing area near Calcutta.

93c. 'Bungalow attached to the House of Maharajah Mutrefeyt Singh'. (Detail of a pencil drawing by Charles D'Oyly, 1825.)

93d. Bungalow in which to deposit rice, erected at the beginning of the 19th century in the fields near Tranquebar.

94a. Detail of a bungalow in Fraser Road, Patna, showing *pucka* walling and bamboo rods covered with tiles (cf. figure 92b).

94b and c. *Pucka* columns and a complicated wooden construction support the roof of this bungalow which was erected at the beginning of the 19th century in the fields near Tranquebar (cf. figure 93d, showing the exterior of the same structure).

95. Bamboo window in a Bengal house.